THE URBANIZATION OF INJUSTICE

THE
URBANIZATION
OF INJUSTICE

edited by
ANDY MERRIFIELD &
ERIK SWYNGEDOUW

NEW YORK UNIVERSITY PRESS
WASHINGTON SQUARE, NEW YORK

First published in the U.S.A. in 1997 by
NEW YORK UNIVERSITY PRESS
Washington Square
New York, N.Y.   10003

CIP data available from the Library of Congress
ISBN 0-8147-5575-5 (clothbound)
ISBN 0-8147-5576-3 (paperbound)

Printed in the United Kingdom

Contents

CONTENTS

Part III Justice and the Cultural Politics of Difference

Preface

This book is the direct outcome of a conference on Social Justice and *Fin de Siècle* Urbanism, commemorating the twentieth anniversary of David Harvey's book *Social Justice and the City*, which took place at Oxford University over two days in March 1994. We would like to thank both speakers and audience alike and apologize to those who we had to turn away because of space restrictions. The event was a lively and intense gathering, none of which would have been possible without the financial aid of the Hume Committee, nor the sterling support of the staff at the School of Geography. We would particularly like to thank Margaret Willis for her tireless administrative assistance and for her patient handling of our own inefficiencies. Thanks, too, to Vanda Allen, Marie McAllister and Pat Woodward for ensuring that the two hectic days ran smoothly and with good humour. We are very grateful to Ruth Borthwick of Lawrence & Wishart for supporting our venture and for encouraging us to have the proceedings published.

This book also reflects in some ways the environment that David Harvey helped create during his stay at Oxford. Together with numerous others, especially Clive Barnett, Adrian Passmore, Michael Samers and Argyro Loukaki, often convening in Jericho's Bookbinders pub, the themes and issues discussed in this book were chewed over and confronted with the politics of our own and other people's daily lives. It was our pleasure to be a part of that vibrant intellectual and political milieu. And while this milieu continues to be nurtured and fostered, albeit in a different guise, it is one where David is sadly missed. This book is therefore dedicated to all those who contributed to make those years such an empowering and emancipatory experience, despite the often ambiguous feelings for the place in which we were living. It is also for that reason that we decided to keep Marshall Berman's slightly idiosyncratic preface to the paper he presented because it both lightened the tone of the conference and nicely captured the ambivalences of an Oxford scene that we have somehow inured over the years.

Andy Merrifield and Erik Swyngedouw, May 1995

Social Justice and the Urban Experience: An Introduction

Andy Merrifield and Erik Swyngedouw

> Justice which is the organic, regulating, sovereign basic principle of societies, which has nevertheless been nothing up to present, but which ought to be everything – what is that if not the stick with which to measure all human affairs, if not the final arbiter to be appealed to in all conflicts?
>
> Friedrich Engels[1]

The ideal of social justice is the bedrock of any democratic society within which citizens can actively participate in a free, tolerant and inclusive political community. Speculations as to what a just society should look like have long been the stuff of political philosophers from the ancient Greeks onwards. Over recent years, it has tended not to preoccupy Marxist thinkers too much, many of whom have either deflected the question or else branded debates around justice (and morality) as bourgeois flirtations.[2] Arguably, Marx himself was no great help in the matter. His writings on justice and injustice were, to say the least, ambiguous and controversial. Geras neatly frames the controversy surrounding Marx and justice, suggesting that all Marxists are unanimous in their acknowledgement that Marx condemned capitalism, but there is dispute as to whether he did in the light of any principle of justice.[3] Marx's line in *The Communist Manifesto* is exemplary in highlighting why so many Marxists have, despite Engels's protestations, thought it irrelevant to theorize justice:

> Law, morality, religion, are to [the working class] so many bourgeois prejudices, behind which lurk in ambush just as many bourgeois interests ... There are, besides, eternal truths, such as Freedom, Justice, etc., that are common to all states of society. But Communism abolishes eternal truths, it abolishes all religion and all morality, instead of constituting them on a new basis.[4]

1

Notwithstanding, in the early 1970s David Harvey used his fledgling Marxism to investigate critically how ideas of social justice and moral philosophy could be related to geographical inquiry. He believed then – and still believes – that principles of justice have profound relevance for understanding the link between spatial form and social processes, and in *Social Justice and the City* proceeded to demonstrate this within urban contexts.[5] In its shift from redistributive paradigms found in liberal formulations (culminating in John Rawls's *A Theory of Justice*) toward revolutionary Marxist formulations, *Social Justice* was a provocative and pathbreaking exploration of urban land use, the problem of ghetto formation, and the circulation of surplus value within urban economies. This shift, in political terms, represented a 'move from the predispositon to regard social justice as a matter of eternal justice and morality to regard it as something contingent upon the social processes operating in society as a whole' (p15).

Harvey's use of Marxism in the pursuit of social justice and for a 'genuinely humanizing urbanism' have important things to tell us about the contemporary capitalist city. Nevertheless, since the publication of *Social Justice*, far-reaching changes have taken place in intellectual and political life. And these transformations maybe necessitate a re-evaluation of the substance of Harvey's argument and of the characteristics of urbanism and social justice generally. This task is fraught with all kinds of dilemmas. Not least is that debates about social justice must now take place in a political-economic atmosphere where free market liberalism has returned to grace; within an intellectual milieu where postmodern modes of thought are dominant; and within an urbanization process which is now thoroughly globalized.

The present volume situates itself within this shifting economic, political, and intellectual reality. The book thereby attempts to reassess what was learned from *Social Justice*, and evaluate what critical scholars continue to learn from more sober postmodernist critiques about 'difference', 'non-totalizing' discourses, and the nature of contemporary urban life. Hence, this book is not some kind of mantra to Harvey's work. Rather, we see it much more as an intervention into a debate that over recent decades has relegated the issue of social justice to the hinterlands of academic inquiry. And this while cities have witnessed a disturbing rise in homelessness, job losses, poverty, housing deprivation, and violence (much of it against women). Indeed, the speed and depth of the urbanization of injustice urges critical analyses not only to rethink the relationship between spatiality, power and justice, but also to push for a political and intellectual agenda that rallies around the development of socially just urban practices. The collection of essays here offer themselves as a response to this behest.

SOCIAL JUSTICE AND CRITICAL SCHOLARSHIP

Over the years, liberal political philosophers have been most active in grappling with the issue of social justice. But justice continues to pivot around some kind of abstract and pristine ideal – invariably devoid of time and place – that normatively tries to plot out the basic constitutive qualities of a 'fair society'. John Rawls's classic liberal disquisition, *A Theory of Justice*, is emblematic here.[6] Twenty years on, Rawls is still at it. His recent *Political Liberalism* takes up the tack of these earlier questions. But Rawls now offers a redefinition of a 'well-ordered society' since the relatively homogeneous society posited in *Theory* is no longer a tenable assumption.[7] Instead, Rawls views a democratic society as 'a plurality of reasonable yet incompatible comprehensive doctrines'. Moreover, Rawls admits that this 'shows that, as used in *Theory*, the idea of a well-ordered society of justice as fairness is unrealistic'[8] (ppxvi-xvii). Still, as Perry Anderson observes in his review of Rawls, the 'contradiction between the postulates of consensus, to which Rawls continually subscribes, and the reality of dissensus, to which his best impulses belong, is incurable.'[9] (In his essay, however, Ira Katznelson further explores Rawls's reformulated liberalism and advocates its importance in relationship to the work of Harvey and Polanyi. And Andy Merrifield situates Rawls alongside Iris Young and Marshall Berman to try to elucidate recent redevelopment plans in Liverpool's Toxteth district.)

Anderson's evaluation here captures very well the omnipresent impasse within the terrain of social justice. In response, we want to suggest that the problematic is maybe best tackled through the 'reality of dissensus' – hence the negativity expressed in the book's title. In other words, by charting the *plurality of injustice* plaguing the present capitalist urban reality we hope to unravel the sorts of dialogues required for the construction of social institutions that ensure freedom, equality and social justice for all. This task is becoming all the more pressing in a context where there is growing recognition that the multiplicity of powers and identities in global cities requires new strategies and politics of emancipation.

Yet this project also incorporates self-reflexivity; self-criticism and honest exchange between radical theorists is a healthy and necessary aspect for formulating agreement and common ground. In this respect we can draw sustenance from Marx's comments on the constitutive qualities of proletarian revolutions which, he maintained, 'criticize themselves constantly, interrupt themselves continually in their own course, come back to the apparently accomplished in order to begin afresh, deride with unmerciful thoroughness the inadequacies, weaknesses and paltrinesses of their first attempts.'[10] Part 1 of the book aims to accomplish such a 'deriding with unmerciful thoroughness' of our own inadequacies within the contested terrain of social justice. Here, theoretical co-ordinates of possibilities and limitations for just and empowering urban politics will be charted. Part II pursues this dialogue concretely in its exploration of urban injustices. Cities are – or at least should be – highly differentiated social spaces expressive of heterogeneity, diversity of activity, excitement, and pleasure. They are arenas for the pursuit of unoppressed activities and desire, but also, as Part II's essays evince, ones replete with danger, oppression and domination. The chapters on the urbanization of injustices in Part II will set the tone for Part III which broadly focuses on culture and the politics of group difference, and how visions of justice (Part 1), and the mechanisms of urban injustices (Part II), can be turned into an enabling urban politics and policy.[11]

Breaching the chasm between the 'realities of dissensus' and the 'possibilities of consensus', however, unavoidably involves some conception of justice to struggle around – even if, in the immediate term, it's only an instrumentalist one. Activists and those involved in the daily round of political organizing have never lost sight of the pressing need to formulate and strategize around socially just interventions. Those committed to practical activism have always operated in environments where exclusion and oppression aren't just concepts and metaphors ready for deconstructive enquiry, but integral components in the grief and pain of everyday life. In Britain, numerous examples come quickly to mind. Consider, for instance, the highly organized campaign against poll tax and the reconstitution of the Anti-Nazi League to combat the unabashed racism in British society. Meanwhile, the proliferation of anti-road protests and broad-based coalitions around environmental and animal rights issues is a further demonstration of the explicit politicization of everyday life issues.

By the same token, such occurrences have taken place alongside a relative retreat by critical intellectuals from active participation. Some who are duly informed by critical theory now indulge in the self-stimulation associated with the pleasures offered by the postmodern turn and the advancement of academic careers. Which isn't to say that some of this work isn't important nor, indeed, revolutionary in terms of its potential political implications. The problem, rather, is that the link between theoretical reformulation and affirmation of a radical alternative to our existing social world has receded from view. And this when society has plunged into generalized market fetishism, and intensified social polarization and silencing. The British Conservative Government's decision in early 1993 to treat gay men as second class citizens by rendering them less equal among equals attests to their enduring marginalization by the forces of reactionary power. Similarly, government policy to extend public order offences to cover land and housing occupations confirms its intention to clamp down on squatters and the young homeless, New Age travellers, ravers and those asserting 'alternative' lifestyles. All of which signals the Government's inadequacy in solving the housing crisis, its fear and loathing of those deemed Other, and its continued assault on basic civil liberties. And this says nothing, too, about the conservative backlash and moral panic on both sides of the Atlantic over the issue of single motherhood.[12]

The problems of formulating and acting upon a coherent empowering politics, furthermore, come disturbingly to the fore in the enervation of an utterly fragmented French intelligentsia to stage an effective attack against the strategies being pursued in cities like Nice and Toulon, where fascist National Front mayors have begun the ethnic cleansing of some urban spaces. Meanwhile, in Paris government policy has used brute force to disperse the homeless, students, academics and workers who had gathered to celebrate the inauguration of a people's university. Thus, even this somewhat feeble popular attempt at confronting the disempowering silencing associated with systematic exclusion and marginalization couldn't be tolerated by the ruling powers that be.

If critical theory has taught us anything in recent years it's shown that reconstructing the past and understanding the present is infused with relations of power that cohere around class, gender, race, ethnicity and affinity group cleavages. To the extent that the past has a hold on the present, radical alternatives attempt to strip away these fetters and probe the conceptual limits of the present. Was it not Marx in *Capital* who once highlighted the power of even the *weakest* prefigurative practice: 'what distinguishes the worst of architects from the best of bees is that the former raises their structure in imagination before erecting it in reality.'[13] Charting the transition, then, from the unjust status quo to an alternative that prioritizes civil liberties and social equality, necessitates some kind of vision of what is acceptable as a just urban life. This vision must readdress the bleak prognosis of right-wing cultural homogenization theorists now scurrying around Fukuyama's 'end of history' clarion call and reaffirm a future that is always up for grabs. But this doesn't mean projecting and formulating a just society around a never never land of tomorrow's Utopia. That was the stuff enshrined in modernization planning concepts of the future. The dilemma with this brand of modernist challenge was that its obsessive preoccupation with 'becoming' proved too flimsy a basis for the construction of a 'better' society – especially when it had to confront the social power of money and property relations.

On the other hand, as Marshall Berman suggests in his defence of modernism, it's nonetheless a *non sequitur* to infer that all universal claims and big ideas are 'con games' warranting rejection. Modernists in the 1980s/90s, Berman reminds us, 'go on struggling to break through to visions of truth and freedom that all modern men and women can embrace. This struggle animates their work, gives it an inner dynamism and a principle of hope.'[14] (Berman in the present collection deepens and problematizes some of those modernist hopes in his discussion on rap music.) Accordingly, a project offering the potential to carve out heterotopian spaces for the celebration of unoppressed differences will necessarily involve turning the tide of the commodity and image fetishism of assorted ruling forces and the theoretical self-indulgence of the academic left. The essays assembled here are maybe united in that they each ground themselves somewhere within this two-pronged desire.

So amidst the theoretical pyrotechnics of contemporary critical thought it is vital that scholars don't lose sight of the grounding of material life. This is made more difficult because of the multi-faceted nature of oppressiveness in contemporary life. Indeed, much unfolds before our eyes in scattered, fragmented and imagined forms: through the lenses of TV cameras, through the patchwork of media-signals, and through the gaze of ever more repressive forms of surveillance. Yet the gimmickry of *reel* life, contra Jean Baudrillard, always belies the deeper grime and hardship of *real* life. Denouncing illusion because reality is said to be no longer possible – which is roughly Baudrillard's line[15] – or turning oppression into text and image and into bits and bytes, may distantiate human beings from each other (didn't the young Marx call this *alienation*?); it doesn't, though, entirely subliminate disempowerment and oppression into a mere series of signs and signifiers. Still, while traditional socialist appeals for equality, democracy and justice become all the more pertinent, they do seem ever more problematical.

THE CONTESTED TERRAIN OF JUSTICE

The meaning of justice itself is certainly never straightforward. For one thing, the formulation of a universal model of justice that is mindful of exploitation, domination and oppression is arguably a utopian hope that no longer holds water in today's highly complex multicultural society. The difficulty here, as Iris Marion Young has illustrated, is that universalist tendencies have in the past presupposed a decidedly unsatisfactory homogeneous public.[16] This leaves no room for the assertion of social group difference, cultural identity, and minority representation. Rawls's latest liberal reformulation has at least picked up on this. According to Young, 'a conception of justice which challenges institutionalized domination and oppression should offer a vision of a heterogeneous public that acknowledges and affirms group differences.'[17] Adopting the standpoint epistemology derived from contemporary feminist thought, Young argues that

> [i]f the theory [of justice] is truly universal and independent, presupposing no particular social situations, institutions, or practices, then it is simply too abstract to be useful in evaluating actual institutions and practices. In order to be a useful measure of actual justice and injustice, it must contain some substantive premises about social life, which are usually derived, explicitly or implicitly, from the actual social context in which the theorizing takes place.[18]

Young's theorization is enabling because it redefines justice away from a purely distributional affair and pinpoints that oppression and domination should be 'primary terms for conceptualizing injustice' (p9). Young posits, furthermore, that justice has no abstract universal meaning, and is therefore in broad agreement with Engels's claim that justice 'varies not only with time and place, but also with the persons concerned.'[19]

Nevertheless, in pursuing such a line caution is warranted. For this understanding can equally create innumerable definitions of what constitutes 'just', thus rendering justice highly vulnerable to manipulation. This was something Marx spotted in his 'Working Day' chapter in *Capital*. For example, Marx castigated Proudhon's ideal of 'eternal justice' and warned that if the 'juridical relations' of commodity production remain unchecked it would still be possible to contextualize justice to defend capitalist rationality.[20] Indeed, Marx demonstrated how the consumption of labour-power and the exploitation of the labourer is deemed just when looked upon from the standpoint of the work contract and laws of exchange. Therein, the capitalist maintains rights as a purchaser of a commodity, but the 'peculiar nature' of the commodity sold 'implies a limit to its consumption ... and the labourer maintains his right as seller when he wishes to reduce the working day'. It was, Marx concluded, an 'antinomy' – a 'right against right, both equally bearing the laws of exchange' – where 'force decides' the outcome. Engels is therefore led to conclude elsewhere that 'always this justice is but the ideologized, idealized expression of the existing economic relations, now from their conservative, and now from their revolutionary angle. The justice of the Greeks and Romans held slavery to be just; the justice of the bourgeois of 1789 demanded the abolition of feudalism on the ground that it was unjust.'[21]

This discomforting logic, moreover, can define as fair – if not just – deteriorating housing stock and homelessness if it is 'idealized' from the standpoint of the dynamics of capitalist landmarkets; and the subordination of women can likewise be argued as just from the vantage point of dominant power relations within patriarchal capitalism. As, indeed, can the cultural oppression of ethnic groups when constructed as Other by the hegemonic occidental gaze. Such a state of affairs is also cross-cut with a further environmental complication: the exploitation of the ecosystem through rainforest annihilation in Amazonia to heat and feed the city may be judged just when viewed from the perceptive of the Latin American urban underclass. In short, the space of justice is highly contested terrain for conflicting social values.[22]

These versions of justice are, however, united in the sense that they derive their meaning through the implementation of *social power*. Plato and Marx both shrewdly recognized this when suggesting that the ruling groups in any society make laws in their own interests and define as 'just' for their subjects simply what is in the interest of themselves. In his *Republic*, Plato has Polemarchus ask Socrates whether justice is nothing more than 'to do good to friends when they are good, and to harm to enemies when they are bad?'[23] Later, Thrasymachus reasons that justice is merely what *is advantageous to the stronger*. Socrates is quick to spot Thrasymachus's insertion of power relations when he too acknowledges that 'justice is in a sense advantageous, but you [Thrasymachus] define advantageous further by the addition of "to the stronger".'[24]

David Harvey confronts this perspective in a compelling defence of Marx's class analysis for restraining the relativism of 'strong' postmodern thought. In this essay, as in his contribution to this volume, Harvey hones his thinking on justice and readdresses the deficiencies of *Social Justice and the City*. Harvey now reconceptualizes a theory of justice that is acutely sensitive toward exploitation, oppression and cultural difference, yet at the same time doesn't jettison universality entirely. On the basis of a horrific fire in 1991 at Imperial Food chicken farm in Hamlet, North Carolina (when twenty-five people mainly African-American women died) Harvey attempts to 'resurrect social justice' from what he calls its 'postmodern death'.[25]

Drawing upon Iris Young's work, Harvey's reformulation embodies a degree of relativism, in terms of cultural difference through 'situatedness'. But Harvey also convincingly emphasizes that universality cannot be avoided if it is to confront the social power of money as the ultimate measure of value under capitalism. This universal condition, Harvey insists, 'prevents groups from imposing their will oppressively on others.'[26] Nonetheless Harvey views universality as open to constant negotiation, though only insofar as it is defined from the standpoint of the oppressed.

So for Harvey universality is construed in dialectical relation with particularity of difference; one defines the other in inexorable unity. As such universality, as Hegel had it, contains particularity, and particularity, 'through its determinateness', contains universality.[27] It makes no sense for critical theory, therefore, to reject universality or so-called 'totalizing theory' in favour of a flimsy kind of relativism. From the dialectical standpoint, meanwhile, universality isn't about totalization or closure; it is an open-ended and emergent construct, acknowledging that each particular difference incorporates in what it is all relations with other particularities to engender a dynamic universality.[28] Thus universality equates to *similarity* not sameness. Similarity, furthermore, implies a commonality which bonds humans together in an inclusive ethical union. In the end, some sort of ethical, universal anchor criterion – a 'principled position' – cannot be done away with in any critical politics.[29]

By the same token, what constitutes a 'principled position' is plagued with considerable problems. Paul Hirst, for example, has recently warned that '[w]e live in a world of differing ethical standards and social objectives, in which a certain social pluralism is the only answer to either perpetual strife or the tyrannical imposition of one set of values'. All the same, adds Hirst, '[w]e also face the necessity of *imposing justified limits* on belief in both the intellectual and the social spheres if the world of knowledge and society as a whole is not to be torn apart by the consequences of certain beliefs'.[30] But in contemporary society what is 'justifiable' is, of course, rather slippery. It is open to excruciating debate and has been so in the history of western intellectual practice. In essence, it has tended to revolve around the profound issue of human 'values'.[31] Though almost inevitably it is a topic that is infused with power relations.

The advent of poststructuralism and postmodernism in radical scholarship has had at once politically enabling and numbing ramifications with respect to grappling with themes of power. At its most rhetorical level, power has been *diluted* to an interrogation of the ways in which particular 'discourses' of power are constructed and reproduced. (As if, say, speaking about torture and being tortured are one and the same.) Under these circumstances, responsibility for articulating critical thought to radical social change – bringing theory to bear on real world struggles – is largely abdicated. Derrida's wry proclamation that 'there's nothing outside the text' is intensely political for literary practices because it shows how real world presences and absences become internalized in specific texts. Lately, though, this reasoning has bizarrely assumed the proportion of some sort of radical call-to-arms; only now all the action and political struggle is located in the library. And it is, so we are told, through the contestation of different 'language-games' and 'discourses' where the path from necessity to freedom lies. The problem here is that these textual excavations on the composition of discourses have so far evaded, and in many instances actively avoided, any translation into a coherent emancipatory political strategy. In a nutshell, responsibility for reconstructing the deconstruction has been averted.

THE URBANIZATION OF INJUSTICE

Intriguing though this stuff may be for critical scholars, it is also intrinsically dangerous in its prospective definition of political action. Decoupling social critique from its political-economic basis is not helpful for dealing with the shifting realities of urban life at the threshold of the new millenium. Consider the pathological tendencies that blight and have become magnified at the urban scale of all advanced capitalist countries over the last decade or so. They all underscore the urgency of formulating some robust and coherent conception of justice. The accelerating and spatially deepening uneven processes of 'creative destruction' leave urban communities uprooted and displaced while propelling others on to new dizzy and commanding heights. Here, Doreen Massey has pointed out that the phenomenon of 'globalization', with its whirl of 'time-space compression' (to use Harvey's term from *The Condition of Postmodernity*), is indeed a double-edged affair. For the privileged – who are able to benefit from new technologies, new fangled multimedia and modes of communication – movement, access, and mobility has been augmented. Needless to say, these developments have been used to reinforce their power and privilege. Meanwhile, there are those on the receiving end of this process – like the impoverished, the aged, the unemployed, and, more specifically, the 'third world' poor – who have increasingly been imprisoned by it.[32]

Within many advanced western cities themselves, new forms of technology have enabled all manner of geopolitical reorganizations. The powerful, for example, are now able to insulate themselves in hermetically sealed enclaves, where gated communities and sophisticated modes of surveillance are the order of the day. Concurrently, the rich and powerful can decant and steer the poor into clearly demarcated zones in the city, where implicit and explicit forms of social control keep them in place. Thus, the efficacy of such a 'militarization of urban space' correlates directly with intensifying time-space compression.[33]

Different groups and individuals consequently bear different relationships to global flows of money, capital, technology and information. In any event, everlasting uncertainty and agitation

11

appears as the dominant motif of late capitalist urbanization. Here, too, the incessant transformation of nature and environmental destruction at all geographical scales betokens apocalyptic ecological disaster. That this accelerating ecological conquest often forms the very basis of the urbanization process itself (in both the underdeveloped and developed world) suggests that the question of a 'just' city must, as David Harvey cogently argues, extend into the realm of environmental justice.

The practices of exploitation by transnational corporate capital, domination and exclusion by state bureaucracies, and oppression by dominant social and cultural forces, has meant that those most disempowered in cities have had to resort to desperate forms of protest. Marshall Berman situates the development of rap music in precisely this context, viewing it as a cry for help by marginalized black youth, and as a no-holds-barred indictment of the social hypocrisy of contemporary urban America. In his chapter, Berman claims rap music's enraged 'shout in the street' can inspire and combine with 'organic intellectuals' to create a cultural street politics of defiance and resistance. And although the danger of reappropriation by big business can quickly turn truth into lie, Berman sees rap music as providing a glimmer of hope for African-American kids living in the urban ruins, where love for place and lust for life conjoin to form an authentic modernism for the 1990s.

Elsewhere in the US, popular struggles organized around homelessness (of the kind Neil Smith illustrates in the present volume) and over the HIV and AIDS virus are reshaping the urban landscape. Moreover, the social inferno in Los Angeles – labelled the 'black intifada' by Mike Davis – in the wake of the Rodney King beating verdict illustrated the fragility of public acquiescence when marginalized citizens confront a deepening economic crisis.[34] By that reckoning, violence would seem the only effective conduit to communicate the voice of the dispossessed and politically disenfranchized. Yet in Los Angeles, although the explosion of voices may have been many and varied, it unanimously resounded jangling cacophony rather than a multicultural harmony. And if, as some pundits suggest, Los Angeles is a crystal ball of capitalism's future, the forlorn dystopia of *Blade Runner* is maybe just around the corner for us all.

Meanwhile, in London's East End worsening poverty and unemployment, coupled with growing disillusionment over the local authority's efforts to spearhead urban renewal and change, has also prompted desperate responses. Random acts of violence against those most vulnerable, such as the racially-motivated attacks against Asian residents, are now commonplace. More disturbingly, these acts of racial hatred seem more organized owing to the growth of the fascist British National Party (BNP). Racist attacks in London's East End – including the near fatal assault of seventeen year old Quddus Ali – have risen 300% since the election victory in September 1993 of BNP councillor Derek Beackon in Millwall. (A seat he subsequently lost in May 1994.) But, as Michael Keith's chapter affirms, a 'vocabulary of resistance' amongst young Bengalis has coalesced, contesting this racism.

Varied as the motivations and constituent qualities of these incidents in Los Angeles and London clearly are, they nonetheless hammer home that acts of contestation and political action (in both its progressive and outright reactionary guises) revolve around the meaning and (re)appropriation of place and space. Empowerment and creative liberation, therefore, necessitate grappling with everyday life and the rituals inscribed in urban life. Henri Lefebvre's proclamation that everyday life is 'the inevitable starting point for the realization of the possible' surely rings true.[35] Lefebvre pointed out how trivial experiences, activities and fleeting moments are colonized by the commodity and dominant social forces and are thus shadowed with mystification. Nevertheless, they remain an elemental source of resistance and social transformation. 'Daily life,' wrote Lefebvre, 'is the screen on which our society projects its light and its shadow, its hollows and its planes, its power and its weakness; political and social activities converge to consolidate, structure and *functionalize* it.'[36]

Lefebvre was likewise right to underscore how every emancipatory and empowering politics inevitably involves a spatial strategy: a struggle not just *in* but *for* a space, a reconquest of spaces expressive of lived difference, of desire, and of the body.[37] Ed Soja draws upon Lefebvre in his elaboration of so-called 'Thirdspace': the lived, interstitial space that is worked out through perception and imagination; a space simultaneously real and imagined, material and metaphorical, ordered and disordered. Making practical sense of 'Thirding', argues Soja, is the way forward for the development of a cultural politics that is 'radically open, and openly radical' in its active recovery of both ourselves and the other and in its promotion of social change. And here, too, city spaces – as vital crucibles of power – are considered as a pivotal axis around which theories of justice and 'radically open' empowerment are constructed.

The city is something akin to a vast and variegated whirlpool replete with all the ambivalence of a space full of opportunity, playfulness and liberating potential, while being entwined with spaces of oppression, exclusion and marginalization.[38] (Doreen Massey explores this tension around a trinity of space, identity and power.) Cities seem to hold the promise of emancipation and freedom whilst skilfully mastering the whip of repression and domination. Sharon Zukin pursues such an ambivalence by arguing that the control of vision is intimately connected with the control of social space. From this perspective, Zukin examines how the cultural strategies of many urban governments, and the concomitant ideological need to impose some form of 'collective vision', have been at the forefront of urban economic policy in the United States over the last decade. And this, says Zukin, has transformed redistributive aspects of collective justice occasionally in rewarding, but frequently in discomforting, directions.

Ironically, relations of power and domination that infuse urban practices and which are contested and fought against in innumerable ways help create the differentiated public spaces that give cities such sweeping vitality. At the same time, these forms of resistance and subversion of dominant values tend only to perpetuate the conservative imagery of cities as places of chaos, disintegration and moral decay rather than as spaces where the prospect of hope, joy, and freedom resides. Guy Debord's manifesto *Society of the Spectacle* revolved around this dialectical nexus of the city as the site of freedom and the space of tyranny and exploitation.[39] His political programme revolved squarely around recapturing the urban, especially as an embodiment of *jouissance*; even though his prophetic vision spotted the coming of the anodyne theme park urbanism of the late capitalist 'spectacular order', with its war of attrition against the public space.

The public space of the city has long been the terrain for struggles, encounters, and protests. These are places symbolic of collective solidarity and of collective experience, where political encounter and dissonance is aired. Historically, people have always come together to argue and demonstrate in the public streets of the city, invariably seeking to reappropriate them and remake society in the image of its citizens. We only have to think of the exuberant force of people power on the streets of Eastern European cities in 1989, and how they helped bring down authoritarian rule. That social change is invariably sanctioned in the streets is currently acknowledged by the British Conservative government, who are paranoid and fearful of any public demonstration seeking to contest their fragile grip on British society.

The Criminal Justice Act, for instance, seeks to crush this vital encounter on the public street. Yet the struggle for empowerment, for dignity, for a more authentic urban life, will not disappear just because it is illegalized. Quite the contrary: this striving will of course go on apace everywhere where injustices reign. And it is our sincerest hope that the collection of essays assembled here might in their disparate ways somehow illuminate this going on.

NOTES

[1] Friedrich Engels, 'The Housing Question', in *Marx & Engels Collected Works, Volume 23*, Lawrence & Wishart, London, p378.

[2] Rodney Peffer's *Marxism, Morality and Social Justice*, Princeton University Press, Princeton, 1990 is a notable exception. Of those Marxists who have engaged in studies of justice and morality, however, the analytical tradition – as epitomized by G.A. Cohen and Jon Elster – is perhaps represented strongest.

[3] See Norman Geras, *Literature of Revolution*, Verso, London, 1986.

[4] Karl Marx and Friedrich Engels, 'The Communist Manifesto', reprinted in R. Tucker (ed), *The Marx-Engels Reader*, Norton, New York, 1978. Quotations are from p482, 489.

[5] David Harvey, *Social Justice and the City*, Johns Hopkins Press, Baltimore, 1973.

[6] John Rawls, *A Theory of Justice*, Harvard University Press, Cambridge, Massachussetts, 1971.

[7] John Rawls, *Political Liberalism*, Columbia University Press, New York, 1993.

[8] *Political Liberalism*, ppxvi-xvii. See Ira Katznelson in this volume for both a critique of Rawls and a defence of the necessity for taking liberalism seriously in the formulation of socially just urban strategies. Within human geography, liberalism and social justice have recently been explored by David Smith's *Geography and Social Justice*, Basil Blackwell, Oxford, 1994.

[9] Perry Anderson, 'On John Rawls', *Dissent*, Winter, 1994, p144.

[10] Karl Marx, *The Eighteenth Brumaire of Louis Bonaparte*, International Publishers, Place?, 1964, p19.

[11] It ought to be stressed that although we recognize that the quickest growing *fin-de-siècle* cities are located in the so-called 'third world' – and as Doreen Massey bleakly emphasizes, around 60% of these peoples will reside in squatter settlements – the book's emphasis is on the injustices and quest for justice prevailing in western cities.

[12] For an illustration of the US's experience here see the debate that ensued in the pages of *Dissent* over Iris Marion Young's article (e.g. 'Making Single Motherhood Normal', *Dissent*, Winter, 1994).

[13] Karl Marx, *Capital I*, International Publishers, New York, 1967, p178.

[14] Marshall Berman, 'Why Modernism Still Matters', in S. Lash and J. Friedman (eds), *Modernity and Identity*, Basil Blackwell, Oxford, 1992, p54.

[15] See Jean Baudrillard, 'The Precession of Simulcra', in *Simulations*, Semiotexte, New York, 1983.

[16] Iris Marion Young, *Justice and the Politics of Difference*, Princeton University Press, Princeton, 1990.

[17] *Ibid.*, p10.

[18] *Ibid.*, p4.

[19] 'The Housing Question', *ibid.*, p381.

[20] See *Capital I*, pp84-85.

[21] 'The Housing Question', *ibid.*, p381.

[22] See Walzer for a defence of pluralism and equality in competing 'spheres of justice'. Michael Walzer, *Spheres of Justice*, Basic Books, New York, 1983.

[23] Plato, *The Republic*, Book One, Terence Irwin (ed), Everyman Edition, London, 1935, p10.

[24] *Ibid.*, p15. Nietzsche echoes this sort of sentiment in *On the Genealogy of Morals: Basic Writings of Nietzsche*, Walter Kaufmann (ed), The Modern Library, New York, 1966. There, he writes that '[j]ustice is the good will among parties of approximately equal power to come to terms with one another, to reach an "understanding" by means of a settlement – and to *compel* parties of lesser power to reach a settlement', (pp506-7. Original emphasis.)

[25] See David Harvey, 'Class Relations, Social Justice and the Politics of Difference', in J. Squires (ed) *Principled Positions: Postmodernism and the Rediscovery of Value*, Lawrence & Wishart, London, 1993.

[26] *Ibid.*, p116.

[27] G.W.F. Hegel, *The Science of Logic*, George Allen & Unwin, London, 1969, p606.

[28] See Bertell Ollman, *Dialectical Investigations*, Routledge, New York, 1993.

[29] Squires (ed) *ibid.*

[30] P. Hirst, 'An Answer to Relativism?' in Squires (ed), p63. Hirst elsewhere tries to resolve such a dilemma via the ideal of an 'associative democracy'. This is an organization that transfers social affairs from the state towards voluntary and democratically self-governing associations. Under this doctrine, government is strengthened in and through civil society, and thus the latter increasingly takes on the qualities of the public sphere (see P. Hirst, 'Associative Democracy', *Dissent*, Spring, 1994, pp241-247).

[31] Dostoevsky's classic novel *Crime and Punishment* (1865/6), for example, explored the theme of values in a fictional sense through an episode of murder in St. Petersburg where the protagonist, Raskolnikov, experimented in the proto-Nietzschean domain of 'beyond good and evil'.

[32] Doreen Massey, 'A Global Sense of Place', in *Space, Place and Gender*, Polity Press, Cambridge, 1994.

[33] See Mike Davis, 'Fortress Los Angeles: The Militarization of Urban Space', in M. Sorkin (ed) *Variations on a Theme Park: The New American City and the End of Public Space*, Noonday, New York, 1992.

[34] See R. Gooding-Williams (ed), *Reading Rodney King/Reading Urban Uprising*, Routledge, New York, 1993; and C. Katz and N. Smith, 'LA Intifada: Interview with Mike Davis', *Social Text*, Number 33, 1992.

16

[35] See H. Lefebvre, *Everyday Life in the Modern World*, Penguin, Harmondsworth, p14.

[36] *Ibid.*, pp64-5. Lefebvre's emphasis.

[37] See, especially, H. Lefebvre, *The Production of Space*, Basil Blackwell, Oxford, 1991.

[38] Elizabeth Wilson, *The Sphinx in the City*, Virago, London, 1991.

[39] Guy Debord, *Society of the Spectacle*, Black & Red Books, Detroit, 1983.

Justice, Politics, and the Creation of Urban Space

Susan Fainstein

The 1970s marked the beginning of a new epoch in discussions of urban space. Although the project of developing theory and empirical research has advanced enormously since the initial writings of that decade, the themes developed then persevere today. In this chapter I use the early works of David Harvey, Manuel Castells, Richard Sennett, and Herbert Gans as a scaffolding for analysing how the issue of social justice has been treated in subsequent years. For the purposes of my argument I classify their approaches into a tripartite typology comprising: (1) political economy; (2) post-structuralism; and (3) urban populism.[1] These three tendencies, while all disparaging of capitalist domination, incorporate understandings of spatial relations and the built environment that differ in their visions of a socially just city and in their proposed strategies for achieving social transformation. Although all three types are built on a vision of social justice, they are vague about their normative frameworks, taking a critical stance without specifying clearly the standards by which they are evaluating the objects of their analyses. Thus, in my description of their definitions of social justice, I am imputing to them positions that are not fully spelled out or defended.[2]

The three perspectives attack the status quo of the capitalist city and seemingly occupy positions on the political left. Nevertheless, assessing their political content is complicated. Only the first is straightforward in giving primary emphasis to the causal connection between economic form, urban development, and social injustice. Consequently it remains alone in taking a traditional left stance derived from the socialist conflation of injustice with economic exploitation and justice with economic equality. Post-structuralism and urban populism are harder to pinpoint; the former, in its celebration of difference, can fade into cultural chauvinism even though its foundation lies in egalitarianism, while the latter often veers into right-wing defence of homeowner privilege and communal exclusionism despite its espousal of the democratic ethos. Indeed, the attractiveness of right-wing versions of identity politics and participatory democracy, which easily become incorporated into post-structuralist and populist political agendas, has constituted a major strategic difficulty for the left ever since the extension of the suffrage. For while the left claims to speak for the mass of people, it lacks the symbolic and material mass appeals of cultural identification and possessive individualism available to the right.

This chapter examines the critique, logic, aims, and weaknesses of each of the three bodies of thought, relying on analyses of a few thinkers to characterize the elements of each type. It identifies the greatest difficulty for the analyses presented in the tension between norms of equality, diversity, and democracy. It then inquires whether a political-economic approach can both maintain a coherent concept of social justice and develop an urban programme with majoritarian appeal. The thought of Karl Mannheim provides the basis for contending that an abstract formulation of urban social justice is possible; Mannheim's argument concerning the possibility of simultaneously holding a categorical ethic and recognizing the partiality embedded in any historical situation is used to justify the endeavour. Finally, the chapter provides examples of types of policies that could advance such an ethic within the present moment, but also recognizes that these policies may sacrifice the interests of some of society's most vulnerable and thus not wholly conform to the ethic proposed.

POLITICAL ECONOMY ANALYSES

Urban political economy encompasses a broad spectrum of viewpoints, ranging from explicitly Marxist to market-oriented approaches. For the purposes of my discussion, I restrict the definition of political-economic analysis to efforts at understanding urban development that start their explanations with economic processes and which criticize capitalist outcomes primarily on the basis of their impacts on the welfare of relatively deprived groups.[3] Political economists vary considerably according to the weight they give to purely economic causes, the extent to which they attribute autonomy to the state and to culture, and the potential that they see for reform within capitalism. Their frameworks need not be, and increasingly are not, Marxist, but there is a strong Marxist influence. Differing from liberal-pluralist analysts, they are sceptical concerning the potential for overcoming serious economic deprivation under capitalism and do not envision the possibility of full human development without the initial satisfaction of material needs.

David Harvey's *Social Justice and the City*[4] and Manuel Castells' *The Urban Question*[5] comprise the foundational works in the political economy tradition of urban analysis. Whatever the differences between Castells and Harvey and the divisions among the many scholars who subsequently elaborated and disputed their initial theses, they and those that followed them in the political-economy vein begin with economic relations and evaluate urban life in terms of a transcendent goal of economic equality.[6] Harvey's approach is to examine the history of urban development, essentially to demonstrate how the inequalities of the capitalist labour process play themselves out in spatial terms and then how the ensuing social space itself exacerbates inequality and exploitation:

> An increase in the total quantity of social surplus produced has historically been associated with the activity of urbanization.... Urban centres have frequently been 'generative' but the need to accomplish primitive accumulation [defined by Harvey as the exploitation of a section of the population in order to gain a surplus product to invest in enlarged reproduction] militates against the process being naturally and reciprocally beneficial as both Adam Smith and Jane Jacobs envision it, for the processes of primitive accumulation are, in Marx's words, 'anything but idyllic'.[7]

Further, in his emphasis on the capitalist property market, Harvey shows how spatial arrangements themselves are used to enhance the profitability of property capital at the expense of urban residents. Echoing Engels, he argues that governmental efforts at urban improvement, whether embodied in Haussmann's reconstruction of Paris or contemporary urban renewal schemes, inevitably recapitulate the miseries of the earlier situation, moving impoverished people out of one slum into another. The crux of Harvey's argument in this book is that, within a capitalist economic system, there is no escape from extremes of inequality and that the built environment must both contribute to and embody the capitalist dynamic, regardless of the programmes of even well-meaning policy-makers.[8]

Castells moves away from Harvey's preoccupation with production and circulation. His emphasis is on collective consumption and the rise of urban social movements that aim at capturing control of the local state and at redistributing the social wage. He roots urban crisis in the clash between the accumulation and legitimation needs of capital, and in a prescient prophecy concerning the future of US cities, predicts 'a new and sinister urban form: the Wild City':

> What could emerge from the current urban crisis is a simplified and heightened version of the exploitative metropolitan model with the addition of massive police repression and control exercised in a rapidly deteriorating economic setting. The suburbs will remain fragmented and isolated, the single-family homes closed off, the families keeping to themselves, the shopping centres more expensive, the highways less well-maintained but people forced to drive further to reach jobs and to obtain services, the central districts still crowded during the office hours but deserted and curfewed after 5 p.m., the city services increasingly crumbling, the public facilities less and less public, the surplus population more and more visible, the drug culture and individual violence necessarily expanding, gang society and high society ruling the bottom and the top in order to keep a 'top and bottom' social order intact, urban movements repressed and discouraged and the urban planners eventually attending more international conferences in the outer, safer world.[9]

Even before his later break with Marxist structuralism, Castells focuses on battles over distribution, on the factors that give rise to social movements, and on the potential for such movements both to encompass coalitions that straddle class divides and to achieve social progress. While alleging that urban conflict is a displacement of workplace-generated antagonisms, he nevertheless concerns himself less with the logic of capital accumulation and pays more attention to overt political conflict than Harvey.

Despite their structuralist analysis, the action agenda of the political economists, as applied to the urban milieu, largely falls well short of calls for full-fledged, class-based revolutionary activity. Defending what Lefebvre termed 'the right to the city',[10] political economists attack schemes that enhance capital accumulation to the detriment of ordinary residents. With varying hopefulness concerning the possibilities for meaningful social action, they endorse community movements that oppose large-scale economic development projects and gentrification. They support construction of housing for low-income people, especially in the form of co-ops or public ownership, criticize 'right to buy' schemes that withdraw housing from the low-income rental stock, favour rent control, and stand up for the rights of tenants, squatters, and homeless people to housing security, even when their interests come into conflict with those of working-class neighbours seeking to protect their own interests in neighbourhood stability.

Political economists focus on substance rather than process; they evaluate the outcomes of actions as they affect social groupings and judge the process that produces these results primarily in terms of its contribution to equality. Nonetheless, even though the form and extent of this allegiance are problematic, the political economy tradition reveals a general commitment to participatory democracy for two reasons. First, programmes generated by the mass of people seem to comprise the only legitimate alternative to elite-dominated decision-making. Second, an analysis that perceives of society as dominated by a small class of the economically dominant leads logically to a conclusion that rule by the relatively deprived majority would result in the defeat of economic privilege.

Political economists have thus rhetorically supported participatory democracy. Each conceivable mode of aggregating popular interests, however, raises difficult questions and has been criticized by them. For example, Katznelson points to the parochialism of neighborhood groups and the inability of community interests to affect the important decisions that determine social outcomes.[11] Castells, despite his dependence on urban social movements as the mechanisms for 'changing the urban meaning', comments that they primarily play a defensive role and are 'not agents of structural social change'.[12] His disgust with the Communist Party prevents him from regarding party structures as more effective vehicles for social transformation. Therefore, he is forced to rely on 'core' – i.e. non-territorial – political movements like environmentalism and feminism as the best alternative even in the face of their evident weaknesses as methods of addressing economic forces.

Harvey finds at most only a glimmer of hope in the varying forms of resistance to capitalist domination that have been stimulated by urbanization:

> Can a co-ordinated attack against the power of capital be mounted out of the individualism of money, the more radical conceptions of community, the progressive elements of new family structures and

gender relations, and the contested but potentially fruitful legitimacy of state power, all in alliance with the class resentments that derive from the conditions of labour and the buying and selling of labour power? The analysis of the conditions that define the urbanization of consciousness suggests that it will take the power of some such alliance to mount a real challenge to the power of capital. *But there is no natural basis of such an alliance and much to divide the potential participants.*[13]

Thus, the abstract commitment to mass equality and democracy that animates the political economy mode of analysis finds no expression in an agreed-upon mode of popular representation within a divided capitalist society.

The most obvious deficiency of the political economy approach is also its greatest strength – its starting point in the economic base of cities. By identifying the economic logic of capitalist urbanization, political economy delineates – I think correctly – the limits of reform and the recurring processes that continuously generate uneven economic development, subordination, and insecurity. But this privileging of the economic in the chain of causal explanation leads to an often mechanical calculation of real interests, as well as a denial of the validity of the subjective perceptions that drive human behaviour.[14] The tendency among political economists, as among economists of other ideological hues, is to equate economic motives with the rational and all other impetuses with the irrational. Thus, somewhat analogously to the way in which psychologists interpret individual aggressive behaviour as projections of underlying weakness, political economists have tended to ignore oppressive behaviour by working-class strata toward other non-elite groups, apparently seeing them as simple displacements of economic insecurity. The assumption is that economic competition is the only contest that really matters, and if it were eliminated other means for asserting superiority would lose their hold.

There are three serious problems with the logic that economic inequality subsumes all forms of subordination. First, both theory and empirical evidence point to the contrary argument. Thus, as Simmel argues, even after the introduction of socialism, individuals would continue to express 'their utterly inevitable passions of greed and envy, of domination and feeling of oppression, on the slight differences in social position that have remained....'[15] Group antagonisms would likely also endure. Recollections of persecution of one group by another or feelings of group superiority based on colour, nationality, or religion will not go away simply because of economic equality. Socialism as it really existed demonstrated that abolition of private property does not dissolve ethnic and gender antagonism and may even increase the importance of symbolic differences.

People's interests are not defined only by their economic position; moreover, other status determinants interact with economic interests, and causality goes in both directions. Max Weber refers to ideal interests, meaning interests in establishing one's own values. Group affiliations involve such ideal aims, but in addition status group membership and gender identification are irretrievably intertwined with real material interests. Networks of influence, based on ethnicity, lineage, gender, or some other 'traditional' relationship combine with the relations of production to generate structures of domination regardless of the mode of property ownership. Marx regarded clientelism and patronage as remnants of traditional societies that would be eradicated by capitalism, while most contemporary political economists simply ignore the question of the non-economic bases of economic power.[16] These forces, however, as well as ordinary corruption endure tenaciously within both socialist and capitalist societies and seem more dependent on culture and political process than on economic system. Their persistence corroborates the correctness of the common view that having access to people in power improves one's chances for material benefits.

A feminist perspective further points to the way in which factors separable from economic relations contribute to subordination both within and outside the economy. Feminists correctly observe that the oppression of women has existed under all economic systems, and the experience of the former Soviet bloc and Communist China shows that full participation by women in production may only partially improve their situation within the household and in a number of respects may cause it to deteriorate.[17] In fact, to the extent that women have improved their economic and social position, this amelioration has largely occurred under bourgeois capitalism.

A second problem of the political economy approach is its silence concerning the need to maintain social order under any economic system.[18] Even among those political economists who have abandoned Marxist structuralism, little mention is made of problems of social hostility except as a product of the capitalist economic system, and the socialist penchant for tracing all forms of domination to economic inequality remains. Whereas liberal political theory has sought ways by which people with differing interests or lifestyles can remain dissimilar and live peacefully together, socialist thought has typically aimed at dissolving differences and thus has not been concerned with the problems of governing antagonistic groups.[19] Liberal thinkers are always vulnerable to the argument that their institutions and procedures function to perpetuate and disguise inequality. But a demonstration that the adjudication systems of liberal democracies are biased against the poor and minorities does not mean that greater equity would result from their dissolution. Harvey does finally recognize this issue when he declares that 'a just planning and policy practice must seek out non-exclusionary and non-militarized forms of social control to contain the increasing levels of both personal and institutionalized violence without destroying capacities for empower-ment and self-expression.'[20] Harvey's simple statement of the problem, however, does not suggest a solution.

Third, an economic programme with redistribution as its central goal lacks strong appeal to popular majorities in societies where the majority feels that pursuit of such a policy would cause it to lose many of its advantages or would threaten aggregate economic prosperity. In particular, it alienates substantial portions of the stable working class, who see their security in homeownership and in separating themselves from the social strata beneath them. Moreover, solidarities based on non-economic communities have more emotional pull and indeed may provide many initially lower-income individuals with greater material gains than structural economic change that dampens class privilege.

The flaws of political economic analysis do not lie primarily in its explanation of urban phenomena as the product of capitalist economic forces. Rather, they stem first from its assurance that the problems it identifies are those that matter (or should matter) most to people; and second, from its political strategy which favours strong democracy but simultaneously rejects the choices of conservative majorities. The question of whether it is possible to retain a political economy approach and accommodate the insights of other traditions will be discussed again later.

THE POST-STRUCTURALIST VIEWPOINT

Post-structuralism is a fuzzy term encompassing a variety of formulations that emphasize contingency over structure in explaining outcomes and that therefore eschew reductionist explanations.[21] The urban post-structuralists emulate the post-modern literary critics in their use of the techniques of cultural criticism, mapping the ways in which spatial relations represent modes of domination, searching out the 'silences' and exclusions in the practices of planners and developers. In their examinations of the symbolic statements expressed by the built environment, the post-structuralists seek to show how urban form functions to manipulate consciousness.

Foucault is frequently identified as the progenitor of this theoretical tendency, but his work evades simple categorization.[22] Contemporary urban critics writing within this tradition nevertheless do take important elements from Foucault's work, especially his methodology of scrutinizing spatial elements for their social content, his insights into the use of space as an instrument of repression, and his elevation of freedom to the top of the pantheon of values.[23] Like Foucault the urban post-structuralists identify the way in which space embodies power without necessarily locating its source in particular groups of people.

The early texts of post-structuralist urbanism are Jane Jacobs's *Death and Life of Great American Cities* and Richard Sennett's *Uses of Disorder*.[24] Within urban studies the importance of post-structuralism lies in its recognition of diverse bases of social affiliation and multiple roots of oppression. This understanding in turn leads to a veneration of diversity. Whereas political-economic thought both predicts and celebrates the disappearance of racial, religious, and ethnic divides, post-structuralism expects and welcomes their persistence. In the words of Richard Sennett:

> It is the mixing of ... diverse elements that provides the materials for the 'otherness' of visibly different life styles in a city; these materials of otherness are exactly what men need to learn about in order to become adults. Unfortunately, now these diverse city groups are each drawn into themselves, nursing their anger against the others without forums of expression. By bringing them together, we will increase the conflicts expressed and decrease the possibility of an eventual explosion of violence.[25]

This theme of diversity runs consistently through the post-structuralist critique of capitalist urbanization. Thus, when identifying the blighting effects of capitalism on urban form, rather than stressing uneven development, as do the political economists, it highlights exclusivity and sterility. Post-structuralists condemn the contemporary city as the product of a white male capitalist elite imposing order on other groups with potentially unruly lifestyles.[26] Subordination is achieved through the mechanisms of city planning, which segregates uses through zoning and which isolates social groupings through the development of large projects and separated suburban communities.[27] At its extreme the drive toward exclusionism expresses itself in the gated communities chronicled by Mike Davis in his description of Los Angeles.[28] In these suburban bourgeois utopias, social homogeneity and property interests combine to create a vicious politics in which middle-class homeowner groups ally themselves with capitalist elites in a battle against progressive taxation and publicly provided social welfare benefits.

Post-structuralist urban critics such as Christine Boyer and Michael Sorkin have 'read' the lineaments of power in the form of the built environment.[29] Frequently referring back to a golden age when the city was more heterogeneous, they excoriate the artificiality and 'false diversity' of theme-part projects.[30] Emphasizing the importance of symbols in determining human consciousness, critics in this vein reject projects like London's Covent Garden and New York's South Street Seaport, which although modelled on the busy marketplaces of earlier times, produce only a simulacrum of urbanism – an 'analogous city'.[31] The purpose of such enterprises is to create an illusion of safety and to foster consumption. Instead of linking the visitor with an authentic past, these imitative schemes project him or her into a fantasy world wherein an ostensibly meaningful existence is available for purchase.[32]

Culture rather than economics becomes the root of political identity in post-structuralist thought. Individuals exist as members of socio-cultural groups from which they draw their identities, derive their welfare, and deploy strategies of resistance and purposeful action. Although post-structuralists posit difference as indissoluble, they regard the particular bases on which it is created and its expressions as socially constructed and therefore subject to change through time and place. This malleability means that social hierarchies within capitalist societies are construed as less fixed than within the political-economic analysis of capitalism. The political aim embedded within the post-structuralist tradition is the empowerment of the least powerful, which may coincide with economic betterment but is by no means limited to it. Indeed, changes in the relations among groups and the overcoming of group domination may not coincide with economic transformations.[33]

One of the strongest statements of the post-structuralist position on difference within the urban milieu is made by Iris Marion Young:

> An alternative to the ideal of community ... [is] an ideal of city life as a vision of social relations affirming group difference. As a normative ideal, city life instantiates social relations of difference without exclusion. Different groups dwell in the city alongside one another, of necessity interacting in city spaces. If city politics is to be democratic and not dominated by the point of view of one group, it must be a politics that takes account of and provides voice for the different groups that dwell together in the city without forming a community.[34]

Young claims that emancipation lies in the rejection of the assimilationist model and the assertion of a 'positive sense of group difference', wherein the group defines itself rather than being defined from the outside.[35] The politics of difference, she contends, 'promotes a notion of group solidarity against the individualism of liberal humanism'.[36]

Post-structuralists thus aim at eradicating social subordination and creating a civil society that allows the free expression of group difference. Strategically such a project fits into the American pluralist framework where ethnicity and interest groups politics have always formed the template for political activity and freedom has been the dominant value. Historically it reflects the experience of black protest movements in American cities and the women's rights movement. It clashes, however, not only with individualistic liberal humanism and assimilationism but also with the concept of the class-based mass party that has been the vehicle for the expansion of the welfare state and the rights of labour in Europe. Indeed, in their effort to transcend Marxist economic reductionism, the post-structuralists seem to have abandoned economic analysis and a recognition of class interests altogether.

Virtually by definition a view of society as consisting of multiple, dissimilar cultural groupings produces a conception of politics as based on coalitions. This is, of course, the standard perception of liberal pluralism, and within that context is wholly desirable. From a left perspective, however, such an approach is problematic. Where exclusion and oppression are identified as prevailing social characteristics of capitalist democracies and hopes for social emancipation come to rest with a coalition out-groups that share little but their antagonism to the extant social hierarchy, expectations for a coherent alternative political force are shaky. Even the identification of the components of such an alliance is difficult. In Harvey's attempt to devise a programme sensitive to post-structuralist arguments, he declares that *'just planning and policy practices must empower rather than deprive the oppressed.'*[37] But who decides who is the oppressed? Without a universalistic discourse, oppression is in the eyes of the beholder. Many members of the American middle class would accept Harvey's dictum but consider themselves oppressed by welfare cheats and high taxes, while their European counterparts construe immigration as representing a similar imposition. Identification of oppressed groups within a pluralistic framework is hardly a simple matter.

Post-structuralist thought hence gives rise to only a weak – and largely oppositional rather than positive – political expression. The socialist dream of a working class united in its common commitment to justice and equality becomes reduced to, at best, demands for tolerance and redistribution with no programme of fundamental economic reconstruction. At worst, post-structuralism leads not to the tolerance and reduction of surplus repression prescribed by its more enlightened philosophers, but to essentialism, unproductive conflict, and new forms of oppression. In some of its versions, it leaves little room for individual deviation from group norms,[38] relegitimating some of the rationales for feudal tyranny that liberal absolutism combatted in the eighteenth century.[39] Most discomforting is the tendency of post-structuralist thought in its feminist and ethnic-culturalist manifestations to take a critical stance toward other groups but to avoid self-criticism.[40] Thus, we have an acceptance of the privileged position of the oppressed and the incapacity to deal with oppression carried out by members of groups that are themselves oppressed. Examples abound, from defense of the abuse of women in communities of color to black anti-Semitism to extreme stereotyping of Western thinkers and traditions by critics of Orientalism.[41]

The goals of both democracy and diversity are particularly difficult to combine in the real world of politics, where popular sentiment for the latter is often lacking. Left critics frequently attack highly popular urban forms, from suburban housing developments to festive markets, on the grounds that they are exclusionary and sterile. But the condemnation of suburbia comprises an assault on a type of living environment for which large numbers of people have a genuine emotional attachment. And the critique of projects designed to titillate consumption smacks of cultural elitism and seems to castigate people for engaging in harmless acts that afford them enjoyment. More seriously, by defending strong group identifications and simultaneously opposing spatial segregation, post-structuralism endorses a situation in which antagonisms are openly expressed and may easily result not in increased understanding of the Other, but in cycles of hostile action and revenge. Sennett seeks to overcome this problem by dismissing the desire of groups to segregate themselves as resulting from lack of experience with a heterogeneous situation:

> If the permeability of cities' neighborhoods were increased, through zoning changes and the need to share power across comfortable ethnic lines, I believe that working-class families would become more comfortable with people unlike themselves.[42]

This argument implies that in order to get people to consent to the new arrangements, they already would have had to experience them. To force the experience, however, is to override democratic considerations and possibly to cause a ratcheting up of animosities.

Sennett uses the example of South Boston's Irish Catholic enclave to demonstrate the xenophobia that ensues from spatial isolation. After he wrote *The Uses of Disorder*, in which this discussion appears, the substance of his fears for South Boston, in fact, became manifest, as that area became the locus of extremely aggressive opposition to school desegregation. This more recent history both supports his argument concerning the effects of isolation and undermines his contention that people should be required to confront the other – forced to be free, as it were. For the court-mandated attempt to break down racial isolation proved largely counter-productive, stimulating massive white flight and leaving a sullen legacy that militated against the genuine integration of the Boston schools.[43] A democratic transition to the desirable end state of tolerance and diversity is extraordinarily difficult to achieve, even in American cities where the melting pot remains a potent ideal and immigration still commands considerable popular sentiment. In Europe, where national cultures are more defined and deeply rooted, the juxtaposition of differing cultural traditions is fraught with tension and the enduring irredentism of Northern Irish Catholics, Spanish Basques, and Bosnian Serbs dispels any illusion that proximity necessarily leads to understanding.

URBAN POPULISM

Urban populism starts with democracy as its central value. This basic orientation encompasses two intertwined but sometimes separate strands. The first consists of a thrust toward economic democracy, aimed in particular at bringing down plutocratic elites. In Todd Swanstrom's words, 'the political analysis offered by urban populism was essentially a streetwise version of elite theory: a small closed elite, stemming from the upper economic class, uses its control over wealth to manipulate government for its own selfish purposes'.[44] The urban populists share the same egalitarian aims as the political economists, but writers and activists in this tradition rarely engage in sophisticated analyses of economic structure and tend to see wealth arising from power rather than vice versa. As a social philosophy urban populism exists less in theory than in practice, where it comprises the agenda of urban political movements that oppose urban redevelopment schemes or call for public ownership of factories and utilities.

While both the political-economy and post-structuralist approaches have difficulty with majoritarian opposition to their aims and thus resort to various contentions of false or untutored consciousness, urban populism begins with popular preference. Thus Gans attacks the schemes of planners that deviate from mass taste: 'The planner has advocated policies that fit the predispositions of the upper middle class, but not those of the rest of the population.'[45] He disparages Jane Jacobs's glorification of diversity and her contention that spatial arrangements are significant determinants of that aim. In a critique that applies also to later writings by, among others, Sennett, Boyer, and Sorkin, he maintains:

> [Jacobs's] argument is built on three fundamental assumptions: that people desire diversity; that diversity is ultimately what makes cities live and that the lack of it makes them die; and that buildings, streets, and the planning principles on which they are based shape human behaviour.... Middle-class people, especially those raising children, do not want working-class – or even Bohemian – neighbourhoods. They do not want the visible vitality of a North End, but rather the quiet and the privacy obtainable in low-density neighbourhoods and elevator apartment houses.[46]

Gans's accusations thus are that Jacobs – and by extension later post-structuralists – succumbs to both an undemocratic desire to impose on others her predisposition to Bohemian colour and a fallacious belief in physical determinism.

Other writers in the urban populist tradition emphasize the elitism of planners and intellectuals in disregarding the traditional affiliations and desires of ordinary people. Harry Boyte, while committed to the aims of diversity and economic equality, attacks Marxists for failing to appreciate the contribution of religion, family, and ethnicity to people's security and well-being.[47] Peter Saunders, incensed by the failure of the British left to comprehend the desire of ordinary people for homeownership, defends Margaret Thatcher's 'Right to Buy' programme in the name of democracy. He asserts:

> The socialist case against owner occupation ... boils down to little more than an ill thought-out commitment to the ultimate value of collectivism coupled with an implicit fear of individualism.... Indeed, it can plausibly be argued that such intensely personal forms of ownership perform important psychological functions for the individual, whether in socialist, capitalist or precapitalist societies.[48]

Saunders argues that widespread homeownership can be achieved without exploitation and indicates how private owners can be prevented from profiting unduly from their possession of property.[49] Gans, Boyte, and Saunders, while seemingly susceptible to charges that they support a majoritarian effort to exploit or suppress powerless minorities, explicitly argue that their form of populism respects minorities. Thus, Gans while demanding that planners respect popular taste, also states that 'democracy is not inviolably equivalent to majority rule' and proposes 'a more egalitarian democracy' that responds to the need of minorities.[50] Boyte declares that 'democratic revolt requires ... an important measure of cultural freedom, meaning both insulation from dominant individualist, authoritarian patterns and also openness to experimentation and diversity'.[51] Saunders calls for the development of 'a coherent socialist theory of individual property ownership' that would abolish relations of exploitation.[52]

Despite their efforts to deny the democratic authoritarianism latent in their arguments, these authors nevertheless fail to confront the genuine inconsistency that afflicts democratic theory in its effort to preserve minority rights. These three writers extol neighbourhood homogeneity, citizen activism, religion, family, ethnic ties, and home in the name of democracy, and even of equality, but their arguments can easily lead to a strongly illiberal, exclusionary politics that does reinforce inequality and minority exclusion. If democratic participation is the principal value underlying the anti-elitist orientation of urban populism, how is it possible to repudiate the injustices perpetrated by homeowner movements in the United States and community-based anti-immigrant mobilizations in Europe? Social theorists who foresaw 'the revolt of the masses' as destructive of civilized values have had endless corroboration in history.[53]

The recourse of democrats who fear the intolerance that can result from majority rule is a theory of rights. As embodied in the first ten amendments of the American Constitution and the Universal Declaration of Human Rights of the United Nations, such a theory protects individuals by attributing to them inalienable rights. The vesting of rights in individuals derives intellectually from concepts of natural law and offers the only logical resolution to the problem of imbuing a democratic philosophy with a transcendent ethic that limits the actions of democratic majorities.

The vulnerability of a theory of rights is in its failure to locate the source of individual rights except in a seemingly natural intuition concerning what is ethical behaviour. Historically liberal democratic theory has particularly stressed property rights as fundamental, and it is, in fact, that emphasis that has cropped up again in American homeowner movements rather than concerns over the exercise of free speech or the protection of privacy. Thus, what is in many respects a fundamentally intolerant movement justifies itself in the name of both democracy and individual rights.

A CONSISTENT THEORY OF URBAN SOCIAL JUSTICE?

Reconciliation of the values of egalitarianism, diversity, and democracy within societies divided by class and communalism presents a supreme challenge to any left agenda. Harvey seeks to meet this challenge by both recognizing the authenticity of multiple publics and specifying a discourse that can unify a popular majority around a positive programme for social change:

> If we accept that fragmented discourses are the only authentic discourses and that no unified discourse is possible, then there is no way to challenge the overall qualities of a social system. To mount that more general challenge we need some kind of unified or unifying set of arguments. For this reason, I chose ... to take a closer look at the particular question of social justice as a basic ideal that might have more universal appeal.[54]

33

In taking this position Harvey maintains that transient coalitions among subordinate groups on particular issues do not suffice as a basis for effective mobilization. Instead he is calling for what Castells would designate as a 'core social movement'. This stance is not based on class, social status (e.g. feminism), or a substantive belief (e.g. environmentalism) but rather on a generalized concept of social justice as defined from the perspective of oppressed groups. Thus, for Harvey social transformation emanates from a coalition of people with a shared moral position in opposition to various forms of oppression.

Harvey enumerates a generalizable set of precepts on which such a movement would be based. It is possible, although he does not do so, to find the roots of his moral propositions in Kant's formulation (his 'categorical imperative') concerning the ethical actions of the individual in society.

> Kant's *first ethical formula* ran as follows: 'Act so that the maxim of thy action may serve as a general rule'; his *second formula* is: 'So act as to treat humanity, whether in thine own person or in that of any other, in every case as an end withal, never as a means only'.... Both formulas presuppose that we actually feel ourselves to be members of a kingdom of personal beings.[55]

In other words one should follow a consistent, generalizable ethic regardless of the specific circumstances; that ethic requires always putting oneself in the place of the other; and its basis is a view of people as sharing a common humanity within a social network. John Rawls later extends Kant's categorical imperative by arguing that it would be freely chosen by individuals in the 'original position' and that its meaning boils down to fairness.[56] Kant's prescription is also elaborated by Georg Simmel, who provides a concept of justice that expands the definition of fairness to encompass the ideals of freedom and equality, although not within a historical context.[57] In Simmel's interpretation, Kant's categorical imperative establishes the ideal of equality, but crucially, equality as a *freely chosen* ideal state: 'Equality supplies freedom, which is the mainspring of all ethics, with its content.'[58]

Such a choice, however, is outside history, where no choices can be made free of material and cultural constraints, as Marx and Engels never failed to point out. Indeed Kant's imperative, even as explicated by Rawls and Simmel, is stated as a pure abstraction rather than as a mandate to transform a complex world of already existing social hierarchies. A programme for social justice devised from a political-economy perspective, however, requires that history be brought into the analysis.

Harvey's ethical propositions are directed at achieving social justice within a political-economic framework that takes into account existing conditions. He essentially accepts the Kantian/Rawlsian contention that fairness comprises the basis for a social ethic, and like Simmel he defines fairness as being comprised by equality.[59] Harvey's use of a Kantian concept of social justice, however, raises fundamental problems, since any attempt to posit a general moral position is suspect within the Marxist tradition in which he places himself. Marx, in his later work, rejected the idealist tendencies of his youth and adopted a stance that Cornel West labels radical historicism: 'The radical historicist approach calls into question the very possibility of an ethics ... that claims to rest upon philosophic notions of rational necessity and/or universal obligations.'[60] Harvey, by not arguing that everyone, if thinking rationally, would adopt equality as his or her aim, does not precisely present an argument that his ethical precepts are either necessary or universal. But he does claim that they comprise 'a basic ideal that might have more universal appeal.'[61] Moreover, he does not specify the groups for whom his assertions are warranted. Crucially, do they include the middle mass of the wealthy nations? Nor does he explain how to overcome resistance to his programme without engaging in acts of repression.

Harvey is not unique among Marxist philosophers in foregoing Marx's strict limitation on foundationalism. As West points out, Marx's followers could not accept the moral relativism inherent in his view and instead sought to ground the value of equality in historical materialism. For Friedrich Engels this quest led to a teleological justification in which actions became moral if they corresponded with the direction of history; while for Georg Lukács they were legitimated by conformity with the interests of the proletariat, which were defined as universal.[62] From the vantage point of the late twentieth century, we can have little confidence in either the inevitable triumph of communism or the universality of proletarian aims – and especially not in the implementation of freedom and equality by the state in the name of the working class. Thus, the approaches of Engels and Lukács to overcoming the issue of moral relativism – an issue also raised by the work of the post-modernists – are clearly inadequate.

According to West, for Marx an individual's concept of justice derives only from his or her position within a moral community, which itself is wholly a historical product.[63] Still, even within this constraint the search for a concept of social justice has a function:

> For the radical historicist, the search for philosophic foundations or grounds for moral principles is but an edifying way of reminding (and possibly further committing) oneself and others to what particular (old or new) moral community or group of believers one belongs to.[64]

Harvey, who does not even go as far as Engels and Lukács in attempting to justify his ethical propositions, might simply be restating Simmel's formulation to the community of those who are already predisposed toward it. He seemingly, however, intends his reach to stretch further when he claims that:

> Justice and rationality take on different meanings across space and time and persons, yet the existence of everyday meanings to which people do attach importance and which to them appear unproblematic, gives the terms a political and mobilizing power that can never be neglected.[65]

FAIRNESS AND HISTORY

Engels, Lukács, and their followers read into history a meaning that is not only unverifiable but easily used to legitimate egregiously inhumane actions. In contrast, the defect of the Kantian approach is its omission of history altogether. Is it possible to develop an argument for fairness that recognizes the historical embededness of identity groups and their particularistic constructions of reality? Can such a formulation avoid the pitfalls of blame and demands for retribution that run at times through everybody's conceptions of fairness and to which individuals who identify strongly with social groupings are particularly prone? Can such a framework be deployed to criticize and transform the capitalist city?

A good place to begin is with Mannheim's 'Sociology of Knowledge'.[66] Mannheim argues for the 'acquisition of perspective' so as to overcome the 'talking past one another' of groups in conflict.[67] He calls for both deconstruction and reconstruction through examining the social origins of ideas and the relationship of modes of interpreting the world to social structure. He names this process 'relationism' and asserts that:

> Relationism does not signify that there are no criteria of rightness and wrongness in a discussion. It does insist, however, that it lies in the nature of certain assertions that they cannot be formulated absolutely, but only in terms of the perspective of a given situation.[68]

Mannheim is arguing that concepts cannot be abstracted from their historical situatedness even while nor forgoing the possibility of a transcendent ethic. At the same time he is calling for demystification and empathy, thereby assuming that this ethic will be reshaped and reinterpreted within differing historical realities. Consciousness derives from group identification *and also* from rational formulations. He assumes that when history is taken into account by all participants, thinking individuals can find a common ground. His is essentially a Hegelian exercise in its acceptance of the concept of the rational subject who is capable of making comparisons and learning. Unlike Hegel, however, Mannheim does not contend that history is reason revealed, and he takes material as well as mental forces into account.

Within Mannheim's conceptualization we can continue to hold up fairness as the key to social justice while developing its content differently depending on our standpoint and historical location. Such an activity requires both self-criticism and criticism of the other. In particular, there is no 'other', whether high or low on the social hierarchy, so privileged as to be immunized from outside criticism.

If the concept of social justice acquires a socio-historical content, the meaning of freedom incorporated within it switches from the liberal formulation of 'freedom from', as well as from the Foucaultian notion of resistance, to a more complex idea incorporating the concept of self-development. Freedom then includes the acceptance of obligations for which, in Nancy Hirschmann's words, 'consent is not only unavailable but of questionable relevance.'[69] Equality likewise shifts its connotations and is measured not by sameness of condition but by reciprocity, communication, and the mutual acceptance of obligation. Indeed some inequalities of power or benefits, stemming from rewards to merit, response to need, or the provision of general welfare, can be interpreted as just.[70]

SOCIAL JUSTICE, ACTION, AND THE CITY

It is easier to recommend an abstract concept of social justice on which members of one's own moral community can agree than to find an expression for it that will attract a mass following. Fairness in the city requires the devising of programmes that do not offend most people's concepts of just rewards, that respond to individual aspirations as well as to a formulation of the social good, and that at a minimum do no harm. How to achieve this without pandering to the forces that wall off homogeneous groups in exclusionary communities, direct unconscionable profits to developers, and reinforce the exploitation of workers is no small task.

The three bodies of thought discussed here each give priority to a value that appears inherent in a concept of social justice. But the tensions among the values of equality, diversity, and democracy endure and cannot be as easily glossed over as the contemporary left, which supports all three, would like. In particular, a commitment to democratic process, in the present historical situation, requires a willingness to accept the outcomes of that process even if they do not favour the most disadvantaged groups.

A movement for social justice, if it is to mobilize large numbers of people, must focus less on the protection of the most deprived and more on broad benefits, less on the rights of the oppressed and more on security. Most people would prefer economic growth, if any of it trickles down to them, to redistribution, if redistribution does not produce an improvement in their standard of living. Strongly targeted redistributional policies may be the most efficient method of attaining broad social benefits, but they are too suspect within the anti-tax sentiment of the present age to constitute an effective rallying point.[71]

A progressive strategy with mass appeal requires supporting urban programmes that help most people. In particular, giving housing preferences to working and lower middle class households, improving access to excellent education for talented lower-income children, and providing venture capital for small business are programmatic options that do not fit well with strongly egalitarian goals but which are popular and would make life better for a considerable sector of the urban population. Combined with an effort to direct investment away from central business districts and into neighbourhoods and to involve people in planning their communities, these actions would broaden the material well-being and reduce the alienation of many city residents, but admittedly at the short-term risk of worsening the situation of those still left out.

In part, whether these approaches amount to a progressive direction depends on their forming part of a national programme to improve the situation of working-class people. If urban strategies targeted at middle

38

strata are not part of a general broadening of economic opportunity, they will produce a zero-sum game between the working-class and the poor. A national programme directed at this goal must focus on the creation of full-time, full-benefit employment at a decent wage. Within the United States this means raising of the minimum wage, portability of health and pension benefits, and the regulation of 'temporary' jobs occupied by long-term employees who receive substandard wages and benefits. In Europe it implies a larger government role as direct sponsor of employment combined with a relaxation of private-sector labour regulations so as to introduce more flexibility into labour markets, along the Swedish model.

Such measures would not address issues of cultural conflict, which require actions within the realm of civil society. Racial and ethnic relations and conflicts over lifestyle are less amenable to becoming the object of a political programme than are questions of material distribution, yet they nevertheless must be the constant subject of critical thinking. People often want to live in situations where they do not have to constantly interact with others pursuing radically different lifestyles. In fact, and contrary to Sennett's prescriptions, the path to greater tolerance may well lie in reduced interaction (although short of the radical separation that has occurred in the US through suburban autonomy). This may mean acceptance of ability grouping (i.e. 'streaming') in schools and neighbourhood homogeneity as long as the larger framework of the school and the city remains heterogeneous.

The task is to figure out and attract people to ways of achieving equality, diversity, and democracy while being sensitive to procedural as well as social norms. Such a programme must not promote the enrichment of the few at the expense of the many and cannot be blind to hostility based on ascriptive attributes. But when one goal precludes another, perhaps there is no alternative to the old Benthamite prescription of 'the greatest good of the greatest number.' Proponents of public policy derived from negotiation express hopes that programmes can be formulated through procedures that accommodate everyone's needs.[72] This viewpoint takes an extraordinarily benign view of social power and social conflict and forgoes the political economist's insight into the substantive content of equality. Nevertheless, it does incorporate Mannheim's thesis concerning the possibility of learning. If it can be combined with a more stringent argument about the material underpinning necessary for participation in the conversation, it can then potentially provide a basis to a governing ethic for the making of an urban agenda.

Acknowledgements

I wish to thank Hooshang Amirahmadi, David Gladstone, Robert Beauregard, Chris Hamnett, Todd Swanstrom, and the editors of this volume for their comments on an earlier draft of this essay.

NOTES

[1] Like all such typologies this one does injustice to the refinements of individual thinkers and ignores the degree to which they synthesize arguments across the intellectual boundaries established here.

[2] In commenting on an early draft of this chapter, Robert Beauregard remarked that 'it is difficult to link these different perspectives to positions on social justice when they are generally silent about it.... In fact, justice is undertheorized, while issues of allocation are used in its stead.' It is, nevertheless, my contention that concepts of social justice are fundamental to the works of the writers discussed here despite their unwillingness to spell out their concepts.

[3] Although often not explicitly socialist, urban political economists operate under the vague aegis of 'democratic socialism' in Europe and 'progressive' scholarship in the US. There is also a conservative branch of political economy, which is rooted in the thought of Adam Smith and which, in its modern manifestation, expresses itself in theories of public choice and rational expectations. I am not including this perspective in my discussion.

[4] Johns Hopkins University Press, Baltimore, 1973.

[5] MIT Press, Cambridge, 1977.

[6] David Harvey deals explicitly with the question of 'a just distribution' in chapter 3 of *Social Justice and the City*. He classifies this chapter, however, as a 'liberal formulation', implying that such a normative discussion cannot be accommodated within the Marxist framework of his later work. Despite, however, the seeming inconsistency of seeking to develop a foundational ethic within a Marxist paradigm, Harvey returns to this issue in his recent work (see David Harvey, 'Social justice, postmodernism and the city', *International Journal of Urban and Regional Research [IJURR]*, 16 [December 1992], pp588-601). The issue of foundationalism will be discussed in the conclusion of this paper.

[7] Harvey, *Social Justice and the City*, p233.

[8] Neil Smith takes up the theme of uneven employment and elaborates it in his work on gentrification. The most money is to be made when the price differentials between desirably located pieces of land are greatest. Consequently capitalists are impelled to first drive down the value of property occupied by poor people until living conditions become untenable, then to clear them out and raise the value by multiples of the original amount. He goes beyond Harvey's work on ghettos and class monopoly rent by deconstructing

the symbolism involved in the takeover of space by gentrifiers and thus employs analytic tools used more often by post-structuralists than political economists. The underlying dynamic that he expounds, however, is fundamentally an economic one and the symbolic level is a legitimation of economic motives rather than an independent causal mechanism. See 'Toward a theory of gentrification: a back to the city movement by capital not people'. *Journal of the American Planning Association*, October 1979, pp538-48, and 'New City, New Frontier: The Lower East Side as Wild, Wild West', in Michael Sorkin (ed), *Variations on a Theme park*, Hill and Wang, New York, 1992.

[9] Castells, *The Urban Question*, pp426-7. Mike Davis's *City of Quartz*, Verso, London, 1990, describes contemporary Los Angeles in a way that seems to fulfil Castells's prediction.

[10] Henri Lefebvre, *La production de l'espace*, Anthropos, Paris, 1974.

[11] Ira Katznelson, *City Trenches*, Pantheon, New York, 1981.

[12] *The City and the Grassroots*, University of California Press, Berkeley, 1983, p329.

[13] David Harvey, *Consciousness and the Urban Experience*, Johns Hopkins University Press, Baltimore, 1985, p274. Italics added.

[14] For example, Bennett Harrison and Barry Bluestone, in their critique of the social impacts of conservative economic policy, comment on the particularly disadvantaged position of women and racial minorities within each category of employment. Nevertheless, their concluding chapter, which contains recommendations for 'further redistribution of wealth to root out poverty and promote equality' focuses entirely on economic measures. (*The Great U-Turn*, Basic Books, New York, 1988).

[15] *The Sociology of Georg Simmel*, Kurt H. Wolff (ed), Free Press, New York, 1950, p75. Ralf Dahrendorf similarly argues the inevitability of hierarchies of power and social differentiation. See his *Class and Class Conflict in Industrial Society*, Stanford University Press, Stanford, 1959.

[16] William Julius Wilson, in his examinations of the causes of ghetto poverty, has made the most significant recent attempt at such a discussion. See *The Declining Significance of Race*, University of Chicago Press, Chicago, 1978, and *The Truly Disadvantaged*, University of Chicago Press, Chicago, 1987.

[17] See Nanette Funk and Magda Mueller (eds), *Gender Politics and Post-Communism*, Routledge, New York, 1993.

[18] A recent, extensive discussion of the problem of order as dealt with by various social theorists is contained in Dennis Wrong, *The Problem of Order*, Macmillan, New York, 1994.

[19] This criticism was most strongly expressed by Max Weber in 'Politics as a Vocation', when he contrasted the ethic of responsibility with the ethic of absolute ends. In Hans Gerth and C. Wright Mills (eds), *From Max Weber*, Oxford University Press, New York, 1958.

[20] Harvey, 'Social Justice, Postmodernism, and the City', p600.

[21] I have chosen to use the term post-structuralist rather than post-modernist, since the latter approach appears to have faded considerably even while certain elements within it linger and have influenced the work of many thinkers. Post-structuralism incorporates feminist and cultural theories that do not necessarily accept the post-modernist emphasis on discourse and rejection of

the Enlightenment tradition. Some of the writers I am including in this category developed their outlooks before the term 'post-structural' came into common usage. Nevertheless, their arguments fit into this general framework.

[22] See his discussion in 'What Is Enlightenment?' in Paul Rabinow (ed), *The Foucault Reader*, Pantheon, New York, 1984, pp32-50, where he rejects categorization of his own thought as either structuralist or anti-structuralist, pro- or anti-Enlightenment; see also Hubert L. Dreyfus and Paul Rabinow, 'Introduction', in Dreyfus and Rabinow (eds), Michel Foucault, *Beyond Structuralism and Hermeneutics*, 2nd ed., University of Chicago Press. Chicago, 1983.

[23] See especially *Discipline and Punish: The Birth of the Prison*, Vintage, New York, 1979; and 'Space, Knowledge, and Power', in Rabinow, (ed), (1984), pp239-56.

[24] Jane Jacobs, *The Death and Life of Great American Cities*, Vintage, New York, 1961; Richard Sennett, *The Uses of Disorder*, Vintage, New York, 1970. These volumes, of course, predate the use of the term post-structuralist and do not involve a theoretical formulation of this philosophic outlook. Nevertheless, their content contains the basic precepts that later became incorporated into post-strucuralist urban criticism.

[25] *Ibid.*, p162.

[26] See Richard Sennett, *The Conscience of the Eye*, Vintage, New York, 1990; Elizabeth Wilson, *The Sphinx in the City*, Virago, London, 1991; Sharon Zukin, *Landscapes of Power*, University of California Press, Berkeley, 1991; Paul Knox (ed), *The Restless Urban Landscape*, Prentice-Hall, Englewood Cliffs, NJ, 1993.

[27] M. Sorkin (ed), *Variations on a Theme Park*, pp205-32; Fishman, *Bourgeois Utopias*, Basic Books, New York, 1987.

[28] Mike Davis, *op.cit.*

[29] See Christine Boyer, 'Cities for Sale: Merchandising History at South Street Seaport', in Sorkin (ed), (1992), pp181-204; Michael Sorkin, 'See You In Disneyland', in *ibid*.

[30] Foucault, in contrast to some of his followers, explicitly eschews any golden age mythology, condemning any 'inclination to seek out some cheap form of archaism or some imaginary past forms of happiness that people did not, in fact, have at all'. ('Space, Knowledge, and Power', in Rabinow (ed), *Foucault Reader*, p248).

[31] Trevor Boddy, 'Underground and Overhead: Building the Analogous City', in Sorkin (ed), (1992), pp123-53. While an important strand of post-structuralist cultural analysis celebrates artificiality and the spectacle, most specifically urban works denounce the creation of urban space for the purpose of commercial exploitation.

[32] In *The City Builders*, (Blackwell, Oxford, 1994), I criticize these critiques for their assumptions concerning a golden age and an authentically urban mileau.

[33] Joan Kelly-Gadol, in a well-known essay, argues that the Renaissance did not improve the lives of women and thus did not constitute a liberating turning point of history for at least half of humanity. ('Did Women Have a Renaissance?' in Renate Bridenthal and Claudia Koonz (eds), *Becoming Visible: Women in European History*, Houghton Mifflin, Boston, 1977,

pp137-64). Other supposedly liberatory activities likewise have left women unaffected or actually worsened their lot. Many have pointed to the subordination of women by New Left men as an important stimulus for the birth of the second wave of feminism.

[34] Iris Marion Young, *Justice and the Politics of Difference*, Princeton University Press, Princeton, 1990. p227.

[35] *Ibid.*, p172.

[36] *Ibid.*, p166.

[37] Harvey, 'Social Justice, Postmodernism and the City', p599. Italic in original.

[38] Young's work seems to allow little leeway for individuals to construct their identities outside their group affiliations. This is not, however, the case for Sennett.

[39] Louis Hartz, in his brilliant analysis of the dialectics of political theory, comments: 'The novel proposition [of the monarchical state] that individuals are genuinely autonomous, and equal within the state, meant that human beings could successfully become unraveled from the meaning of their prior associations. Formerly [i.e. in the feudal era] corporate attachment had defined personality; in the breakdown of the old order individuals would be redefined. (*The Necessity of Choice: Nineteenth-Century Political Thought*, edited, compiled, and prepared by Paul Roazen, Transaction, New Brunswick, NJ, 1990. p29).

[40] See Toril Moi, *Sexual/Textual Politics*, Routledge, London, 1985.

[41] Hooshang Amirahmadi terms this practice 'reverse Orientalism'.

[42] *The Uses of Disorder*, p194.

[43] See J. Anthony Lukas, *Common Ground*, Knopf, New York, 1985.

[44] Todd Swanstrom, *The Crisis of Growth Politics*, Temple University Press, Philadelphia, 1985, p129.

[45] Herbert Gans, *People and Plans*, Basic Books, New York, 1968, p21.

[46] *Ibid.*, pp28-9.

[47] Harry C. Boyte, *The Backyard Revolution*, Temple University Press, Philadelphia, 1980, Chap. 1

[48] Peter Saunders, 'The Sociological Significance of Private Property Rights in Means of Consumption', *International Journal of Urban and Regional Research*, 8(2)(1984). p219.

[49] *Ibid.*, pp218-23.

[50] Herbert Gans, *More Equality*, Pantheon, New York, 1973, pp138, 139. Italic in original.

[51] Boyte, *op.cit.*, pp38-9.

[52] 'Beyond Housing Classes', p223.

[53] See José Ortega y Gasset, *The Revolt of the Masses*, Norton, New York, 1932.

[54] 'Social Justice, Postmodernism and the City', p594.

[55] Harald Höffding, *A History of Modern Philosophy*, Volume 2, Dover, New York, 1955, p86. Italic in original.

[56] John Rawls, *A Theory of Justice*, Harvard University Press, Cambridge, Massachusetts, 1971, pp251-7.

[57] Simmel points out that in the nineteenth century the link that Kant made

between freedom and equality was severed. 'Crudely ... these ideals may be identified as the tendencies toward equality without freedom, and toward freedom without equality'. The former was taken up by socialism, the latter by liberal individualism. (*The Sociology of Georg Simmel*, p73).

[58] *Ibid.*, p72.

[59] 'Social Justice, Postmodernism and the City', pp594-600. Harvey does not state this as his purpose. Rather, it is my reading of the article that equates his view of social justice with fairness.

[60] Cornel West, *The Ethical Dimensions of Marxist Thought*, Monthly Review Press, New York, 1991, p1.

[61] 'Social Justice, Postmodernism and the City', p594.

[62] West, *op.cit.*

[63] *Ibid.*, pp98-9.

[64] *Ibid.*, p.2.

[65] 'Social Justice, Postmodernism and the City', p598.

[66] Contained in Karl Mannheim, *Ideology and Utopia*, Harcourt, Brace, & World, New York, 1936.

[67] *Ibid.*, p281.

[68] *Ibid.*, p283.

[69] Nancy J. Hirschmann, *Rethinking Obligation: A Feminist Method for Political Theory*, Cornell University Press, Ithaca, 1992, p235.

[70] See W.G. Runciman, *Relative Deprivation and Social Justice*, University of California Press, Berkeley, 1966; G. Simmel, *Sociology of Georg Simmel*, 1950, pp73-8.

[71] It is widely believed that the British Labour Party lost the 1992 election bcause it had indicated that it would increase taxes on the middle class.

[72] See Patsy Healey, 'Planning through Debate: The Communicative Turn in Planning Theory', *Town Planning Review*, 63 (2), 1992, pp143-62.

Social Justice, Liberalism, and the City: Considerations on David Harvey, John Rawls, and Karl Polanyi

Ira Katznelson

David Harvey's *Social Justice and the City* appeared two years after John Rawls published *A Theory of Justice*.[1] Respectively, these texts transformed the fields of urban studies and normative political theory. Harvey's text mobilized a renewal of the urban field by turning it away from surface and relatively trivial questions to engage the social and economic processes that structure space. Rawls re-established the capacity of abstract, deductive liberal thought to engage problems that matter, including issues of social justice, after a period in which political philosophers had become obsessed with technique at the expense of substance.

References to Rawls dot Harvey's text. He deployed them to make two points, one quite specific, the other concerned with his project of re-orienting the work urban geographers perform. The more focused claim bears on the insufficiency of an orientation to social justice, of which Rawls's theory is exemplary, that does not take issues of production into account. In effect, Harvey took up issues raised by the second of Rawls's two famous principles of justice which dealt with the conditions under which inequalities can be judged legitimate.[2]

More generally, Harvey treated Rawls as emblematic of liberal approaches he wished to supplant. He recommended the movement 'from a predisposition,' like that of Rawls, 'to regard social justice as a matter of eternal justice and morality to regard it as something contingent upon the social processes operating in society as a whole.' Harvey recorded his frustration with the limits of 'liberal formulations' and his manifest excitement in discovering the possibilities of 'socialist (Marxist) conceptions of the problem' of justice.[3] He treated these options as mutually exclusive: liberalism *or* socialism.

Social Justice is framed by four main orienting concerns. It opens by announcing attempts to overcome 'an artificial separation of methodology from philosophy'; to rethink space by focusing on 'how it is that different human practices create and make use of distinctive conceptualizations of space'; to reject concepts of social justice 'as a matter of eternal justice and morality',[4] and, to develop a relational view of urbanism 'as a vantage point from which to capture some salient features in the social processes operating in society as a whole – it becomes, as it were, a mirror in which other aspects of society can be reflected'.[5] Many of us who work on urban themes have been roused and nourished by the challenges embedded in these orienting ideas for the past two decades.[6]

These gains, however, have been purchased at the cost of leaving the domain of 'liberal formulations' entirely behind. Harvey did so, first, by insisting on the integrative power of a closed and holistic Marxism; second, by entirely ignoring the level of liberalism entailed in Rawls's first principle of justice, the one concerned with the equal distribution of political rights and liberties.[7] It is the second of these matters I wish to focus on here; that is, on the relationship between political liberalism and the city.

Some of my reasons for turning to this theme Harvey left behind are very similar to those he identified in *Social Justice*. I, too, should like to secure a close tie between methodology and philosophy, reconsider urban space, deepen our conceptions of social justice, and treat the city as a privileged and condensed perspective from which to grapple with large scale processes. I see an engagement between liberalism and the city as providing means to these ends. But some of my reasons may also be different from his.

The orientation to Marxist theory, subjects, and themes has imposed a critical constraint on the capacity of urban studies to address quite a wide swath of political questions central to our times about which the Marxist tradition either has been silent or tendentious. Marx's critique of liberal categories and rights as shams and as barriers to the creation of human subjects capable of acting effectively within a capitalist framework was thoroughgoing. So much so, that if we remain wholly within a Marxist framework it is not possible to credit the significance of such matters as the organization of conditions for the rival representation of interests or, more generally, for desirable rules of transaction to govern relations between the state and civil society.

At least since Locke, issues of this kind have fallen centrally within liberalism's sphere. Notwithstanding the masking qualities of this tradition, our century's experience of a variety of illiberal doctrines and political arrangements surely counsels us to beware any versions of socialism, republicanism, feminism, communitarianism or other critical standpoints from which to confront the power relations and complacencies of the *status quo* unless they are firmly embedded within liberal political premises and institutional practices. From its founding in early modern Europe as a code of religious toleration and as a shield against unbridled state sovereignty, liberalism has been eclectic, perhaps even promiscuous, in its programmatic orientations. Liberalism has demonstrated a capacity to bond both with capitalist and socialist impulses, with moral pluralism and monism, with appreciations of deep difference as well as with racism and very ugly versions of nationalism. If liberalism is untidy, it also is flexible.[8] Decent politics depend on a rejection of the choice about *whether* to have a liberal polity composed of individual citizens who possess the trump cards of civil and political rights.[9] The quality of our politics rests instead on the answers we discover to the question of *what kind* of liberalism we wish to have.

In this sphere of contention, various sharp critiques of liberalism, including, but not only, Marxist ones have a vital role to play in the creation of a liberalism capable of a high degree of social justice, and of recognizing and valorizing, as well as containing, deep differences based on blood and kin or on values and incommensurable ways of life. At a time when the majority of successor states to the Soviet Union and former members of the Warsaw Pact either are at war with each other or engaged in civil war, and at a time when the West is marked by racist populism, the task of building such a capable liberalism is more pressing than ever.

In recent years, say since the publication of John Rawls's

A Theory of Justice, there has been an explosion of liberal political theory. To its discredit, far too much of this work has been wilfully unconcerned with moving beyond the superficial assumptions about capitalism and markets Harvey upbraided in *Social Justice*. Much liberal theory also has searched for ideal principles suspended outside of, and apart from, specific times and places. Such a disembodied and a-historical liberalism has been insufficiently attuned to institutions and has been credulous about the character and identities of political actors. Nonetheless, liberal theory as it has developed in the past two decades or so deserves our close attention because it currently constitutes the only serious site for deliberation about the principles and convictions that might help craft desirable political regimes based on liberal foundations. Quite simply, we lack compelling alternatives.

A contrapuntal engagement of liberalism with the city, I should like to suggest, is potentially important for the manner in which it could help remedy liberal theory's insouciance with regard to issues of deep inequality and difference as well as its unrooted character.[10] At the same time, studies of the city could profit from the widening in the scope of its questions entailed in the relationship of liberalism and the city.

Students of the city presently offer two main foci of emphasis: a continuing elaboration of materialist analysis under the auspices of political economy perspectives largely drawn from Marxism, and an anti-materialist, anti-essentialist focus on culture, discourse, identity and realms of power such as the family and sexuality once relegated mistakenly to the zone of the private, as if they have nothing to do with political capacity. The tension between these impulses has been enormously productive, and it has helped produce exceptionally stimulating thinking, such as Mark Gottdiener's return to Lefebvrian considerations of space and David Harvey's grappling with postmodernity.[11] But this duopoly also has left urban studies burdened with a great zone of silence in the area of institutional-political analysis, including work on rights, constitutionalism, representation, and law. These omissions cost us a great deal, including the possibility of crafting persuasive accounts of how people who live in cities unregulated by the kind of strong moral compulsion that governed and standardised behaviour in medieval Christendom actually can live together in spite of vast differences in condition, interest, and value.

Of course, within the disciplinary subfield of urban politics, especially in the United States, work on political themes goes on all the time, but it tends to be narrow, a-theoretical, and sublimely uninformed by the innovations in urban studies that *Social Justice and the City* helped kick off; or even by any degree of self-consciousness about key thematic encounters within liberalism about such issues as the divide between public and private, individual and group rights (including those for ethnic and racial minorities), moral pluralism, entry rules to liberal citizenship, and the legitimate scope of state capacity. In turn, all of these issues have been considered by liberal political theorists and their critics, but almost wholly without a spatial or urban imagination of any kind. Surely it is possible to do better.

At our own *fin-de-siècle*, we need liberalism, but not just any liberalism. How might the compound of liberalism and the city promote a liberalism of depth and complexity? To clear ground for the pursuit of this question, I should like, first, by way of a reading of Rawls, to accent the cost of placelessness for contemporary liberal theory; second, to underscore that key themes in western liberalism and urban development have been tightly intertwined in doctrine and in practice; thus, third, to stress how attention to this relationship promises a remedy for some of liberalism's key weaknesses and an elongation of the area occupied by studies of the city. After all, although liberalism has been thought without the city, it cannot be thought about as a historical construct without the city; nor can urban studies achieve its potential unless it is open to probings about just those historical separations as between property and sovereignty, the state and civil society, and the religious and the secular, inscribed in cities, which have provided political liberalism with its central objects for deliberation.

LIBERALISM WITHOUT THE CITY

To its detriment liberalism has been thought without the city. Indeed, a good chunk of liberal theory has matured without specific reference to history or to place, except as an idealized construct. Most political theorists at work since the publication of *A Theory of Justice* have practiced what Michael Walzer calls the path of invention, where moral and political principles are fashioned as part of an analytical exercise written as if from nowhere. Arguments in this mode of work stand or fall on their own terms, without appeal either to the authority of past philosophers or the practices and political culture of the societies and groups within which they are embedded.[12]

Rawls's masterwork takes just this form of analytical reason. The well-known centrepiece elements of his text include the placement of moral actors in an imaginary situation outside of any concrete context. Deprived of information about the particularities of their communal, economic, social, or political circumstances, they are charged with the task of designing principles of justice behind this 'veil of ignorance'.

There are individuals in *A Theory of Justice* and there is society at the level of the state but there are no groups with standing and rights in the intermediate zone between state and society.[13] Actors are stripped of context and particularity. They are all presumed to share a capacity to reason of the post-Enlightenment kind on the basis of commensurable standards. Rawls presumed that reasonable actors set in a reasonable process would produce reasonable principles to guide reasonable policies and action. There is little place in this view for deep conflicts of world views and values or for either the nobility or abominations that can flow from profoundly felt particularistic identities. Rawls's social liberalism invited a confusion between a preference for a certain kind of universalism with a claim that it actually exists as the basis for moral and political reasoning. In this way, history and context enter, as it were, by the back door without examination or notice.

Of course, there is something odd about these working assumptions when they are located within liberalism's long lineage. Liberalism as a doctrine and as a set of institutional devices was created to grapple with beliefs that are more than diverse, but are charged, intractable, and characterized at times by huge asymmetries of power. The abstractions of Locke, for example, never constituted a stepping away from context and danger; nor did they elide the problem of building institutions capable of coping with and shaping a world characterized by deep ethical conflict and political division. Liberalism has searched for rules and procedures, in the here and now, to discover a balance between the acceptance of authority by convention as necessary for the creation of order and the maintenance of judgment, conscience, and choice. As opposed to various approaches that have sought to justify the imposition of authority, key elements in the liberal political imaginary are bound up with the identification of a fulcrum point for the joining of authority and consent, not in settings where universalism is taken for granted or in which agents are disembodied actors, but where identity and belief exert strong partial claims. As Steven Lukes notes, for liberalism, there was

> no recurrent renewal of consent, but rather the establishment of a way of thinking about government and authority which suggested a basis of consent, setting indeterminate and flexible limits to the power of governments. Society came to be seen as 'civil society' – the 'natural' arena in which individuals pursued their 'civil interests', which it was the function of authority to secure. And power was seen by Locke, as by Hobbes, as personal and coercive control. Hence the liberal project of both restraining the coercive power of government while claiming its authority to be based on consent and to promote the general interest.[14]

Within this framework, of course, there is a tension between the abstract equality of citizenship and the thick and textured vision of civil society constituted by individuals and groups with clashing, at times incommensurable, interests, practices, and beliefs. The centrepiece of liberalism, in this view, is the attempt to recognize and tame moral and religious conflict 'by accommodating it within the framework of the modern nation-state. The case for religious toleration was central to its development; and out of that there developed the crucial but complex thought that civil society is an arena of conflicts, which should be co-ordinated and regulated by the constitutional state.'[15] What is not certain but deeply contested is both the possibility of discovering such a balance between conflict and regulation in areas where bases for compromise are not shared and whether the discovery of any such balance necessarily entails either a politics of exclusion or an imposed flattening of profound difference. These are not questions that can be answered wholly in the sphere of logical deduction, outside history.

In recent years, Rawls has been turning to a reckoning with difference, and in so doing, he has strained against the limits of his way of working.[16] He now identifies 'the problem of political liberalism' in terms of the questions,

> How is it possible that there may exist over time a stable and just society of free and equal citizens profoundly divided by reasonable religious, philosophical, and moral doctrines? What are the fair terms of social co-operation between citizens characterized as free and equal yet divided by profound doctrinal conflict? ... *Political liberalism starts by taking to heart the absolute depth of that irreconcilable latent conflict.*[17]
> [emphasis added]

This problem is new for Rawls. While affirming liberal constitutional premises, no longer are ethical principles seen to reflect a shared morality or the reduction of people to individualist abstractions with broadly common motivations. Instead, the focus is on the conditions required for a decent public life in recognition of human complexity, variety, and possibility. No longer are there principles of justice advanced as matters of morality shared by all. Rather, they are treated as those principles that make a public political life possible based on an 'overlapping consensus' drawn from vastly different commitments and identities which, in fact, are not compatible. This is an approach grounded not in the flattening of difference but in the mutual accommodation of difference within a common public frame.

These formulations raise, but also beg, some quite fundamental issues. If the plurality of ethical views and groups is to define a public sphere where an overlapping consensus obtains, but only 'reasonable' views are admitted to this game, how is reasonable to be defined? Must people modify their deeply-held identities and preferences in order to be fit to be admitted to the liberal contest? Can views be reasonable in the now much more private sphere but not reasonable when inserted in the public? Rawls still seems to want to point toward a broadly consensual public arena without much clamour and a civil society that is diverse but which proceeds mainly by way of the separate pursuit of ways of life by distinctive social groupings. This assumption about hermetically-sealed zones of public and private, as a practical matter, seems hopelessly abstract. Further, can a single conception of justice survive the introduction of deep difference into Rawls's now much thicker social liberalism?

Rawls's portrait of human actors remains entirely rationalist. Though he smells, and fears, human propensities for non-rational solidarities and destructiveness (these, I hasten to add, are not reducible one to the other), the spirit of Hobbes and what Judith Shklar called 'a liberalism of fear' never make an appearance.[18] What is to happen when fraternity turns into chauvinism or when solidarity begats a war of all against all? Recognizing ethical pluralism, Rawls wants to keep incommensurability outside the public realm and admit to it only when reasonable and capable of contributing to his overlapping consensus. This remains a reduction in the direction of abstractness and disembodiedness.

Like most theorists who spend a lot of time developing and refining doctrines, Rawls entirely abjures the realm of institutional innovation.

I find it odd as a political scientist who does not earn his living teaching political theory to read theoretical texts that betray no interest either in actually existing institutional arrangements aimed at securing the doctrine's goals, or in literatures on groups and interest representation that of necessity have to grapple with these questions. Terms concerned with public deliberation take the place of these forms of analysis and prescription. The alternative, as Stuart Hampshire pointed out in a review of *Political Liberalism*, is a movement away from the text's misplaced rationalism toward a rationalism of institutions grounded in that part of the lineage of political thought – Montaigne, Machiavelli, Hobbes – that can ground liberalism in an appreciation of the ubiquity of conflict. 'Nowhere,' Hampshire writes, 'is there evidence, whether in the individual soul or in society, of a sovereign reason which can secure a consensus, the end of conflict, a uniform order, a harmony of interests, the heavenly city of the philosophers.'[19] Instead we must face the choice of constructing no institutions to fashion order, authoritarian ones, or democratic institutions devoted to negotiation, compromise, arbitration, and provisional outcomes.

LIBERALISM AND THE CITY

The Jerusalemite monks and sisters of St Gervais in Paris distribute a broadsheet to visitors explaining their work of urban refuge and rescue. They make it clear they wish to turn their backs on the English and French traditions of political liberalism, especially as these have developed since the Enlightenment, and on what they see as the valueless despair of the modern city. They have rightly understood that liberalism and the city are tightly coiled (from their perspective, liberalism and the city together compose one of modernity's most doleful songs).

Today, this kind of affirmation has an odd ring, whereas earlier in the century it would have seemed as obvious as it does to the community of St Gervais. A good deal of work by urbanists, notably by the Chicago School of sociology, was concerned with the impact of urban growth and differentiation on the capacities of liberal institutions and norms to accommodate a remarkable diversity of classes, races, and immigrant groups as they came to be arrayed in city space. Questions of multiculturalism and difference again have come to the fore, of course, and not just in urban studies. But about liberalism's qualities and capacities as a doctrine created to promote religious toleration and act as a prophylactic against predatory state power urbanists have grown silent.

This has been a loss on both sides of the divide of liberalism and the city. The repair of liberalism's various omissions and shortcomings can be advanced, I believe, by the kind of spatial and processual imagination that highlights the implications of the social geography of the city at different places and times. On both sides of Harvey's socialist and liberal divide, urbanists, more than any other scholarly community, have been concerned with the complex imbrication of space, class, and culture; with space and inequality; with an elaborated understanding of markets to include housing and real estate as well as capital and labour; with the implications of spatial differentiation for collective action; with order and protest and the control and regulation of spaces and people; and with the links between macro- and micro-processes elaborated at different spatial scales. These accomplishments and sensibilities – even though they have not been deployed to develop liberal political thought or doctrine – provide a vastly under-exploited resource. But this is an asset that can be deployed only if its potential is recognized by those interested in liberalism; and, in turn, if urbanists are willing to return to the 'liberal domain'. The current lack of mutuality is easy enough to explain. If Rawls and Harvey on social justice, each in his own way, revivified fields of inquiry, they and their successors have done so without any engagement to speak of.[20] The turn to Marxism within urban studies defined liberalism as Other; liberal theorists, to the extent they might have attended to studies of the city at all, would have discovered just this representation of their work. Yet the grounds for rich mutual learning are plentiful.

This claim is premised on a provocative homology. Of the vast array of definitions and approaches to cities we possess, the dual theme of concentration and differentiation predominates. Cities are places that compress and intensify. They raise population densities, amass fixed and liquid capital, crowd built-environments, amplify production, link form to power, facilitate administration and the development of multi-branched networks of communication and control, and provide locations for the defragmentation of sovereignty.[21] At the same time, cities and urban space differentiate: both in the patterns of demarcation and encirclement that distinguish between city and country and between insiders and outsiders, and in the internal social geography that inscribes separations of functions, groups, cultures, and ways of life.

Likewise, political liberalism has been concerned from the start with concentration and differentiation; in particular, with the creation and implications of the indivisibly sovereign modern state and with the break-up of a unitary Christianity; with the constitution of a citizenry of equals and with distinctions between people considered eligible to enter the liberal realm and those who are not.

Yet more than a homology, the two antinomies of concentration and differentiation characteristic of liberalism and the city are bound tightly one to the other. It is impossible to conceive of the development of liberalism without the prior growth and development of cities. Liberalism maps a world in which property has been divided from sovereignty, the person of the ruler from the institutions of rule, the zone of private life from the public sphere, and the realm of faith from the realm of physical coercion. Liberalism makes assumptions about the equal standing of members eligible to participate in a polity within a demarcated territorial zone, and it theorizes those institutions and rules that join the state to the economy and the state to civil society. Some of these elements first appeared in nascent and very rudimentary form in Europe's towns after the eleventh century, which, as differentiated zones within feudalism, defined a special legal status for town dwellers, provided protected locations for the development of autonomous law, governance, and civic associations, and made possible a political and civic pluralization with such new sources of power as universities and non-noble merchant wealth.[22] But these elements developed far more inclusively and decisively after the sixteenth century when the organic imagery and regulation/integration of feudal urban centres were supplanted by far more internally differentiated cities that were inserted into larger state units of sovereignty and protection, and, in turn, interjected into Europe's assertive overseas ambitions.[23] City institutions and spatial arrangements, drawing both on the art of perspective and the new sciences of precision, now provided more elaborated bases for conceptions of separate private and public spheres and for the division of authority between 'public rulers' and such 'private' actors as male heads of household and owners of workshops. Under these conditions of transformed urban settings marked both by the concentration of large-scale processes and by a complex differentiated social geography, unitary notions of medieval Aristotelianism no longer could hold sway. Drawing on resources already available in fresh aspects of political thought developed within the towns of the later middle ages, liberalism was born in these circumstances as a quest for new foundations for politics and regimes.[24]

By the eighteenth century, the ordered and symmetric aesthetic and architecture of absolutist capitals imposed a novel differentiation. Growing, if still very rudimentary and unevenly distributed, divisions between residence and work (the private home, in the sense of private from business, made its appearance) and between the increasingly homogeneous life-spaces of social classes (which included the first high-prestige all-residential areas) became far more pronounced than in earlier cities. Zones of commerce and manufacturing, moreover, increasingly came to be distinguishable from zones of governance and state power.[25] These spatial dynamics motored by the development of grids and markets in urban land, the extension of property ownership, and systematic planning on behalf of order and the display and protection of state power energized the links connecting rapid urban growth to the elaboration of state power and military capacity and the acceleration of trade and conquest. This powerful synergism also contributed both to the enhancement of religious authority (by way of the growing wealth of religious establishments and as a result of fusions between national and religious identities) and to its potential reduction to the realm of private conscience and individual choice.

The congestion of political, economic, and religious power in these cities provided spatial and processual bases for the elaboration of liberalism's notions of toleration and desire to put and keep powers in their place by implementing rules to circumscribe state authority, develop institutions to represent civil society-based interests in the state and thus curb its absolute autonomy, and chart a reduction in the scope of religious claims from those capable of authoritatively ordering every aspect of human life to competing preferential matters of faith. Ironically, the loss of local freedom to the courts of kings and to increasingly uniform state administration problematized the ties between rulers and others to provide a focus for an urban-generated liberalism. Cities, moreover, were sites for the creation of citizens and for demands of citizenship. They contained the most important institutions, including parliaments and law courts, that established the potential for political pluralism and rights.[26] Cities became centres for information and secularized print. Even if city speech was not free by today's standards, it was far freer than previously. Independent ideas and thought now mattered. Further, cities were physically bounded and closed. Their form divided insiders from outsiders. Unlike the

Greek *polis*, they distinguished between the rights and standing of inhabitants and those in the open countryside. Across the scope of Europe's territories, and despite considerable variation in types of urban settings and strong local identities, something of a common urban culture began to link cities by way of networks of communication, language, trade, ideas, experience, architecture and artistic sensibilities. In this way, city forms and practices facilitated the development of conceptions of identity whose polar contrasts helped liberalism distinguish in doctrine and on the ground between those who possessed the requisite character and characteristics to join its ken and those who did not. But as markets extended over larger areas and as states controlled larger, more secure, areas and succeeded in defining identities and nationality, cities also became more porous, open to flows of people, capital, communication, and ideas. Without this dynamism, liberalism's insistence on human autonomy and choice would have been merely speculative (as, of course, it was for the vast majority of city dwellers before the democratization generated by the American and French Revolutions).

Liberalism and the city, in short, compose a compelling couplet. They have been deeply intertwined for centuries. Liberalism was inconceivable either as a set of ideas or as a set of practices without the urbanization of early modern Europe. It required the multiple, intricate world made possible by the new qualities and social relations of city space. Not surprisingly, its imagery often drew on the normative and metaphysical reservoir of representations of the city as being in possession of high moral qualities as sites of refuge and locations for political emancipation and free citizenship.

THE CITY WITHOUT LIBERALISM

It is this subject matter that has lacked attention and analysis, and not just for the foundational period in early modern Europe. The positivist impulse in urban studies – whether in geography, sociology, or other fields – has taken its postulates about choice and its market imagery so for granted that it has denuded the 'liberal' side of David Harvey's divide, from which he recoiled with good reason. On the 'socialist' side, these issues have been understood either as secondary or they have been left unexamined. Furthermore, just as Marxism's intellectual development suffered from its silence about cities and space during the long period from Engels to Lefebvre, so liberalism as political theory continues to pay a non-trivial price for its comparable disinterest. What Harvey labelled as liberal urban studies continue to prosper in the sense of dominating the field in quantity of work, but as far as I can tell they have had almost no impact on the thought of the theorists who have tried to make sense of liberalism's politics and possibilities.

Harvey's contrast between liberal and socialist formulations was not designed as a comparison of equivalents. In addition to the opposition of surface and depth, he also intended the movement from one to the other epistemic grounding to prolapse the familiar distinction between spatial forms and social processes. Within the liberal domain as he had experienced it, the two had appeared as irreconcilable. Within the socialist one, however, 'spatial forms are there seen not as inanimate objects within which the social process unfolds, but as things which "contain" social processes in the same manner that social processes *are* spatial'.[27] Similarly, in *Marxism and the City*, I opposed the social process formulations of Marxism to the more lank differentiation approaches of mainstream urbanism, which tended to collapse the object of urban differentiation with its causes. But it would be a mistake to simply identify the contrast between differentiation and social process approaches as identical to that dividing liberal and socialist conceptions. As Weber's brilliant social process analysis of medieval towns and governance demonstrates, it is possible to mount such accounts on both sides of Harvey's divide.[28] Rather than choose between them, as in his attempt to move to better and stronger ground, I prefer to insist, first, on the possibility of a social process approach to the analysis of liberalism (as well Marxism) and the city; and, second, that a rotation in our axes of attention and explanation can be salutary.[29] I shall conclude with an example of what I have in mind, turning initially back to Harvey.

Social Justice and the City culminates in a magisterial chapter on 'Urbanism and the City'. Aside from the work of Marx, it pivots on the scholarship of Karl Polanyi, especially his economic anthropology.[30] Harvey draws on Polyani's typology of types of economic integration and, by connecting it with Marx on surplus value, discusses their links with urbanism. 'It is the central thesis of this essay', Harvey wrote, 'that by bringing together the conceptual frameworks surrounding (1) the surplus concept, (2) the mode of economic integration concept and (3) concepts of spatial integration, we will arrive at an overall framework for interpreting urbanism and its tangible expression, the city'.[31]

The typology Harvey deploys distinguishes between reciprocity (the exchange of goods, favours, and services among people in a group in accordance with social custom); redistribution (the flow of goods in and out of a centre to support the lifestyle of elites); and market exchange (characterized by bargaining over prices rather than set prices). Reciprocity as the dominant mode of exchange is incompatible with urbanism; redistribution only supports an urbanism of central places; while markets together with the extraction of surplus value facilitate concentrations of surplus labour value. The city thus is conceptualized as the locale for disposing of surplus product, and the space economy is the site for the circulation of surplus value.

Harvey's artful combination of Polanyi's macro-history with quite an orthodox reading of Marx's *Capital* took three steps. First, it elaborated Polanyi's typology; then it deployed the concept of surplus value and showed how it is linked to space; last, it argued that 'the relationships between the modes of economic integration, the creation of the social surplus and the various forms of urbanism' with the development of the notion of 'the concept of the "balance of influence" among the different modes of economic integration in a particular period'.[32] Harvey deployed this engagement of Marx and Polanyi to describe, analytically, the current situation. 'The contemporary metropolis', he argues, 'is a veritable palimpsest of social forms constructed in the image of reciprocity, redistribution, and market exchange. Surplus value, as it is socially defined under the capitalist order, circulates within society, moving freely along some channels while being reduced to a mere trickle among others.'[33]

This effort, like a good deal of subsequent work by Harvey, combines a fertile and flexible analytical approach with stringently applied Marxist criteria. Like any other such effort, it possesses the defects of its virtues. Its insistence on supplanting liberal formulations has the effect of reading Polanyi only partially and, as a result, of eliding a close analysis of key issues – especially as they concern residential differentiation – that Harvey himself wishes to explore.

Polanyi was not just the materialist historian of economic exchange deployed by Harvey, but one of this century's most acute analysts of the doctrine and institutions of modern liberalism. *The Great Transformation*, in particular, is concerned to establish the *political* origins of our times by demonstrating that the movement from prior mechanisms of economic integration to markets was an institutional process organized by states acting in accordance with the policy dictates of liberal theory. Polanyi further shows how the combination of economic and political liberalism proved unstable because the very same people who had to make their way within labour markets also were citizens, with rights and the vote, who insisted the state protect them from the ravages of the marketplace. Liberalism, on this reading, is inherently multiplex and contradictory. Understanding the first four decades of the twentieth century in these terms, Polanyi lamented the breakdown of the liberal order and sought to reconstruct it in order to avoid the nasty combination of global war, economic depression, and anti-liberal 'totalitarian dictatorships' of the right and the left.[34]

Polanyi, in short, was a liberal realist. His grounded analyses occupied intellectual and normative space located, as it were, between Harvey, who understands the tight constraints of different economic forms, and Rawls, who searches at a high level of abstraction for theory capable of connecting economic and political liberalism to deliver both stability and social justice. What Rawls sought to figure out was how to introduce equality into the heart of a liberal order in spite of its capitalist grounding and how to shape political institutions and public policies in such a way as to make it possible for people who differ in class, moral, and group terms to live together under common decent rules.

Harvey's deliberate decision to supersede liberalism thus cost the ability to tap into the linkages characteristic of the work of Polanyi and with it our capacity to connect with, rather than override, the concerns raised by Rawls and other recent liberal thinkers about justice, pluralism, and social peace. Earlier, I lamented the price exacted for political morality. I should like to close by suggesting that it also has been considerable for questions more usually found at the centre of materialist approaches to the city.

Consider housing and spatial differentiation by way of an example. Harvey briefly takes up these matters near the end of 'Urbanism and the City':

> Since the self-regulating market leads different income groups to occupy different locations we can view the geographical patterns in urban residential structure as a tangible geographical expression of a structural condition in the capitalist economy. Residential segregation in the contemporary metropolis is therefore fundamentally different from the residential segregation exhibited in typical redistributive cities which was largely symbolic.[35]

Harvey, of course, has returned to these issues in later scholarship, but always with the orientation of showing how urban social geography is shaped fundamentally by capitalism at work. The political enters this work, as it does here, in functional terms; and variations are explained as the products of the continuing presence of reciprocity and redistribution as countervailing forces. But in this rendering, the challenges posed by Polanyi and Rawls are left out of consideration. Having decided to suppress the liberal dimension, Harvey has no choice but to overlook how the working out of liberal political institutions actually shaped the development of independent, quasi-autonomous, housing markets or how, under conditions of spatial differentiation, residents of the city map urban space and discover ways to live together, negotiate relationships, and fight for change under conditions that stop short of revolution or the wholesale transformation of the mode of production.

A full Polanyian analysis of housing and spatial segregation, rather than the partial one Harvey provides, perforce would contain a more multiple account of the origins and reproduction of housing markets, more attention to the politics of spatial contest treated not only as holdovers from older communitarian traditions romantically understood, more notice of group pluralism in more than the single dimension of class, more of a concentration on law and public policy, and more of an orientation to the mutual impact of institutions, political norms, and patterns of identity and agency. And it would focus on questions of working-class formation not only in relation to the impact of capitalist exploitation but by considering 'the worker' at home, at work, and as a citizen.

In these respects, I really am doing no more than reiterating and extending the agenda on housing and space announced a decade ago by Christian Topalov.[36] Bearing Harvey's important work in mind, he criticized research on urbanization and the production of housing for having treated the conflict between labour and capital only in a very formalistic way in functionalist accounts which leave workers out as historical actors. Instead, he called for concrete historical studies of transformations of ways of work and ways of life, understanding that both spheres are sites of struggle tied to economic, political, and spatial development. By treating ways of life as ways both of compliance and resistance, Topalov advocated studies of linkages between social history, social policy, and the welfare state. To this I wish to advocate a more explicit focus on liberal institutions, doctrine, and norms in light of our ever more clear understanding that western working classes – especially, but not exclusively, in Britain and the United States – have interacted with and have been shaped by the liberal as much as the socialist tradition.[37] Even with respect to subjects at the heart of materialist urban studies, much conceptual and empirical enrichment can be secured by attending to issues central to liberal political thought and to a focus on institutions, rules, law, and negotiation so basic to political liberalism.

NOTES

[1] David Harvey, *Social Justice and the City*, Edward Arnold, London, 1973; John Rawls, *A Theory of Justice*, Harvard University Press, Cambridge, Massachusetts, 1971.

[2] It 'holds that social and economic inequalities, for example inequalities of wealth and authority, are just only if they result in compensating benefits for everyone, and in particular for the least advantaged members of society'. Rawls, *ibid.*, pp14-15.

[3] Harvey, *op.cit.*, p15.

[4] Harvey obviously had in mind the then recently published treatise by John Rawls, *op.cit.*

[5] Harvey, *op.cit.*, pp11, 13, 14, 15. Harvey's relational approach regarded space 'in the manner of Leibniz, as being contained *in* objects in the sense that an object can be said to exist only insofar as it contains and represents within itself relationships to other objects.' (p13)

[6] For my views, see Ira Katznelson, *Marxism and the City*, Clarendon Press, Oxford, 1992, especially chapters 1 and 3.

[7] 'Each person is to have an equal right to the most basic extensive total system of equal basic liberties compatible with a similar system of liberty for all.' Rawls, *op.cit.*, p302.

[8] 'It can comprehend Nozick, who thinks anything other than a minimum state is a recipe for tyranny, and Rawls, who is prepared to advocate a fair amount of redistributive intervention. But the flexibility of liberalism is also its strength.' Peter Pulzer, 'Ideologues', *London Review of Books*, 20 February 1986, p9.

[9] The formulation of rights as trump cards for persons against various sources of tyranny can be found in Ronald Dworkin, 'Liberalism', in Stuart Hampshire, (ed), *Public and Private Morality*, Cambridge University Press, Cambridge, 1978.

[10] The latter is a criticism frequently mounted by communitarian critics. See, for a lucid example, Michael Walzer, *Interpretation and Social Criticism*, Harvard University Press, Cambridge, Massachusetts, 1987.

[11] Mark Gottdiener, *The Social Production of Urban Space*, University of Texas Press, Austin, 1985; David Harvey, *The Condition of Postmodernity*, Blackwell, Oxford, 1989.

[12] Walzer, op.cit., p3; Tom Nagel, *The View from Nowhere*, Oxford University Press, Oxford, 1986. To this impulse, Walzer opposes his preferred option, the role of the theorist as a social critic from somewhere who follows the path of interpretation.

[13] This point was made well before multiculturalist critiques became fashionable by Vernon Van Dyke, 'Justice as Fairness', *American Political Science Review*, June 1975.

[14] Steven Lukes, *Moral Conflict and Politics*, Clarendon Press, Oxford, 1991, pp111-112.

[15] Lukes, *ibid.*, p17.

[16] These have now been collected and revised in John Rawls, *Political Liberalism*, Columbia University Press, New York, 1993.

[17] Rawls, *Political Liberalism*, ppxxv-xxvi.

[18] Judith N. Shklar, 'The Liberalism of Fear', in Nancy L. Rosenblum, (ed), *Liberalism and the Moral Life*, Harvard University Press, Cambridge, Massachusetts, 1989.

[19] Stuart Hampshire, 'Liberalism: The New Twist', *New York Review of Books*, August 12, 1993, p46.

[20] Recall the famous 1956 formulation of Peter Laslett in the first in a series of edited books devoted to its revival, that 'for the moment, anyway, political philosophy is now dead.' Laslett and his new collaborator W.G. Runciman cited this declaration in the third, 1969, volume that featured an essay by Rawls on 'Distributive Justice' and was marked by what they now saw as a renewal getting underway. Peter Laslett and W.G. Runciman, (eds), *Philosophy, Politics, and Society*, Third Series, Basil Blackwell, Oxford, 1969. The state of urban theory in this period could have been described in the same terms as Laslett's 1956 dispirited view of the situation of political philosophy.

[21] Of course, not all cities concentrate elements and processes equally. Thus Charles Tilly, who 'schematizes the relationship between cities and states as an interaction of capital and coercion', notes that 'the distinction applies to individual cities; European ports such as Amsterdam and Barcelona typically wallowed in capital while having relatively thin coercive apparatuses; seats of monarchy such as Berlin and Madrid, on the other hand, stood much higher with respect to coercion than to capital'. Charles Tilly, *Coercion, Capital, and European States, AD990-1990*, Basil Blackwell, Oxford, 1990, p56.

[22] A useful discussion of the civic imagery and political theory of medieval Europe can be found in Antony Black, *Political Thought in Europe, 1250-1450*, Cambridge University Press, Cambridge, 1992, chapter 4.

[23] In time, these produced important new urban settlements overseas, which, in some places, provided important extra-European sites for the elaboration of liberal political thought and practices.

[24] A provocative discussion along these lines can be found in Andrezej Rapaczynski, *Nature and Politics: Liberalism in the Philosophies of Hobbes, Locke, and Rousseau*, Cornell University Press, Ithaca, New York, 1987.

[25] There is a massive literature on these subjects. A useful recent volume focusing on the reorganization of the physical city is Leonardo Benevolo, *The European City*, Basil Blackwell, Oxford, 1993.

[26] The financial and commercial institutions in these cities also concentrated in

specific buildings and locations, congesting the class power with which state rulers had to negotiate rather than merely coerce.

[27] Harvey, *op.cit.*, pp10-11.

[28] Ira Katznelson, *ibid.*, Chapter One.

[29] My guide in this respect is Albert Hirschman's brilliant analysis of 'Rival Interpretations of Market Society', in which he invites us to ponder whether quite different theories and approaches might not either have their subjects, moments, or places of relative truth, and whether dialectical combinations of theories and approaches might not yield better understandings than any single one on its own terms. Albert O. Hirschman, 'Rival Interpretations of Market Society: Civilizing, Destructive, or Feeble?', *Journal of Economic Literature*, December 1982, p1483. It was with an amended version of this citation, with 'Marxism' substituted in brackets for 'social science', that I concluded *Marxism and the City*, p308.

[30] Karl Polanyi, *The Great Transformation: The Political and Economic Origins of Our Time*, Beacon Books, Boston, 1944; and G. Dalton (ed), *Primitive, Archaic, and Modern Economies: Essays of Karl Polanyi*, Beacon Books, Boston, 1968.

[31] Harvey, *op.cit.*, pp245-246.

[32] Harvey, *ibid.*, p240.

[33] Harvey, *ibid.*, p245.

[34] Polanyi, *op.cit.*, p28.

[35] Harvey, *op.cit.*, p273.

[36] Christian Topalov, 'Social Policies from Below: A Call for Comparative Historical Studies', *International Journal of Urban and Regional Research*, 9 (2), 1985.

[37] See, for discussions, Eugenio F. Biagini, *Liberty, Retrenchment, and Reform: Popular Radicalism in the Age of Gladstone, 1860–1880*, Cambridge University Press, Cambridge, 1992; Eugenio F. Biagini and Alastair Reid (eds), *Currents of Radicalism: Popular Radicalism, Organised Labour and Party Politics in Britain, 1850–1914*, Cambridge University Press, Cambridge, 1991; and John Breuilly, *Labour and Liberalism in Nineteenth-Century Europe: Essays in Comparative History*, Manchester University Press, Manchester, 1992.

The Environment of Justice

David Harvey

The bourgoisie has only one solution to its pollution problems: it moves them around

(saying adapted from Friedrich Engels)

I THE MOVEMENT FOR ENVIRONMENTAL JUSTICE

The Economist (September 8 1992) reported on a leaked World Bank internal memorandum (dated 12 December 1991) from the pen of Lawrence Summers, a Harvard economist of considerable reputation (nephew of Paul Samuelson and son-in-law of Kenneth Arrow, both Nobel prize-winners in economics). Summers, an oft-quoted advisor to Democratic Presidential candidates, then chief economist of the World Bank and subsequently Undersecretary of State for Trade in the Clinton Administration wrote:

> Just between you and me, shouldn't the World Bank be encouraging more migration of the dirty industries to the LDC's (Lesser-Developed Countries)? I can think of three reasons:
> (1) The measurement of the costs of health-impairing pollution depends on the foregone earnings from increased morbidity and mortality. From this point of view a given amount of health-impairing pollution should be done in the country with the lowest cost, which will be the country with the lowest wages. I think the economic logic behind dumping a load of toxic waste in the lowest-wage country is impeccable and we should face up to that.
> (2) The costs of pollution are likely to be non-linear as the initial increments of pollution probably have very low cost. I've always thought that under-populated countries in Africa are vastly *under-*polluted; their (air pollution) is probably vastly inefficiently low compared to Los Angeles or Mexico City. Only the lamentable facts that so much pollution is generated by non-tradable industries (transport, electrical generation) and that the unit transport costs of solid

waste are so high prevent world welfare-enhancing trade in air pollution and waste.

(3) The demand for a clean environment for aesthetic and health reasons is likely to have very high income elasticity. The concern over an agent that causes a one in a million change in the odds of prostate cancer is obviously going to be much higher in a country where people survive to get prostate cancer than in a country where under-5 mortality is 200 per thousand. Also, much of the concern over industrial atmosphere discharge is about visibility of particulates. These discharges may have little direct health impact. Clearly trade in goods that embody aesthetic pollution concerns could be welfare enhancing. While production is mobile the consumption of pretty air is a non-tradable.

The Washington Office of Greenpeace faxed copies of the memo around the world. Environmental groups had, and continue to have a field day. The World Bank, already a strong focus for criticism for its lack of environmental concerns, was put very much on the defensive at the very moment it was seeking to influence the Rio Summit on the Environment through publication of its 1992 Report on Development and the Environment. Brazil's Secretary of the Environment described Summers's reasoning as 'perfectly logical but totally insane'. Summers was featured in *People Magazine* in its special Earth Day issue as one of the top eight 'enemies of the earth' and even *The Financial Times* thought it time to 'save planet earth from economists'.[1] *The Economist*, however, editorialised that his economic logic was indeed 'impeccable'.

The Summers memo appears to endorse 'toxic colonialism' or 'toxic imperialism'. The final paragraph of the memo points out, however, that the problem with all of these arguments is that they 'could be turned around and used more or less effectively against every Bank proposal.' This suggests that Summers was not himself endorsing such ideas but trying to point out to his colleagues the logical consequences of their own mode of thought. While this may exculpate Summers somewhat, it broadens the questions the memo raised to a whole mode of discourse about environmental issues.

So what objections can be raised? To begin with, the class situatedness of the argument is transparent. Affluent groups, including most professional economists (median weekly earnings of $889 in the USA in 1994)[2] do not have to accept toxic wastes on their own doorstep to survive whereas child care workers ($158 per week), janitors and cleaners ($293 per week) and sewing machine operators ($316 per week) do not have the same range of choice. The logic also pays scant attention to questions of distributive justice, except in the narrowest sense that trade in toxics is meant to be 'welfare-enhancing' for all. This presumes that one way to raise incomes of the poor is to pay them to absorb toxins (largely generated on behalf of the rich). Any negative health impacts, it should be noted, will then be visited on those least able to deal with them. Since most of the poor and the disempowered are people of colour, the impact is racially discriminatory. And if we care to think about it at all, there is a symbolic dimension, a kind of 'cultural imperialism' embedded in the whole proposal – are we not presuming that only trashy people can stomach trash? The question of stigmatization of the Other through, in this instance, association of racially marked others with pollution, defilement, impurity and degradation becomes a part of the political equation. If, as Douglas claims, 'some pollutions are used as analogies for expressing a general view of the social order', and if 'pollution beliefs can be used in a dialogue of claims and counter-claims to status', then claims about pollution as 'matter out of place' cannot be separated from claims about the impurities and dangers of 'people out of place.'[3]

Questions of how and why 'wastes' in general and hazardous wastes in particular are produced in the first place are, of course, never even mentioned in discussions of the Summers's sort. Yet, as Commoner has, among others, again and again emphasized, the question of *prevention* surely should take precedence over disposal and cure of any side-effects.[4] But posing that question requires a discursive shift on to the far more politically charged terrain of critique of the general characteristics of the mode of production and consumption in which we live.

Though the 'impeccable economic logic' advanced by Summers is not hard to deconstruct as the characteristic discourse of a particular kind of political-economic power and its discriminatory practices, it unfortunately approximates as a description of what usually happens. The market mechanism 'naturally' works that way. Property values are lower close to noxious facilities and that is where the poor and the disadvantaged are by and large forced by their impoverished circumstances to live. The insertion of a noxious facility causes less disturbance to property values in low income areas so that an 'optimal' lowest cost location strategy for any noxious facility points to where the poor live. Furthermore, a small transfer payment to cover negative effects may be very significant to and therefore more easily accepted by the poor, but largely irrelevant to the rich, leading to what I long ago referred to as the 'intriguing paradox' in which 'the rich are unlikely to give up an amenity "at any price" whereas the poor who are least able to sustain the loss are likely to sacrifice it for a trifling sum.'[5] If, as is usually the case, areas where low-income, disempowered and marginalised Others live are also zones of poor political organization, and weak political resistance, then the symbolic, political and economic logic for the location of noxious facilities works in exactly the way that the Summers's memo envisages.

As a consequence, one of the best predictors of the location of toxic waste dumps in the United States is a geographical concentration of people of low-income and colour. The dumping of toxic wastes in indigenous Indian reservations or in communities of colour (African-American or Hispanic) across much of the South and West of the United States is now well documented. Even more remarkable, are the bidding wars between, for example, different native American groups or lesser-developed countries to accommodate the waste in return for money incomes. While that practice might be better understood in the case of dictators or military regimes who receive all the benefits while visiting the costs on their own populations, it is not unknown for reasonably democratic debate to generate a political consensus in favour of accepting toxic waste facilities on the grounds that this generates otherwise unavailable income and employment. In Alabama's 'Blackbelt' the question of hazardous land fills in Sumter County is politically contested: those who have most to lose from denying the facility, in terms of jobs and incomes (the poor and people of colour), are in this instance at odds with the middle class and often white environmentalists who seek to close such facilities down.[7] The same conflict holds in Mississippi.[8] The political economy of waste creation and circulation under capitalism incorporates Summers's logic, including some of its inherent social contradictions.

The practice of that logic has sparked militant resistance. In the United States, the movement for environmental justice and against environmental racism has become a significant political force. It is a political movement that has been long in gestation, owing its most recent reincarnation to two particular incidents. First, the celebrated case of Love Canal in 1977, when houses built on top of an infilled-canal in Buffalo, New York, found their basements full of noxious liquids with serious health effects on resident children.[9] This led to the formation of a Citizen's Clearing House for Hazardous Waste which, according to Taylor, now works with over 7,000 community and grass-roots groups nationwide. The second arose out of the 1982 protests in Warren County, North Carolina, when a mostly African-American community was selected as the site for burial of soil contaminated with PCB's. The vigour of the protests (multiple arrests of well-known civil rights figures) and the involvement of a wide range of organizations focused attention on what soon came to be known as 'environmental racism'. In 1991, a very dispersed and highly localised movement came together around the First National People of Color Environmental Leadership Summit held in Washington, DC. There it adopted a manifesto defining environmental justice in no less than 17 different clauses. I select just a few:

> *Environmental justice:*
> 'affirms the sacredness of Mother Earth, ecological unity and the interdependence of all species, and the right to be free from ecological destruction.
> 'mandates the right to ethical, balanced and responsible uses of land and renewable resources in the interest of a sustainable planet for humans and other living things.
> 'demands the cessation of the production of toxins, hazardous wastes, and radioactive materials, and that all past and current producers be held strictly accountable to the people for detoxification and the containment at the point of production.
> 'affirms the need for urban and rural ecological policies to clean up and rebuild our cities and rural areas in balance with nature, honouring the cultural integrity of all our communities, and providing fair access for all to the full range of resources.
> 'opposes the destructive operations of multi-national corporations ... military occupation, repression and exploitation of lands, peoples and cultures, and other life forms.
> 'requires that we, as individuals, make personal and consumer choices to consume as little of Mother Earth's resources and to produce as little waste as possible; and make the conscious decision to challenge and reprioritize our lifestyles to insure the health of the natural world for present and future generations'

I shall return to these principles later, though it is not hard to see how many professionals might regard them as just as 'insane' as Summers's memo, while lacking the virtue of elementary let alone 'impeccable' logic. The militant local struggles for environmental justice that coalesced to advance these theses created sufficient national political ferment, however, to force the Environmental Protection Agency (EPA), even in its most recalcitrant Reagan–Bush years, to take up the issue of environmental equity. The EPA's 1992 report on that issue conceded that there were problems of unequal exposure of minority and low-income populations to environmental risks, but asserted that there was not enough hard information to substantiate effective discrimination (except in the case of lead poisoning). In February 1994, however, the Clinton administration – responding to its constituencies of environmentalists, minorities and the poor – issued an executive order to all federal agencies to ensure that programmes would not unfairly inflict environmental harm on the poor and minorities. This means that the environmental needs of low-income and minority communities must be fairly addressed and that environmental issues can be adjudicated in terms of civil rights.

That move did not pacify many in the environmental justice movement in part because they recognized that co-optation into such a legal-political quagmire would be the kiss of death. The reason that hardly any new hazardous waste sites have been opened these last ten years has to do precisely with the fact that movements against such sites have been organised outside of 'channels'. For this reason too, the environmental justice movement has frequently been at odds with the main environmental groups (such as Friends of the Earth, The Sierra Club, the Environmental Defense Fund, etc – usually referred to as 'the Big Ten'). The division here reflects class, race and gender. People of colour and working-class women have been most active in the grass roots movement whereas the Big Ten are dominated, in membership but more particularly in organization, by white, middle-class professional men. The sort of distinction in allegiance and membership has been playfully characterised as follows:

> Citizen's Clearinghouse – 'typical member: quit the church choir to organize toxic dump protest.' Natural Resources Defense Council – 'typical member: Andover '63, Yale '67, Harvard Law '70, Pentagon anti-war marches '68, '69, '70.' Environmental Defense Fund – 'typical member: lawyer with a green conscience and a red Miata ...'[10]

This does not imply that all forms of co-operation are ruled out – Greenpeace helped the Concerned Citizens of South Central Los Angeles (organised primarily by women) to fight off the LANCER mass-burn incinerator (designed to serve 1.4 million people throughout the city) that was to be located in a poor and heavily minority community.[11] Nevertheless, the environmental justice movement preserves its fiercely independent 'militant particularism'.[12] It rejects government and broadly 'bourgeois' attempts at co-optation and absorption into a middle-class and professional-based resistance to that impeccable economic logic of environmental hazards that the circulation of capital defines.

What we encounter here, are radically different discourses within which environmental issues get framed and from which political and social action follows. But discourses, as Foucault correctly argues, are forms of power that have institutional bases. The discourse of the World Bank is therefore radically different from that of some local community. With this in mind, let me outline what seem to be the dominant forms of discourse about the environment in the late twentieth century and then to go on to try and locate the environmental justice discourse in relation to such dominant power relations.

II THE 'STANDARD VIEW' OF ENVIRONMENTAL MANAGEMENT

Capitalism has frequently encountered environmental problems. Over the last two centuries or so institutions, scientific understandings, public policies and regulatory practices have been evolved to deal with them. These practices have converged over time on to something that I will call 'the standard view' of environmental management in advanced capitalist societies.

In the standard view, the general approach to environmental problems is to intervene only 'after the event'. This strategy in part stems from the belief that no general environmental concerns should stand in the way of 'progress' (more precisely, capital accumulation) and that any 'after the event' environmental difficulties can be effectively cleaned up if need be. This implies no irreversibility problems of the sort that arise with species extinction or habitat destruction and that a 'remedial science' exists to cope with any difficulties that do arise. This 'after the event' emphasis means that environmental issues are essentially regarded as 'incidents' – the result of 'errors' and 'mistakes' (often based on ignorance) – that should be dealt with on a case-by-case and hence fragmented basis. The preference is for environmental clean-ups and 'end of pipe' solutions (e.g. the installation of scrubbers on smokestacks, catalytic converters in cars, etc.) rather than for preemptive or proactive interventions.

The only general problem admitted under the standard view is so-called 'market failure' which occurs because firms (or other

71

economic entities such as governments and households) can 'externalise' costs by free use of the environment for procuring resources or for waste disposal. The theory of the firm developed in neoclassical economics effectively describes why it might be economically rational for individual firms to plunder common resources like fisheries (the famous 'tragedy of the commons' argument advanced by Hardin), to pollute, to expose workers to toxic hazards and consumers to environmental degradation under conditions of market failure. It then becomes the task of the state to evolve a regulatory framework that either forces firms to internalise the external costs (generate a more perfect market that factors in all real costs including those attributable to environmental degradation) or to mandate standards that firms (or other entities) must meet with respect to resource management, occupational safety and health, environmental impacts and the like. It also becomes the task of the state to provide those public goods and public infrastructures conducive to environmentally sound conditions of public health and sanitation. Periodically, as was the case in the Progressive era and in the early stages of the New Deal, this leads to the idea of considerable state intervention to ensure the proper conservation and efficient management of national resources, thus challenging the rights of private property in the interests of a state-managed class strategy for capital accumulation.

All state interventions, the logical tool of environmental management, are typically limited under the standard view by two important considerations. First, intervention should occur only when there is clear evidence of serious damage through market failure and preferably when that damage can be quantified (eg in money terms). This requires strong scientific evidence of connections between, for example, exposure to asbestos in the workplace and cancers developing twenty years later or power plant emissions and acidification of lakes hundreds of miles away. And it also requires careful measurement of costs of pollution and resource depletion because the second constraint is that there is thought to be a zero-sum trade-off between economic growth (capital accumulation) and environmental quality. To be overly solicitous with respect to the latter is to forgo unnecessarily the benefits of the former. This is the domain of monetised cost-benefit analysis which now plays such an important role in shaping environmental politics under the standard view.

Getting to the heart of what the trade-offs might be (theoretically and empirically) requires a particular combination of engineering and economic expertise coupled with scientific understandings of ecological processes. The translation of the environmental problem into the domain of expert discourses permits the internalization of environmental politics and regulatory activity largely within the embrace of the state apparatus or, more loosely, under the influence of corporate finance of research and development. It becomes an application of bureaucratic-technocratic rationality under the dual influence of the state and corporations, in which the rough and tumble of democratic politics is generally viewed as getting in the way of proper, rational and sensible regulatory activities. The preferred strategy, except in those periods of euphoric state strategising, is to negotiate out solutions between the state and the private sector often on an *ad hoc* and case-by-case basis.

Under the standard view, the basic rights of private property and of profit maximization are not fundamentally challenged. Concerns for environmental justice (if they exist at all) are kept strictly subservient to concerns for economic efficiency, continuous growth and capital accumulation. The view that economic growth is fundamental to human development is never challenged. The right of humanity to engage in extensive environmental modifications is tacitly accepted as sacrosanct (turning the standard view into a doctrine complicitous with the hubristic version of the domination of nature thesis). The only serious question is how best to manage the environment for capital accumulation, economic efficiency and growth. From this standpoint, negative externality effects (including those on health and welfare) deserve to be countered (provided no serious barriers are created to further accumulation) and serious attention should be given to proper conservation and wise use of resources. Given the framework, ecological issues within the standard view are generally viewed as a concern of the nation state, in some instances devolving powers to lower levels of government. National politics and cultural traditions (for example, with respect to the importance of wilderness or the forest) then typically play an important role in affecting the way in which the standard view gets worked out and presented in different nation states and even in different localities. Put in the prevailing terms of economics, socially-based and often locally specific preferences for environmental qualities can be factored into the argument as a particular manifestation of consumer preference.

A powerful and persuasive array of discourses are embedded

(sometimes without even knowing it) within this standard view and its associated practices, institutions, beliefs and powers. Environmental economics, environmental engineering, environmental law, planning and policy analysis, as well as a wide range of scientific endeavours are ranged broadly in support of it. Such discourses are perfectly acceptable to the dominant forms of political-economic power precisely because there is no challenge implied within them to the hegemony of capital accumulation. Financial and logistical support therefore flows from the state and corporations to those promoting such environmental discourses, making them distinctive discourses of power.

The standard view has a considerable history. Beginning with the extensive public health measures in nineteenth century urban settings and following through to present day efforts to improve air and water quality in many areas of the advanced capitalist world, the working out of the standard view has not been without a substantial record of successes to its credit. Were this not the case, it would long ago have been abandoned. At its best, even some of its seemingly negative features have a virtuous side: the *ad hoc* and fragmented approach has sometimes permitted a degree of local and particularist sensitivity to consumer preferences and considerable flexibility in environmental interventions. But there are, plainly, serious limitations to the effectiveness of the standard approach and in recent years some of its more glaring internal contradictions have spawned the search for some alternative way to look at environmental issues.

III ECOLOGICAL MODERNIZATION

An alternative thesis of 'ecological modernization' can sometimes be detected as shifts of emphasis within the standard view.[13] But in other instances it now stands out, particularly in the rhetoric of some of the main environmental pressure groups, as a clear discursive alternative. And in recent years there are signs of its adoption/co-optation by certain institutionalised configurations of political-economic power.

Ecological modernization depends upon and promotes a belief that economic activity systematically produces environmental harm (disruptions of 'nature') and that society should therefore adopt a proactive stance with respect to environmental regulation and ecological controls. Prevention is regarded as preferable to cure. This means that the *ad hoc*, fragmented and bureaucratic approach to state regulation should be replaced by a far more systematic set of policies, institutional arrangements, and regulatory practices. The future, it is argued, cannot be expected to look after itself and some sorts of calculations are necessary to configure what would be a good strategy for sustainable economic growth and economic development in the long run. The key word in this formulation is 'sustainability'. And even though there are multiple definitions of what this might mean (and all sorts of rhetorical devices deployed by opponents to make the term meaningless or render it harmless – no one, after all, can be in favour of 'unsustainability'), the concept nevertheless lies at the heart of the politics of ecological modernization.

This shift in emphasis is justified in a variety of ways. The irreversibility problem, marginalised in the standard view, becomes much more prominent, not only with respect to biodiversity but also with respect to the elimination of whole habitats, permanent resource depletion, desertification, deforestation and the like. High orders of environmental *risk* are emphasised coupled with a rising recognition that unintended ecological consequences of human activity can be far-reaching, long-lasting and potentially damaging. Beck's formulation of the idea that we now live in a 'risk society' (largely a consequence of an accelerating pace of seemingly uncontrollable technological change) has proven a useful and influential adjunct to the discursive thrust to define a risk-minimizing politics of ecological modernization.

The role of scientists in promoting the discursive shift from the standard view to ecological modernization was important.[14] It was science that revealed global problems (acid rain, global warming and ozone holes) demanding wide-ranging collective action beyond nation state borders, thereby posing a challenge (legal, institutional and cultural) to the closed bureaucratic rationality of the nation state. And some individual scientists pushed the knowledge of ecological systems and interrelatedness to the point where the unintended consequences of human activities could be seen to be far more widespread, irreversible and potentially serious than had previously been recognised. This made the 'business as usual' and 'after the fact' approach of the standard view appear more and more inadequate. This kind of science provided crucial support to many environmental pressure groups, many of whom initially viewed scientific rationality with scepticism and distrust, given their roots in the 'romantic' and aesthetic traditions of, say, Wordsworth and Thoreau. The thesis of ecological modernization has now become deeply entrenched within many segments of the environmental movement. The effects, as we shall see, have been somewhat contradictory. On the one hand, ecological modernization provides a common discursive basis for a contested rapprochement between them and dominant forms of political-economic power. But on the other, it presumes a certain kind of rationality that lessens the force of more purely moral arguments and exposes much of the environmental movement to the dangers of political co-optation.

The general persuasiveness of the ecological modernization thesis rests, however, on one other radical discursive shift. This refuses to see the supposed trade off between environmental concerns and economic growth in zero-sum terms. What are known as 'win-win' examples of ecological control are increasingly emphasised. Given the power of money, it is vital to show that ecological modernization can be profitable. Environmental care, it is argued, often contributes to efficiency (through more efficient fuel use, for example) improved productivity and lower costs (through soil conservation practices, for example) and long-term preservation of the resource base for capital accumulation. If, furthermore, pollution is merely being moved around (from air to water to land) under standard practices, then aggregate efficiency is being impaired in the long-run if, as is increasingly the case, there are fewer and fewer empty 'sinks' within which pollutants can costlessly be absorbed. And if, to take the parallel case of supposedly 'natural' resources, depletion is occurring too fast to allow for smooth market adjustment and measured technological change, then costly disruption to economic growth may be in the wind. To some degree the search for 'win-win' solutions has also been prompted by environmental litigation, environmental impact legislation and, in some sectors, like those directly associated with occupational and consumer safety and health, by extraordinarily high compensation awards for injured parties. The costliness of recent clean-up efforts – the 'superfund' experience in the United States to clean up hazardous waste sites being perhaps the best example – has also pushed many to take a new look at prevention.

Environmental equity (distributive justice) has a stronger role to play in ecological modernization arguments. This is in part due to the inroads made by the environmental justice movement and various other movements around the world expressive of what Martinez-Allier calls 'the environmentalism of the poor.'[15] But leaving these aside, co-operation is required to gain support for proactive environmental initiatives so that the question of environmental justice has to be integrated into the search for long-term sustainability, partly as a pragmatic adaptation to the internationalism of several key contemporary ecological issues: sovereign nation states, including those that are poor, have to agree to a certain regulatory environment on, for example, carbon emissions and CFC use, and, furthermore, enforce its provisions. Negotiating with China and India is politically quite different from negotiating the location of a hazardous waste site in Mississippi. So some sort of configuration has to be envisaged in which ecological modernization contributes both to growth and global distributive justice simultaneously. How, and if, that can be done is at the heart of deeply contentious debates. There are also signs of a discursive shift, perhaps fashioned as a response to the contentiousness of the distributive justice issue, in which economic *development* (improvement in human capacities and conditions) is seen as quite distinctive from economic *growth* (the increase in output of goods and services). If governments can be persuaded to take the former path then the competitive challenge to the hegemony of the advanced capitalist powers with respect to capital accumulation through economic growth will be lessened.

One side-consequence of these shifts is that environmental management is no longer seen to be the exclusive provenance of governments or the nation state. The nation state, while clearly still important, should be supplemented by strong international organizations as well as local governments. The general import of the Rio conference was to give far greater powers to international organizations (like the World Bank and the United Nations Environmental Programme) and to set up local government mandates for environmental quality. Many layers of government operating at many different scales should be implicated as partners in the search for better paths of environmental management. This move to construct some sort of hierarchy of powers tacitly recognizes the diverse scales at which environmental issues can arise. While very little of this has actually been worked out in practice, a discursive shift from the nation state towards some sort of recognition of the scalar layering of environmental issues can certainly be detected.

If the spatio-temporal understanding of the environmental-ecological issue has shifted, then so has its social context. Equity struggles are involved, economic growth is no longer equated with economic development and politics becomes much more integral to environmental management as opposed to the tradition of national bureaucratic technical decision making. A wide range of forces in civil society (non-governmental organizations, pressure groups, community agents) can become involved. The debate over 'values' can then become much more explicit, preparing the ground for a veritable industry of philosophical reflection devoted to 'environmental ethics.' And much more open and democratic as well as wide-ranging discussions of environmental issues become possible. It is precisely at this interface that the fine line between incorporation and open contestation again and again gets crossed and re-crossed, with legal, scientific and economic discourses, institutions and practices becoming a deeply implicated and contested terrain.

A discursive shift of the sort I am here describing is never neatly executed or accomplished. In portraying the general characteristics of the ecological modernization thesis in this systematic way, I am exaggerating both its coherence and its difference from the standard view. The raggedness of the environmental-ecological debate of the last twenty years defies any such simple characterization. But the debate in the public realm has been much more open to ecological modernization arguments than was previously the case. And as often happens with a public discourse in formation, all sorts of interventions and openings have occurred, through which quite a bit of radicalisation has been achieved. Some radical environmental groups have been partially drawn to the ecological modernization thesis, sometimes as a tactic because it provides convenient and more generally persuasive public arguments with which to pursue other objectives, but sometimes as a matter of deeper conviction, viewing it as the only way to move a deeply entrenched capitalism towards ecological sanity and a modicum of global justice. And there is some evidence that the nascent European bureaucracy in Brussels saw ecological modernization as a means of empowerment against narrower national and corporate interests. Socialists, for their part, could take to the argument as a way of combining traditional commitments to growth and equity with rational planning under socialist control. Commoner's *Making Peace with the Planet Earth* and Leff's *Green Production: Toward an Environmental Rationality* can be read as left wing versions of this thesis. I shall come back to this particular line of thinking by way of conclusion.

But the discourse would not have the purchase it evidently has had without a significant tranche of support from the heartland of contemporary political-economic power. The rising tide of affluence in the advanced capitalist countries after World War Two increased middle-class interest in environmental qualities and amenities, 'nature' tourism, and deepened concerns about environmental dangers to health. While this lent an indelible bourgeois aesthetic and politics to much of the environmental movement, it nevertheless pushed environmental issues on to the political agenda where they could not easily be controlled as a mere adjunct of bourgeois fashion. The health connection, as Hays points out, became particularly salient and peculiarly open-ended in relation to environmental concerns in the United States after 1950 or so. Systematic environmental concern for everything from landscape despoliation, heritage and wilderness preservation, control of air and water quality, exposure to toxics, waste disposal and regulation of consumer products, became much easier to voice given middle-class acceptance of such issues as fundamental to its own qualities of life. *The Limits to Growth* published in 1972, which in many respects was a powerful warning shot to say that the standard view was inadequate, was supported by the Club of Rome (an influential group of bankers and industrialists) and the *Brundtland Report* (WCED) of 1987, which consolidated the ecological modernization discourse in important ways, bringing the question of 'sustainability' to the fore, was an effort supported by many government officials, industrialists, financiers and scientists. And since that time, major world institutions, such as the World Bank, which previously paid no attention whatsoever to environmental issues, corporations (like IBM and even Monsanto), and powerful establishment politicians, like Margaret Thatcher and Al Gore, have been converted to some version of the ecological modernization thesis.

The shift towards a discourse of ecological modernization was in part reactive to these social and scientific trends coupled with the political pressure from organised environmentalism. But there were other more sinister forces at work to make the discourse more subtly appealing to political-economic power. The severe recession of 1973-5, the subsequent slow-down in economic growth and rise of widespread structural unemployment, made an appeal to some notion of natural limits to growth more attractive. Scapegoating natural limits rather than the internal contradictions of capitalism is a well-tried tactic. When faced with a crisis, said Marx of Ricardo, he 'takes refuge in organic chemistry'. This particular way of thinking put particular blame on population growth, again and again raising the spectre of Malthus, thereby reducing much of the ecological-environmental problem to a simple population problem. But this essentially reactionary political approach was paralleled in *The Limits to Growth* and *The Brundtland Report* by concerns for natural limits to capital accumulation (and, hence, for employment possibilities and rising standards of affluence world-wide). The rhetoric of 'sustainable development' could then be attached to the ideal of a growth economy that had to respect natural limits. Demands for higher wages or more rapid economic growth in poorer parts of the world were countered by appeal to certain immutable laws of nature, thus diverting attention from the far more mutable laws of entrenched class and imperialist privilege. The supposed sheer physical inability of the planet to support global populations with aspirations to a living standard of Sweden or Switzerland became an important political argument.

The evident failures of capitalist modernization in many developing countries also made the rhetoric of ecological modernization more attractive. In many developing countries this meant a partial return to traditional methods as more ecologically sensitive and hence more efficient. The World Bank took to blaming the governments of Africa for the failure of its own development projects there and then sought to decentralize the process of development to see if indigenous methods led by indigenous peoples, with women cast in a much more central role, could work so as to pay off the accumulating debts built up precisely through World Bank-imposed western-style development.

Finally, many corporations, like IBM saw that a great deal of profit was to be had from superior environmental technologies and stricter global environmental regulation. For the advanced capitalist nations, struggling to remain competitive, the imposition of strong environmental regulations demanding high technology solutions promised not only a competitive advantage to their own industries, but also a strong export market for the more environmentally friendly technology they had developed (the environmental clean-up in Eastern Europe has proved particularly lucrative). If only a small fragment of corporate capital thought this way, it was nevertheless a significant dissident voice arguing for ecological modernization from within a powerful segment of the bourgeoisie. Global environmental management 'for the good of the planet' and to maintain 'the health' of planet earth could also be conveniently used to make claims on behalf of major governments and corporations for their exclusive and technologically advanced management of all the world's resources. So while a good deal of corporate capture of the ecological modernization rhetoric (particularly via 'green consumerism') could be found, there are also positive reasons for some segments of corporate capital to align themselves with a movement that emphasised certain kinds of technological change coupled with highly centralized global environmental management practices.

As a discourse, ecological modernization internalises conflict. It has a radical edge, paying serious attention to environmental-ecological issues and most particularly to the accumulation of scientific evidence of environmental impacts, without challenging the capitalist economic system head on. It is reformist in its objectives rather than revolutionary and poses no deeply uncomfortable questions to the perpetuation of capital accumulation, though it does imply strict regulation of private property rights. But the difficulty is that such a discourse can rather too easily be corrupted into yet another discursive representation of dominant forms of economic power. It can be appropriated by multinational corporations to legitimize a global grab to manage all the world's resources. Indeed, it is not impossible to imagine a world in which big industry (certain segments), big governments (including the World Bank) and establishment, high-tech big science can get to dominate the world even more than they currently do in the name of 'sustainability,' ecological modernization and appropriate global management of the supposedly fragile health of planet earth.

IV 'WISE USE' AND THE DEFENCE OF PRIVATE PROPERTY

Ecological modernization is by no means a dominant discourse. There is a strong desire to smother it (together with anything other than the minimalist version of the standard view) in many quarters. While some corporations are favourably disposed towards it, most are not. But by far the most powerful conflict is with the rights of private property. The whole idea of ecological modernization, and the planned government-led or collective interventions it presupposes, is anathema to the libertarian wing of conservative politics. And through the 'wise use' movement, particularly focused in the American West, it has found a right wing equivalent of the environmental justice movement with which to attack not only ecological modernization but anything except minimalist appeal to the standard view.

The 'wise use' movement draws in fact on a long tradition of environmental activism. The appropriation of the term 'wise use' is not merely an opportunistic rhetorical device with which to counter any form of governmental intervention or regulation. The tradition has its origins in classical liberal theories, particularly those generally attributed to Locke, and their translation into political-economic practices, most particularly in the United States with its tradition of Jeffersonian democracy. The argument is in part based on the inalienable right of individuals to mix their labour with the land in such a way as to 'make the earth fruitful and to multiply.' But it is also strongly based on the view that private property owners have every incentive in the world to maintain and sustain the ecological conditions of productivity that furnish them with a living and that, left to their own devices, they will more likely pass on the land to their offspring in an improved rather than deteriorated condition. Arthur Young, an influential commentator on agricultural affairs in late-eighteenth-century England, put it this way: 'on an annual rental a man will turn a garden into a desert: but give a man a fourteen year lease and he will turn a desert into a garden.'

This was, of course, exactly the sentiment that led William Lloyd to propose 'the tragedy of the commons' thesis in 1833. And some commentators on Hardin's influential restatement of that idea have treated it as a plea for private property arrangements as the best protection against those abuses of the commons which governments by their very nature are powerless to prevent.[16] Even if Hardin does not himself follow that line of reasoning, it has not been hard for legal scholars and for theoreticians to argue that the taking away of private property rights without full compensation for environmental reasons is unjustified and that the wisest and best organizational form for ensuring proper use of the land is a highly decentralized property-owning democracy. Von Hayek, Nozick and a whole host of contemporary economists and legal scholars would agree.

V ENVIRONMENTAL JUSTICE AND THE DEFENCE OF THE POOR

The environmental justice movement advances a discourse radically at odds with the standard view and with that of ecological modernization and is profoundly at odds with the wise use movement. Of all the discourses considered here, it has proven far less amenable to corporate or governmental co-optation. Four issues stand out:

(1) Inequalities in protection against environmental hazards have been felt in very tangible ways in enough instances, such as Love Canal, to make compensation for and elimination of such inequalities a pressing material (largely health) issue for many. Putting the inequalities at the top of the environmental agenda directly challenges the dominant discourses (be they of the standard, ecological modernization or wise use variety).

(2) 'Expert' and 'professional' discourses have frequently been mobilised by dominant forms of political-economic power to either deny, question or diminish what were either known or strongly felt to be serious health effects deriving from unequal exposure. The resultant climate of suspicion towards expert and professional discourses (and the form of rationality they frequently espouse) underlies the search for an alternative rationality (even, if necessary, 'irrationality') with which to approach environmental hazards. While science, medicine, economics and the law may remain important ingredients within the discourse of environmental justice, they are not therefore ever permitted to frame the arguments *in toto*.

(3) The environmental justice movement puts the survival of people in general, and of the poor and marginalised in particular, at the centre of its concerns. The marginalised, disempowered and racially-marked positions of many of those most affected, together with the strong involvement of women as dominant carers for the children who have suffered most from, for example, the consequences of lead paint poisoning or leukemia, have forced otherwise disempowered individuals to seek empowerment outside of prevailing institutions. The coupling of the search for empowerment and personal self-respect on the one hand with environmentalist goals on the other means that the movement for environmental justice twins ecological with social justice goals in quite unique ways. In so doing, the movement opens itself to distinctive positionalities from which injustice can differentially be measured.

(4) Doing battle with the lack of self-respect that comes from 'being associated with trash' lends a very emotive symbolic angle to the discourse and highlights the racial and discriminatory aspects to the problem. This ultimately pushes discussion far beyond the scientific evidence on health effects, cost-benefit schedules or 'parts per billion' on to the thorny, volatile and morally charged terrain of symbolic violence, 'cultural imperialism' and personalised revolt against the association of 'pollution' in its symbolic sense of defilement and degradation with dangerous social disorder and supposed racial impurities of certain groups in the population.

These conditions of production of an environmental justice movement in the United States account for some of its central features. The focus on particular kinds of pollution – toxics and dangerous contaminants – loads the discussion towards symbolic questions, making clear that the issue is as much about 'claims and counter-claims to status,' as it is about pollution *per se*.[17] This is what gives the movement so much of its moral force and capacity for moral outrage. But the corollary, as Szasz points out, is that the movement relies heavily upon symbolic politics and powerful icons of pollution incidents.[18] Toxics in someone's basement at Love Canal in Buffalo, New York is a much more powerful issue from this perspective, even though it involves a very small number of people, than the diffuse cloud of ozone concentrations in major cities that effects millions every summer throughout much of the United States. In the case of Love Canal, there was an identifiable enemy (a negligent corporation), a direct and unmistakable effect (nasty liquids in the basement, sick children and worried suburban mothers), a clear threat to public trust in government, a legal capacity to demand personal compensation, an undefinable fear of the unknown, and an excellent opportunity for dramatization that the media could and did use with relish. In the case of ozone concentration, the enemy is everyone who drives: governments have very little mandate to intervene in people's driving habits, the effects are diffuse, demands for compensation hard to mount, and the capacity for dramatization limited making for very little media coverage. The resultant bias in choice of targets permits critics to charge that the emphases of the environmental justice movement are misplaced, that its politics is based on an iconography of fear, and that the movement has more to do with moral outrage than the science of impacts. Such criticisms are often justifiable by certain standards (such as those espoused by mainstream environmentalists), but precisely for that reason are largely beside the point.

The refusal to cast discussion in monetary terms reflects an intuitive or experiential understanding of how it is that seemingly fair market exchange always leads to the least privileged falling under the disciplinary sway of the more privileged and that *costs* are always visited on those who have to bow to money discipline while *benefits* always go to those who enjoy the personal authority conferred by wealth. There is an acute recognition within the environmental justice movement that the game is lost for the poor and marginalised as soon as any problem is cast in terms of the asymmetry of monetary exchange. Money is always a form of social power and an instrument of discipline in social relations rather than a neutral universal equivalent with which to calculate 'welfare-enhancing benefits.'

This active denial of the neutrality of the monetary calculus perhaps accounts for the somewhat medieval tone of the declaration on environmental justice adopted at the 1991 conference. The affirmation of 'the sacredness of Mother Earth, ecological unity and the interdependence of all species, and the right to be free from ecological destruction' parallels in interesting ways Gurevich's characterization of medieval justice as:

> at one and the same time a moral and a cosmic principle, to which all human activity must be subordinated. Any departure from this principle is equivalent to transgression of the divine order of things and of natural law.... social justice (is) that by which the harmony of the whole is sustained, and which denies none their due deserts.[19]

I do not present this parallel in order to undermine, but rather to suggest that the principles of environmental justice, though cast in a somewhat unfamiliar mould to many of us, would be familiar to those upon whom what Benton calls 'the liberal illusion', has yet to do its insidious work.[20]

The environmental justice movement has, by and large, seen through this illusory state of affairs. But this means that it also has to do battle with the liberal illusion and its pervasive effects as well as with direct forms of ecological harm. In so doing, some have indeed been led into backward looking praise for the medieval world (a golden age of integration with nature when human societies trod so lightly on the earth that all was well between humans and nature) and sidewards looking admiration for those marginalised peoples who have not yet been fully brought within the global political economy of technologically advanced and bureaucratically rationalised capitalism.

The affirmation of the 'sacredness of Mother Earth' and other rhetoric of that sort is, I want to suggest, both problematic and empowering. It is empowering precisely because it permits issues to be judged in terms of moral absolutes, of good and evil, right and wrong. By posing matters in terms of the defilement, violation or even 'rape' of a sacred Mother Earth, the environmental justice movement adopts a non-negotiable position of intense moral rectitude untouchable by legal, scientific or other rationalistic discourse. It permits the assertion, in quasi-religious language, of the widespread view that the proper approach is to ask, in Lois Gibbs's words, 'what is morally correct?' rather than 'what is legally, scientifically and pragmatically possible?'

It also permits, through the medium of social protest, the articulation of ideas about a moral economy of collective provision and collective responsibility as opposed to a set of distributive relations within the political economy of profit. While the 'moral economy' being proposed is definitely not that of the traditional peasant, the very grounding of the discourse in a language of sacredness and moral absolutes creates a certain homology between, say, struggles over exposure to environmental hazards in urban areas, nativist beliefs on the relation to nature and peasant movements throughout the developing world such as that of the Chipko or the Amazon rubber tappers. It is therefore not surprising to find that 'the fundamental right to political, economic, cultural and environmental self-determination of all peoples' is asserted as one of the principles of environmental justice.

It is precisely through this discursive strategy that links can then be found between the environmental justice movement as shaped within the specific conditions of the United States, and the broader movement that Martinez-Allier refers to as 'the environmentalism of the poor.' These movements fundamentally concern either the defense of livelihoods and of communal access to 'natural' resources threatened by commodification, state takeovers, and private property arrangements, or more dynamic movements (both *in situ* and migratory) arising as a response to ecological scarcities, threats to survival and destruction of long-standing ways of life. But, as with the environmental justice movement, the symbolic dimension, the struggle for empowerment, for recognition and respect and above all for emancipation from the oppressions of material want and domination of others, inevitably has a powerful role to play, making the environmentalism of the poor focus upon survivability in all of its senses.

From this standpoint, it is not hard to understand the fierce critique of 'sustainable development' and 'ecological modernization' (in its corrupted form) launched by Sachs:

> The eco-cratic view likes universalist ecological rules, just as the developmentalist liked universalist economic rules. Both pass over the rights of local communities to be in charge of their resources and to build a meaningful society. The conservation of nature (should be) intimately related to rights of communal ownership, traditional ways of knowing, cultural autonomy, religious rituals, and freedom from state-centred development.[21]

Doctrines of cultural autonomy and dispersion, of tradition and difference, nevertheless carry with them a more universal message which permits a loose alliance of forces around alternative strategies of development (or even, in some instances, growth) that focus as much upon diversity and geographical difference as upon the necessary homogeneities of global market integrations. What seems to be at work here is the conversion of ideals learned through intense ecologically-based militant particularism into some universal principles of environmental justice. The environmental justice movement, like other 'militant particularist' movements:

> has tried to connect particular struggles to a general struggle in one quite special way. It has set out, as a movement, to make real what is at first sight the extraordinary claim that the defence and advancement of certain particular interests, properly brought together, are in fact the general interest.[22]

This connection is nowhere more apparent than in the shift from 'Not-in-my-back-yard' politics to 'Not-in-Anyone's-Back-Yard' principles in the United States. This is not the only leap that the environmental justice movement is prepared to make. The environment itself gets to be redefined to include 'the totality of life conditions in our communities – air and water, safe jobs for all at decent wages, housing, education, health care, humane prisons, equity, justice'.[23] And this leads straight back to the connection between environmental and social justice, particularly in urban settings which is where most people now live in the advanced capitalist world.

VI ENVIRONMENTAL JUSTICE AND THE CITY

The long-standing hostility of what now passes in the public eye for the environmental movement to the very existence of cities has created a blindspot of startling proportions. Usually depicted as the high-point of the pollution and plundering of planet earth, cities (where nearly half the world's population now lives) are either ignored or denigrated in the deep ecology literature as well as in that wing of environmentalism that focuses primarily on 'nature' as wilderness, species and habitat preservation. Theoretically, the movement may claim that everything is related to everything else, but it then marginalises or ignores a large segment of the practical ecosystem. Furthermore, if biocentic thinking is correct and the boundary between human activity and ecosystemic activities must be collapsed, then this means not only that ecological processes have to be incorporated into our understanding of social life: it also means that flows of money and of commodities and the transformative actions of human beings (in the building of urban systems) have to be understood as fundamentally ecological processes.

The environmental justice movement, with its emphasis upon marginalised and impoverished populations exposed to hazardous ecological circumstances, freely acknowledges these connections. Many of the issues with which it is confronted are specifically urban in character. Consequently, the principles it has enunciated include the mandate to address environmental justice in the city by the cleaning up and rebuilding of urban environments.

In so doing, the environmental justice movement connects back into a much neglected facet of environmental politics. Gottlieb correctly seeks to interpret environmentalism as part of a complex of social movements that arose in response to rapid urbanization and industrialization, accelerating strongly after World War Two.[24] He re-inscribes in environmental history (and its hegemonic discourses) a whole set of urban environmental concerns that conventional accounts conveniently misplace. Gottlieb suggests a way to take the supposed 'holism' of the environmental movement at its word and to overcome a long-standing ideological predilection to oppose city and country in ways that denigrate the former and romanticize the latter.

Consider, for example, the case of lead paint poisoning, an issue that has been of major concern for environmental justice advocates. Lead has been known to be a highly toxic substance for hundreds of years (the Romans understood the problem well, lead featured large in the pioneering work of Alice Hamilton on industrial toxicology at the beginning of this century and the problems associated with lead-based paints in residential areas were well-known by the 1920s). Yet the use of lead continued to expand well into the 1970s (particularly lead-based additives to gasoline) and lead-based paints were banned only in 1978, after repeated and conclusive studies had shown a strong relation between them and serious brain damage in children. But the lead-based paints almost universally deployed in houses before 1950 have remained as a serious environmental hazard. Since its effects were largely concentrated in areas of housing dilapidation and poor maintenance, the lead paint problem was increasingly seen (incorrectly) as an exclusively inner city problem. Largely for that reason, the problem did not command the sort of urgency of action that lead-based additives in gasoline commanded through their impacts across all class and race lines. So on an issue where, as early as the 1960s, 'the epidemiology was clear, its victims could be predicted, its health effects could be identified, and its treatment was known to the medical profession', little or nothing was done.[25]

The reason for the lack of action over nearly twenty years goes back to that infernal economic logic that Summers so brilliantly encapsulated: the costs of lead-removal would either drive rents up or render inner city landlordism for the poor so unprofitable as to exacerbate already serious problems of housing-abandonment in inner city areas. In either case, one consequence is greater homelessness, implying a social choice for the poor between living with lead paint or being on the street. To this is now added another wrinkle – liability suits against landlords after proven exposure of children to lead poisoning (some compensation awards have gone as high as $500,000) have led insurers to deny coverage in many inner city areas. That leads to even more housing abandonment as landlords prefer to leave a building vacant rather than have it occupied and face personal liability if an occupant suffers from the paint. The state has sought to broker some sort of compromise but again and again agreements break down and legislation falters in the face of the 'twin tragedies: childhood lead poisoning and the disappearance of affordable housing'.[26]

But isn't this where we all came in? Did not the 1947 Housing Act in the United States affirm the *right* of everyone 'to a decent house in a suitable living environment'? The *Report of the National Commission on Urban Problems* published by US Government in 1968 in the wake of the assassination of Martin Luther King, not only lamented the failure to progress towards such a goal but focused particularly on the failure to define what a 'suitable living environment' might mean. In seeking to rectify that ommission, the Presidential Commission not only focused on the environment of jobs, racial discrimination, poor social infrastructures (particularly education) and accessibility (particularly transportation) but also inserted a strong chapter on more conventional environmental issues:

> America will surely fail to build a good urban society unless we begin to have a new respect – *reverence* is not too strong a word – for the natural environment that surrounds us.... None of us can afford to be ignorant or silent about what the despoilers are doing to our environment. We must respond to growing reports of smog-choked cities, air pollution alerts, communities drying up, industries fleeing, people thirsting for lack of water supply, lakes dying, bird species threatened by chemical poisoning, and all life jeopardized by radiation waste hazards.

In seeking solutions to housing questions, the Commission went on to argue that:

> it is impossible to conceive of good housing downwind from a factory spewing ashes and noxious gases, in neighbourhoods so poorly served by local government that trash and filth dominate the scene, in sections where open sewers or seepage from septic tanks spread disease, or adjacent to rivers or ponds that would poison or infect anyone who used the water for swimming.[27]

But this was a rare historical conjuncture. The dominant forms of power were forced to take closer look at the wide ranging environmental conditions underlying the political unrest in the inner cities of the United States at the same time as a whole range of aesthetic, health and environmental quality questions were being placed upon the political agenda by the middle class, aided and abetted by a restless student movement which, from Paris to Mexico City and from Santa Barbara to Tokyo, was raising profound questions including that of our alienated relation to nature. At that time, therefore, it was a matter of almost common consensus that social and environmental justice concerns were inseparable from each other in urban settings (see *Social Justice and the City*, chapter 2). Only since then, has the environmental issue been weened away from its urban basis.[28]

It has, however, taken the mutiple and diversified efforts of the environmental justice movement to revive and keep alive such long-standing concerns. Consider, for example, the case of Chicago's notorious Southeast Side. Home to 150,000 people, mostly African-American and Hispanic, it has '50 active or closed commercial hazardous waste landfills, 100 factories (including seven chemical plants and five steel mills), and 103 abandoned toxic waste dumps.' Altgeld Gardens, a segregated African-American community in the area, 'is surrounded on all four sides with the most toxic facilities in all of Chicago, and, no surprise, has one of the highest cancer rates in the United States'.[29] But the seriousness of such environmental hazards has long been obvious. Various workers associated with The Hull House Settlement organised by Jane Addams in the 1890s quickly recognised that much of Chicago was nothing short of an urban-environmental catastrophe that demanded immediate and swift remedies if public health was to be protected and a modicum of social justice achieved. They also recognised, as the contemporary environmental justice movement has rediscovered, that the only path to improvement was empowerment of the poor and working classes in the face of a recalcitrant, obdurate and often corrupt corporate power structure (Sara Paretsky's novel *Bloodshot* captures the contemporary dimensions of that struggle most graphically).

But the whole question of the link between environmental and social justice in a rapidly urbanizing world does not stop at the borders of communities differentially impacted by exposure to environmental hazards. Urbanizing processes are much more multilayered than that, as are the environmental and social justice issues with which they are associated. Changing patterns of urban organization simultaneously produce configurations of uneven social and economic development at different scales coupled with multiple displacements of environmental issues to different scales. Highly localised urban smogs are reduced at the expense of a regionalised acid deposition problem. Middle-class commuters escape toxic zones and urban heat islands only to contribute to global warming and high metropolitan concentrations of ozone in summer. The health and quality of urban food provision is much improved by resort to packaging practices (an extraordinary growth industry since 1945) that create an immense plastics and paper waste disposal problem. Battery-driven cars are advocated as a solution to ozone producing automobiles, but there is lead in those batteries. Electrical power contributes to the cleanliness and health of urban environments only at the expense of massive carbon dioxide, nitrous oxides and sulphur emissions that give rise to acid deposition and global warming. Refrigeration cuts down on food contamination, dysentry and disease but the CFCs deplete the ozone layer.

In all of these issues, the activities of urbanization pose a distinctive set of environmental problems and foment a wide range of environmental consequences that have uneven social impacts. Furthermore, the immense concentrations of population now occurring throughout the world create their own milieu in which distinctive and often new hazards can all too easily flourish. The epidemiology of diseases shifts. Measles epidemics occur for the most part only in urban concentrations of more than 250,000 people and outbreaks of plague – such as the pneumonic plague that shattered Surat in India in 1994 and the Ebola virus that hit urban concentration in Zaire in 1995 – take the course they do in part because of the form that contemporary urbanization takes. Yet only recently has the link between urbanization and environmental questions begun to be explored in any systematic way.[30] How to do that in ways that are sensitive to social justice questions, in the midst of the complex scalar layering of environmental and developmental issues (local, metropolitan, regional, global), has hardly begun to be integrated into any environmental discourses. Certainly, the complexity of the issues will make for an abundance of confusion and argument.

But amidst all of the disagreements, both actual and potential, as to how environmental justice might be established, the one solid foundational argument to which all proponents again and again return, is the primacy of social relations and of the justice of those relations. Commoner summarises it this way:

> When any environmental problem is probed to its origin, it reveals an inescapable truth – that the real root cause is to be found in how (people) interact with each other; that the debt to nature…. cannot be paid person by person, in recycled bottles or ecologically sound habits, but in the ancient coin of social justice.[31]

But of what metal is that ancient coin?

VII PRINCIPLES OF JUSTICE AND ENVIRONMENTS OF DIFFERENCE

A comparison of environmental discourses and principles of social justice, suggests a crude set of pairings. Utilitarian theories of justice are strongly associated with the standard view. The intermingling of both such discourses in the advanced capitalist societies is fairly evident, making this by far the most prevalent and hegemonic mode of thinking for regulating institutional behaviours, political action and material practices. Ecological modernization, particularly in terms of its concerns for the rights of future generations, seems more compatible with some sort of social contract view and I think it is significant that several attempts to adapt the Rawlsian version of the social contract have emerged in recent years.[32] Wise use doctrine appeals directly to libertarian views and draws much of its strength precisely from that association. The environmental justice movement, by contrast, frequently invokes egalitarian principles (sometimes individualistic but more frequently communitarian) in its demands for a more equitable distribution of environmental advantages and burdens.

Each of these broadly anthropocentric theoretical positions, interestingly, has its biocentric analogue. The libertarian view produces strong doctrines of animal rights when extended on to the terrain of rights accorded to all 'subjects of a life'.[33] The utilitarian view can be extended to accord rights to as many species as possible in terms of their ability to flourish and to multiply. Radical egalitarianism across all species and habitats characterises the deep ecology movement while the contractarian view suggests a strong appreciation for rights of the less well-off (endangered species) as well as a conservative approach to habitat transformation (justified only if it is to the benefit of the least advantaged species).

It is on this sort of terrain that we now find an essentially irresolvable debate on the proper form of environmental ethics unfolding. And the arguments can be bitter: for example, concern for whole ecosystems and habitats as against the rights of individual organisms is tantamount to fascism in Regan's view.[34] We are then left with a case of determining which is the most socially just theory of social justice. In the case of lead paint poisoning in Baltimore City, for example, the conflict is not between just and unjust solutions but between different conceptions of justice. Libertarian views put the rights of private property owners (and their contractual position vis-à-vis consumers of housing services) at a premium and what happens between the parties is a private matter. Utilitarians would treat the problem as a public health nuisance that ought to be cleaned up insofar as it imposes intolerable burdens (while leaving open the Achilles's heel that the greatest happiness of the greatest number might be consistent with inflicting damage on a minority, particularly when the cost of doing otherwise is burdensome for the majority). Contractarians of a Rawlsian persuasion would take it more as a question of an inequality of exposure that benefits no one, and most certainly not the least privileged. If none of us knew (and Rawls presumes a 'veil of ignorance' as essential to the derivation of his theory) what our location or position in life might be (ie whether or not we would be in a lead paint environment) all parties would presumably choose to eliminate the hazard altogether. Egalitarians would treat differential exposure to lead paint hazards as an affront to their principles. But the egalitarian principle is not so helpful when it comes to allocating the cost of remediation. Should the poor pay for the clean up of their own rather dirty environments on an equal footing with the rich who live in cleanlier circumstances? Non-funded federal mandates with respect to clean water and sewage treatment in the United States, for example, will impose enormous financial burdens on older cities where the less affluent live, making this an intractable problem for environmental justice if the raw equality principle is adhered to rigorously.

These are all valid theoretical positions. Each can be subjected to philosophical critique. Benton thus provides a deep and trenchant analysis of animal rights and social justice theories, de Shalit subjects the contractarian theory to a sympathetic critique and Wenz examines the whole spectrum of possible theories of environmental justice only to decide that 'each theory failed when taken by itself.'[35] We are therefore confronted with a plurality of theories of justice, all equally plausible and all equally lacking in one way or other. We are, Wenz notes, 'attracted to using one theory in one kind of situation and a different theory in a different kind of situation' and in a conflict, such as that surrounding lead paint poisoning, different groups will resort to different concepts of justice to bolster their position (the property owners use the libertarian rhetoric and the defenders of children typically use a contractarian rhetoric). Wenz's answer to this situation is to abandon the search for coherence among moral judgements and for a singular theory applicable to all environmental questions. Instead, he proposes a much more flexible pluralistic theory which combines principles from many separate theories applicable to a diversity of environmental issues arising at different scales. The difficulty with such a solution is evident: why one particular blend of principles rather than another? And what is to prevent the vaunted flexibility of some pluralistic discourse on environmental justice being perverted by acts of power to the material advantage of the already elite and powerful? Trade in toxics, as Summers argued, can indeed be welfare-enhancing for all given certain suppositions about how to theorize just outcomes from trade. Class struggle is then over exactly which principles of justice shall prevail.

At this point, I find myself returning to some of the basic formulations laid out in *Social Justice and the City* more than twenty years ago. There I argued that it was vital to move from 'a predisposition to regard social justice as a matter of eternal justice and morality to regard it as something contingent upon the social processes operating in society as a whole.' The practice of the environmental justice movement has its origins in the inequalities of power and the way those inequalities have distinctive environmental consequences for the marginalised and the impoverished, for those who may be freely denigrated as 'others' or as 'people out of place.' The principles of justice it enunciates are embedded in a particular experiential world and environmental objectives are coupled with a struggle for recognition, respect, and empowerment.

But as a movement embedded in multiple 'militant particularisms', it has to find a way to cross that problematic divide between action that is deeply embedded in local experience, power conditions and social relations to a much more general movement. And, like the working-class movement, it has proven, in Williams words, 'always insufficiently aware of the quite systematic obstacles which stood in the way'.[35] The move from tangible solidarities felt as patterns of social bonding in affective and knowable communities to a more abstract set of conceptions with universal meaning involves a move from one level of abstraction – attached to place – to quite different levels of abstraction capable of reaching across a space in which communities could not be known in the same unmediated ways. Furthermore, principles developed out of the experience of Love Canal or the fight in Warren County do not necessarily travel to places where environmental and social conditions are radically different. And in that move from the particular to the general something was bound to be lost. In comes, Williams notes, 'the politics of negation, the politics of differentiation, the politics of abstract analysis. And these, whether we liked them or not, were now necessary even to understand what was happening.'

But it is exactly here that some of the empowering rhetoric of

95

environmental justice itself becomes a liability. Appealing to 'the sacredness of Mother Earth', for example, does not help arbitrate complex conflicts over how to organize material production and distribution in a world grown dependent upon sophisticated market interrelations and commodity production through capital accumulation. The demand to cease the production of *all* toxins, hazardous wastes, and radioactive materials, if taken literally, would prove disastrous to the public health and well-being of large segments of the population, including the poor. And the right to be free of ecological destruction is posed so strongly as a negative right that it appears to preclude the positive right to transform the earth in ways conducive to the well-being of the poor, the marginalised and the oppressed. To be sure, the environmental justice movement does incorporate positive rights particularly with respect to the rights of all people to 'political, cultural and environmental self-determination', but at this point the internal contradictions within the movement become blatant.

At this conjuncture, therefore, all of those militant particularist movements around the world that loosely come together under the umbrella of environmental justice and the environmentalism of the poor are faced with a critical choice. They can either ignore the contradiction, remain within the confines of their own particularist militancies – fighting an incinerator here, a toxic waste dump there, a World Bank dam project somewhere else and commercial logging in yet another place – or they can treat the contradictions as a fecund nexus to create a more transcendent and universal politics. If they take the latter path, they have to find a discourse of universality and generality that unites the emancipatory quest for social justice with a strong recognition that social justice is impossible without environmental justice (and *vice versa*). But any such discourse has to transcend the narrow solidarities and particular affinities shaped in particular places – the preferred milieu of most grass-roots environmental activism – and adopt a politics of abstraction capable of reaching out across space, across the multiple environmental and social conditions that constitute the geography of difference in a contemporary world that capitalism has intensely shaped to its own purposes over the last two hundred years.

The abstractions cannot rest solely upon a moral politics dedicated to protecting the sanctity of Mother Earth. It has to deal in the material and institutional issues of how to organize production and distribution in general, how to confront the realities of global power politics and how to displace the hegemonic powers of capitalism not simply with dispersed, autonomous, localised and essentially communitarian solutions (apologists for which can be found on both right and left ends of the political spectrum), but with a rather more complex politics that recognises how environmental and social justice must be sought by a rational ordering of activities at different scales. The reinsertion of the idea of 'rational ordering' indicates that such a movement will have no option, as it broadens out from its militant particularist base – but to reclaim for itself a non-coopted and non-perverted version of the theses of ecological modernization. On the one hand that means embracing and subsuming the highly geographically differentiated desire for cultural autonomy and dispersion, for the proliferation of tradition and difference within a more global politics, but on the other hand making the quest for environmental and social justice central rather than peripheral concerns.

For that to happen, the environmental justice movement has to radicalize the ecological modernization discourse itself. And that requires confronting the fundamental underlying process (and their associated power structures, social relations, institutional configurations, discourses and belief systems) that generate environmental and social injustices. Here, I revert to another key moment in the argument advanced in *Social Justice and the City* (pp136-7): it is vital, when encountering a serious problem, not merely to try to solve the problem in itself but to confront and transform the processes that gave rise to the problem in the first place. Then, as now, the fundamental problem is that of unrelenting capital accumulation and the extraordinary asymmetries of money and political power that are embedded in that process. Alternative modes of production, consumption and distribution as well as alternative modes of environmental transformation have to be explored if the discursive spaces of the environmental justice movement and the theses of ecological modernization are to be conjoined in a programme of radical political action.

Acknowledgement: Much of this chapter could not have been written without the stimulus of supervising Maarten Hajer's doctoral dissertation work in Oxford. That dissertation is now published under the title: *The Politics of Environmental Discourse: Ecological Modernization and the Policy Process*.

NOTES

[1] B. Rich, *Mortgaging the Earth: the World Bank, Environmental Impoverishment and the Crisis of Development*, Beacon Press, Boston, 1993.
[2] L. Uchitelle, 'For many, a slower climb up the payroll pecking order, *New York Times*, May 15 1995.
[3] M. Douglas, *Purity and Danger: an Analysis of the Concepts of Pollution and Taboo*, Routledge, London, 1984.
[4] B. Commoner, *Making Peace with the Planet*, Pantheon, New York, 1990.
[5] D. Harvey, *Social Justice and the City*, Edward Arnold, London, 1973, p81.
[6] See, for example, B. Bryant and P. Mohai (eds), *Race and the Incidence of Environmental Hazards*, Westview Press, Boulder, Colorado, 1992; R. Hoffrichter (ed), *Toxic Struggles: the Theory and Practice of Environmental Justice*, New Society Publishers, Philadelphia, 1993.
[7] C. Bailey, C. Faupel and J. Guudlach, 'Environmental Politics in Alabama's Blackbelt', in R. Bullard (ed), *Dumping in Dixie: Race, Class and Environmental Hazards*, Westview Press, Boulder, Colorado, 1990.
[8] K. Schneider, 'Plan for toxic dump pits Blacks against Blacks', *New York Times*, December 13 1993.
[9] L. Gibbs, *Love Canal, My Story*, State University of New York Press, Albany, New York, 1982; A. Levine, *Love Canal: Science, Politics and People*, Heath & Co, Lexington, Massachusetts, 1982.
[10] W. Greider, *Who Will Tell the People?*, Simon & Schuster, New York, 1992.
[11] M. Blumberg and R. Gottlieb, *War on Waste: Can America Win its Battle with Garbage?*, Island Press, Washington DC, 1989.
[12] D. Harvey, 'Militant Particularism and Global Ambition: the Conceptual Politics of Place, Space and Environment in the Work of Raymond Williams', *Social Text*, Volume 42.
[13] M. Hajer, *The Politics of Environmental Discourse: Ecological Modernization and the Policy Process*, Oxford University Press, Oxford, 1995.
[14] K. Litfin, *Ozone Discourses: Science and Politics in Global Environmental Co-operations*, Columbia University Press, New York, 1994.
[15] J. Martinez-Allier, 'Ecology and the Poor: a Neglected Dimension of Latin American History', *Journal of Latin American Studies*, Volume 23, 1990.
[16] G. Hardin, 'The Tragedy of the Commons', *Science*, Volume 162, 1968.
[17] M. Douglas, *op.cit.*, p3.
[18] A. Szasz, *Ecopopulism: Toxic Waste and the Movement for Environmental Justice*, University of Minnesota Press, Minneapolis, 1994.
[19] A. Gurevich, *Categories of Medieval Culture*, Routledge, London, 1985.
[20] T. Benton, *Natural Relations: Ecology, Animal Rights and Social Justice*, Verso, London, 1993.
[21] W. Sachs, *Global Economy: A New Arena of Political Conflict*, Zed Press, London, 1993.
[22] R. Williams, *Resources of Hope*, Verso, London, 1989, p115.
[23] Southern Organizing Committee for Economic and Social Justice 1992; cited in Szasz, 1994, p51.
[24] R. Gottlieb, *Forcing the Spring: the Transformation of the American Environmental Movement*, Island Press, Washington DC, 1993.

[25] *Ibid.*, p224-50.

[26] T. Wheeler, 'Bill may cut lead poisoning's deadly toll,' *Baltimore Sun*, February 27 1994.

[27] Report of the National Commission on Urban Problems, US Government, Washington DC, 1968.

[28] R. Walker, 'Nature in the City: San Francisco's Radical Conservatism', paper delivered at the Human Geography Symposium in Honor of Reds Wolman, Johns Hopkins University, Baltimore, 1995.

[29] R. Bullard (ed), *Unequal Protection: Environmental Justice and Communities of Color*, Sierra Club, San Francisco, 1994, pp14-15, 279-80.

[30] H. Giradet, *The Gaia Atlas of Cities*, Gaia Books, London, 1992; and see P. McCarney, 'Urban Research in the Developing World: Four Approaches to the Environment of Cities', in E. Stren (ed), *Urban Research in the Developing World*, University of Toronto Press, Toronto, 1995.

[31] Cited in Sachs, *op.cit.*, p224.

[32] P. Wenz, *Environmental Justice*, State University of New York Press, Albany, New York 1988.

[33] T. Regan, *The Case for Animal Rights*, University of California Press, Berkeley 1983.

[34] Benton, *op.cit.*, p3.

[35] Wenz, *op.cit.*

[36] Williams (1989), *op.cit.*, p115.

Space/Power, Identity/Difference: Tensions in the City

Doreen Massey

TWO POINTS TO BEGIN WITH

1

By the year 2,000, on current estimates, one half of the world's population will live, not just in cities, but in mega-cities. That is to say, about 3,000 million people will be living in urban areas each of which is home to many millions of people.[1] At this very moment between 20 and 30 million people a year are leaving the countryside and moving into towns and cities.

Most of the mega-cities of the new millennium will be in 'the Third World'. By the year 2,000, it is projected, only three of the world's twenty biggest cities will be in the current industrialised countries of 'the First World'. *Seventeen* will be in what is called the Third World. Moreover, increasing proportions of the populations of those cities will live in squatter settlements, in *favelas*, in parachute cities ... By the year 2,000 it is estimated that 60% of the urban population of Asia will be living like this. This, for the bulk of the world's city-dwellers in the year 2,000, will be the face of *fin de siècle* urbanism.

I make this point, in part, simply because we should remember it. When so much of our intellectual, and even political, discourse is of the excitements and desperations of Los Angeles and New York, Paris and London it is salutary to bear in mind the relative unimportance of these places, in quantitative terms, in the context of world-wide twenty-first-century city life.

But the point is also salutary in that it makes one wonder yet again what it is we mean by 'a city'. In the year 2,000, the top ten cities of the world in terms of size of population are projected to be:

1. Tokyo
2. São Paulo
3. Bombay
4. Shanghai
5. Lagos
6. Mexico City
7. Beijing
8. Dacca
9. New York
10. Jakarta

How can one define the commonalities which lie behind such variety? Evidently each of these cities is an immense conglomeration of people. More interestingly perhaps, each is also a magnetic focus of the geography of social relations. They pull in to themselves, and are the foci for the diffusion of, networks of transport and communication, the complexities of the movement of people both within and between nations, the invention, interchange and export of media and cultural forms, the focus of the imagination of millions and the seat of longing for elsewhere – the thoughts of the home-village in the mind of the exiled urban migrant. All these cities, too, are essentially open, they are meeting-places, places without walls.

Yet if these characteristics are the commonality of cities, they each live out these commonalities in very different ways. Tokyo, London and New York are very different kinds of foci in the global geography of power relations from Lagos, Dakar or Dacca. London, Tokyo, New York and Los Angeles are centres from which emanate social relations of control and command around the world, and at the same time they are absorbers of goods and food products from the whole planet. Dakar has a third of Senegal's population and is certainly a centre of control within its own country. But it is low down in the networks and chains of command in the global organisation of social power. Moreover, while the planet as a whole is organised to feed London, Berlin, Los Angeles ... Dakar to a significant degree lives locally. It functions, in a very important sense, in an intimate and individualised relation to the countryside which spreads out around it. Each day people arrive with rice and other crops. It is a long time since London lived off the market-gardens of the Home Counties.

Clearly, cities vary. Above all perhaps, they are very unequally placed within the global geometry of power. Yet what they all are are highly complex articulations of the social relations which construct global time-space. Or, at any rate, that is how I want to think of them here.

2

My second point is that we know so much already. This is in no way an argument against further research. It is merely to establish, maybe to admit, that we already understand a great deal about many of the problems which afflict great cities, and we can also say quite a lot about their potential solution, or at least amelioration. In many cities of the Third World there are simple and evident needs: for clean water and clean air, for basic housing and healthcare, for the most minimal of public infrastructure. In many cities of First World countries many of those same needs remain (maybe increasingly so, after a decade and a half of politico-economic neoliberalism) and the lack of public transport, the degradation and/or privatisation of public space and the social and spatial polarisation of populations are ever-growing problems. The reason so little is presently being done in the face of all this is not a lack of knowledge.

It is, on the one hand, the brute fact of political opposition to any of the policies which might address the causes of these problems and, on the other hand, perhaps our own and others' collective failure to communicate and make real to a wider public what we have learned.

An example is in order here. For this latter point has just been nicely, and forcibly, demonstrated by recent developments on the world stage. One argument which has been incontrovertibly established is that the economic bases of cities, their characters and their liveability, cannot be explained in terms of the city itself alone. Rather, any understanding or explanation of the city needs to be set in a wider canvass, what goes on in them needs to be interpreted in the context of the broader scheme of things. It is years ago now, way back in the days of the then new radical geography, in the late-1960s and 70s that we first strongly made that point. It was to become a major theme-tune: that you can't blame the victim, that what we understood popularly – and often in parliamentary politics too – as 'the problems of the cities' needed to be understood, in part, as the phenomena of more general social processes. We argued, in other words, that wider social relations had to be addressed if anything was to be done about what was then the relatively confined problem of the inner city. It is an argument which has become so accepted as hardly to bear repeating.

And yet it has just happened again. That argument has, effectively, been once again ignored on what may turn out to be a disastrous scale. I am thinking here of the signing of the North American Free Trade Agreement (NAFTA), of the agreement of the Uruguay round of GATT – and even of the Single European Act in its present form. Thus, to take one example, NAFTA looks set to have major repercussions for Mexican agriculture, especially that which currently takes place on *ejido* land (land held communally by townships) and that which is in the hands of small producers. Coffee, corn and sugar, at present grown on about half of Mexico's arable land, will face new competition. Presently about three-and-a-half million households grow corn and in the past have received about double the US price for their product, a system aimed at both feeding the cities and at maintaining the rural population. 'Free trade' with a neighbour that boasts one of the world's largest grain surpluses will make it impossible for such systems of production to compete and, most likely, to survive. Estimates of the possible consequent displacement of people from the Mexican countryside range from 700,000 upwards to a figure of many millions.[2] They will go to the cities, to Mexico City, to the *maquiladora*-land of the north or, if they can get across the border and California does not throw them out again, to Los Angeles. The state of Chiapas in southern Mexico is among the vulnerable areas, and the leader of the Zapatistas whose guerilla uprising exploded on the day that NAFTA was inaugurated has argued that it is 'the death warrant for the indigenous people of Mexico'.

Meanwhile on another continent, and in the context of another trade agreement – this time GATT – in Dakar those individual connections between town and country will be severed. No longer will the small farms enable the multiple-income families to feed both themselves and the cities. Life in both city and countryside, and the daily, weekly, yearly geographies of traders between them will both be affected.

What GATT and NAFTA represent, in other words, is a potentially massive reorganisation of the world geography of social relations, in which cities are deeply implicated. While multinational companies are freed even more to roam the globe – their already existing power forcing down borders and thereby further increasing their power – the local production and trade relations of peasants and small farmers are undermined. More people leave the land and make for the cities. Yet they cannot go to just any city. 'Free trade' does not go so far as that. The US border and the EU border still remain closed to such people from outside. (This is, of course, one reason why New York and Los

Angeles, London and Paris are not higher-up the projected size-rankings of the cities of the new millennium.) And so it is that yet more people arrive in unprepared, polluted, Mexico City.

This is a real, global, spatial reorganisation. Some barriers are torn down; others are maintained. New spaces are created (of global trade, of new *favelas*); others are destroyed (the spaces of more integrated national economies, and those of small-scale agriculture). Some identities (the hybrid-Mayan cultures of Chiapas, perhaps) come under threat from such spatial reorganisations, while those who already have more strength within the shifting power-geometry can wall themselves more tightly in (Californians approving Proposition 187, for instance).[3] Moreover, this reorganisation of the power-geometry of social relations will focus that geometry even more on cities and mega-cities.

World population is now about 5.3 billion people, of whom roughly 2.9 billion currently live in rural areas. If GATT 'succeeds' in agriculture, and if the required transformation of agricultural production takes place, then – it has been estimated – some 1.9 billion people will have to leave the land.[4] Under current conditions in all probability they will move to towns and cities – where they will consume internationally-produced (and probably cheaper) products ... their place within the world-seen-as-social-relations will have changed. Commenting upon this is not intended to broach any debates about the benefits of urbanism or the dangers of rural idiocy. The fact is, simply, that the cities, and our economic and social systems more generally, are not prepared. Maybe the Zapatistas of Chiapas, farmers in India fighting Cargill and GATT, even French farmers, are part of urban resistance in a wider sense: a refusal to become part of the armies of the world's *fin-de-siècle* urban poor.

What is going on here is a demonstration of the intimate interconnections of spatiality and power. 'Social space' can helpfully be understood as a social product, as constituted out of social relations, social interactions. Moreover, precisely because it *is* constituted out of social relations, spatiality is always and everywhere an expression and a medium of power. What all these recent developments represent is a reorganisation of that spatiality of power which stands to have major implications for cities everywhere.

Space/Power, Identity/Difference

WITHIN THE CITY

That interrelation of space and power continues and becomes more intense and complex within the city itself.

The language, and often the fact, of cities is frequently one of extremes. On the one hand high opera, on the other the mingling of the popular cultures of the world. Here precious, chi-chi restaurants and a few blocks away food kitchens. Some of these polarisations are, perhaps, frequently over-drawn; most people's lives are still lived somewhere in the middle. Yet there is one central tension in the city which is undoubtedly real. On the one hand cities are places of freedom and escape. You can come here to get away from the constraints of small communities. Here you can find the advantages of multiplicity and of complexity, of the potential for mixing and the ability to disappear, here you can do your own thing, be anonymous. And yet for others, or for other aspects of identity, all that multiplicity and chaos can become a source of danger, vulnerability and oppression. It can close down the possibility of self-expression. Cities, in their various forms, can be a context both for the freedom of expression of some identities and for the extinction of the expression of others. Some 'differences' may flourish while others are repressed. One of the central questions in the making of liveable cities must be how we can maintain the advantage of the first of these characteristics without falling into the oppressions of the second. What I want to argue here is that one way into this dilemma may be found by thinking through the relationship (or the myriad of potential relationships) between identity/difference, spatiality, and power. By thinking through the active interlinkages between these terms it may be possible to explore some of the potential dimensions of a democratic politics of spatiality.

One good way of testing out one's ideas is by making them confront the challenge of the ordinary. Away from the drama of the juxtaposition of homelessness with millionaire penthouses, are they able to have any useful purchase on the (apparently) more humdrum happenings of middling daily life?

The vast estates of public housing (some of it now privatised) which form such a significant part of the acreage of many British cities are just such places. They are home to millions of people. They are not the kind of place to which most of the drama-critics and novelists of the city find themselves much attracted. Yet, as much as the destitute inner areas and the gleaming towers of multinational capital, they have been caught in the vice of recent decades of global restructuring and neoliberal politics.

Over recent years many of these estates have shifted their places somewhat within the global power geometry. They are still utterly tied-in to globalisation, whether through the videos hired by the night, the international cleaning company on contract to the local council under the national imposition of compulsory competitive tendering, or simply through the range of consumer goods brought home. Yet at the same time many of these estates have also seen their spatial connections in some ways becoming more local. The places have, to some extent, become more closed-in on themselves. Large numbers of jobs off the estate have been lost, especially for men, and unemployment has risen. Cuts in public transport in some areas have increased the difficulty, and the price, of movement in and out. Sometimes even some of the big stores have withdrawn, finally defeated by lack of demand or by vandalism.

This shift in the location of the estates in the context of broader spatial relations has led on occasions to complex renegotiations of spatiality and power within the estate itself. There have been disruptions to the pre-existing relations between spatiality and identity/difference and new modes of negotiating these interrelations have arisen.

One detailed recent study of some parts of these estates is Bea Campbell's *Goliath*, an intimate and insightful investigation of those areas which became the setting in 1991 for outbreaks of rioting.[5] It is a book which provides a window into the complexity of relations between identity and spatiality and how these are criss-crossed by and constructed through a multitude of dimensions of power – of gender, of generation, of policing, of ethnicity. Two small examples drawn from this study of the riot neighbourhoods enable these relationships to be explored.

Example One

One immediate and important effect of the loss of jobs in previously-established sectors of industry was that the spatial range of the lives of many men was dramatically altered. They no longer went off the estate each day to work.

One of the ways in which many of these men had been accustomed to establish their identities, and in particular their identities in relation to women (their local Other) was through the degree and nature of their relative mobility. The men had left the confines of the estate every day; they had worked in different, and more spatially dispersed, workplaces from the women. The fact of this relatively greater mobility and especially that it was a daily demonstration of their power to leave, had been one of the central axes of their self conception as men. It was a significant element in that set of characteristics which these people had internalised, in the particularity of this social setting, as being essential to the establishment of what they saw as masculinity. (In contrast, Campbell explores in detail the various ways in which it had also been essential, and by a variety of means ensured, that the women of the estate remained relatively immobilised. Spatial stability, not to say constriction, was interpreted as being an essential element in the establishment of that much sought after characteristic: respectability.) The significant point for the argument here is that there had been intimate connections between (i) the gender-dimensions of identity and difference, (ii) spatiality, and (iii) power, and that, in the context of national and international economic and political shifts, those previously established connections had been destroyed.

Under the previous socio-spatial arrangement, many men's attitude to the estate had been like their relationship with home; both the estate and the home were places which the men left and to which they returned, but within which they didn't fully participate. When, as Campbell puts it 'their patrons – the owners of private capital – walked away' (p322), and many men were left unemployed, all this geometry of power disintegrated. Capital's desertion removed from the men 'their licensed means of episodic escape' (p320). It was a situation which threatened to consign them, spatially, to what they interpreted as the world of women: the estate and the home. The response of the men, in a significant proportion of cases, was a refusal to co-operate. They refused to co-operate within the home. They refused to co-operate in fatherhood. They became itinerant (another, even if more local, demonstration of the power of their mobility?) between wives, mothers and girlfriends. And they refused to co-operate at the level of the estate: in the forms of resistance and community survival being organised by residents who saw the place as a basis for fighting back, as a place through which some kind of political identification could be established. They rejected the possibility of co-operation in this form of spatiality.

There are some who have interpreted such dislocations and re-negotiations as a crisis of masculinity, the classic argument running along fairly straightforward lines: men lose their jobs → they become confined to the home, without a role → their masculinity is undermined. The problem with the most frequently proposed version of this approach is that it assumes an essential masculinity. And from such an assumption there is no way out – men and a singular, pre-given masculinity are inevitably and necessarily associated. Together they demand, for their ability to flourish 'normally', a particular relation to space, a particular form of spatiality. The implication is that we just have to accept it.

But that is not the only way of interpreting these events. The far more satisfactory alternative is to argue against any notion of essential identities. Thus, Chantal Mouffe, for instance, says of political practice that it 'does not consist in defending the rights of preconstituted identities, but rather in constituting those identities themselves in a precarious and always vulnerable terrain.'[6] This is a formulation of identity which can be extended beyond the field of political practice. It sees (the various aspects of) identity as the product of social circumstances, outcomes of and responses to specific articulations of social interactions. There is, however, one caveat which might be entered concerning the formulation as spelled out in that quotation. For while to insist so strongly on the lack of 'preconstituted identities' is certainly important in establishing a non-essentialist approach, it can be problematical if it implies that identities are somehow formed out of nothing, or that there is a series of instantaneously-formed identities. On the contrary, there is always a preceding history, and a history which is brought to, and which is part of the raw material for, each new situation.

All this is relevant to what happened on the estates. The recently unemployed men were facing a challenge to an aspect of their previously constituted identities. The disruption to their lives had revealed, as well as undermined, some of the bases on which these identities had been built. One of these bases was a crucial relationship between the construction of spatiality and the construction of (that particular form of) masculinity. It was a specific relationship, particular to these times and places. And it had broken down. The men found themselves confronted with the need to construct new

108

identities; moreover these would be identities in which – given both the wider social context and the prevailing understanding of women as being the nearest available Other – the construction of a 'masculinity' in some form or another was likely to play a part. (Not all men would respond in the same way, but the pressure to conform to *some* socially-recognised masculinity must have been considerable.) They were thus now faced with the task of negotiating another identity and another masculinity, but in the context of a spatiality which no longer offered the same opportunities for establishing their difference. The possibility of participation in a gender-inclusive spatiality of estate and home was, by many of them, rejected, and they began to negotiate within the constraints of their more confined spatiality another (equally precarious and vulnerable) form of detachment and mobility.

In both old and new identities spatiality was a key term in the attempt to accomplish and establish 'difference'.

Example Two

The argument can be pursued further by taking another example, this time concerning a group of the younger men, and a set of events which took place on a particular estate. The central characters in this story are young men who became known as 'TWOCcers'. The verb to 'TWOC' was coined in this period to refer to an activity (Taking Without the Owner's Consent) which rose briefly to prominence in the national tabloids and psyche and for a short period was the focus of a small moral panic. The objects which were so taken, without the owners' consent, were cars. The activity consisted of taking a suitably sharp car and driving it sometimes on the open road sometimes for display but always at great speed, and quite often quite dangerously. It was an activity which hit the headlines, caught the imagination, and then faded again from the public view; and it was interpreted in a variety of ways. One such interpretation understood TWOCcing as a response to the impact of recession. The loss of employment and of financial resources was seen as having immobilised these young men, as having threatened to enclose them spatially – as in the case of the older men discussed in the previous example, the recession threatened to lock them into a world which, basically, they held in very low esteem. Once again, there is a relationship being hinted at here between identity and spatiality.

The cars, and the way they were handled, offered an opportunity to break the bounds of these constraints. The space of the car itself had an immediate effect: Campbell quotes a consumer psychologist on the subject of what happens 'when men step into a car, "they step into a private world in which they feel invulnerable. They feel grander, more powerful, they have no feeling of their own vulnerability, and so there is nothing to stop them doing what they do" ' (p263). Inside this private space of invulnerability the lads demonstrated to the world their mobility, through the speed at which they drove, and their agility, through display-performances of handbrake turns and suchlike. And indeed one of the essences of it all was performance. On one of the estates, displays of dramatic driving were held. They took place in the square near the shopping centre, after ten at night.

This 'square near the shopping centre after ten at night' was a time-space transformed by the activities of these young men. By day it was the square near the shopping centre; after ten it was an arena of display, a classic time-space of enunciation. And this transformation of a bit of space was part and parcel, for these lads, of establishing a powerful identity.

Here, at night, was a space-time whose particularity was established in part by wider references and connections. Many of the cars were, at least in part, foreign-made models. A wide range of globally-designed electronics was used to communicate, to monitor, even to video the performance. The correct, internationally accredited, youth culture clothes had to be worn. In all these ways, this place, like every place, was an open space, its specificity established by a particular mixture and articulation of links to the wider world. And yet the aim of the TWOCcers was to bound it, to command and control it, to establish exclusive use of it. As a shopping centre and public square it was a space open to all. After 10 o'clock it belonged implicitly to one group. 'We don't do it at three o'clock in the afternoon, because that would be dangerous, but we do it any time after ten o'clock. Anyone who came into Blackbird Leys (near Oxford) after that would know that as soon as they hit the shops they had to beware, because a car could pop out from anywhere. It's not a no-go area, it's just that people know they've got to be careful and that the driver is the one who's calling the shots' (cited in Campbell, p256).

Here was a clear establishment of an 'us' and a 'them' which demarcated both space-time and personal identity. It was part of a wider crisis of public space on the estate: 'the erosion of *co-operative* use of public space, its tyrannical appropriation and degradation by the lads who terrorised the men, women and children with whom they shared space' (p320). And such moves to establish exclusivity further debilitated any efforts to organise resistance to the deterioration of material and imaginary life. Moreover, it closed off possibilities for *other* peoples' construction of *their* identities, including collective identities, through sitting, talking, mingling outdoors in the square.

It was the making and claiming, as part of the establishment of a group identity – the establishment of their 'difference' – of an envelope of space-time which was exclusive, bounded, and constituted through relations of dominance and subordination.

A whole host of issues is raised by such stories. Before drawing out the main conclusions I want to raise just two sub-themes.

First, the episode of TWOCcing, just like the more generalised inability of some of the men to identify with the estates, emphasises the problems inherent in any attempt to equate the notion of 'community' with spatially local areas. Such equations have been made across the political spectrum from right to left for decades, and continue today. What they assume, usually implicitly, is an internal coherence and a homogeneity of interests within small geographical areas. Episodes such as these blow such assumptions apart. What they reveal are the fractures and contradictions, the deep conflicts of interest which can exist within such places. In that sense, the attempts even within the estates to build bases of resistance need also to be analysed for their assumptions about the commonality or not of the interests of different groups. Estate-based alliances would have to be just that, alliances which recognised the differences and conflicts between the various social groups.

Such episodes also reveal how the places themselves are so differently interpreted by different groups – by some as locales in which to construct some kind of life, maybe even some kind of resistance; by others as places of deadly entrapment. Geographical places themselves, in this case 'the estates', do not have single uncontested, identities. To assume that they do, by assuming a community of interest, is to ignore much of what goes on within them and to adopt a politics which, as Bea Campbell points out, is doomed to failure. It is also to ignore the fact that so much of politics and political practice these days is in fact *not* based on spatial community in that sense. This is not to say that it is not heavily influenced by spatiality – indeed spatiality may still be an important axis of organisation – but it will not necessarily be the spatiality of the internally coherent, spatially contiguous, local community.

Second, these episodes point to the social significance of spatial mobility. But it is a complex significance. Clearly there is frequently a relationship between spatial mobility and social power. The potential mobility of multinational corporations is one of their key bargaining counters, in relation both to employees and to national governments; the fact of this mobility lies behind their power in current negotiations over 'free trade' – their existing socio-spatial power being wielded to win changes in the organisation of global economic space which will reinforce that power still further. In the cities set within this world structure of the spatiality of power, the men who have been thrown out of work feel disempowered because of the new constraints on their mobility; both they and the TWOCcers seek to re-establish it some other way. The power to move, and – the real point – to move more than others, is of huge social significance. Indeed, that it is *relative* mobility which is at issue is underlined in both of these instances (at such different spatial scales, involving such apparently different actors) by the need of some, the relatively mobile/powerful to stabilise the identities of others in part by tying them down in place. So capital is freer to roam the world than is labour; Mexicans must wait in Mexico for capital to come to them. And the ideal, if not fact, of womanhood on the estates has in the past been centred on a smaller place/space than that of masculinity. The relationship between the home, restricted life, and respectability may effectively have used the containment of potential mobility as a means of curtailing social power.

And yet, of course, the relationship between spatial mobility and social power is by no means a simple positive one. Many of the most mobile in this world – low-wage economic migrants, political refugees – are deeply powerless.[7] And, on the other hand, restriction to a spatial base may be used as an organising principle for fighting back – as some of the women on the estates, though unsuccessfully perhaps precisely because of the internal divisions, tried to do. Moreover, the apparently positive power of mobility and its significance in some instances in the establishment of identity exists in a strange counterpoint to the establishment of difference/identity through the construction of essentialist views of place or identification with such socially-constructed places as 'home' or 'homeland'. And yet, to complicate things still further, it might be hypothesised that the romanticisation of place is most frequently undertaken by those who have left (migrants thinking of home) or by those with the power to leave (the ex-urban 'villagers' whose weeks are spent in the world of globalisation, enabling a return at weekends to the secure stability of a rural idyll).

But if the relation is not simple, it is none the less clear that there *is* a relation between spatial mobility, social power and the construction of identities. And it is a relation which intertwines with a host of very ordinary policy issues which are at the heart – or which should be at the heart – of political debate about the future social form of cities: issues of public transport, of safety on the streets, and of the importance of crowded and genuinely open public space.

SPACE, POWER AND IDENTITY IN THE CITY

What, then, of the tension in the city, between the delights of anonymity offered by metropolitan multiplicity and the relative lack of imposed community controls on the one hand, and the isolations and the terrors of going out at night, say, on the other? What are the possibilities of a democracy with multiplicity, and in particular for a democratic politics of spatiality?

Both general everyday knowledge and the evidence of the particular examples just explored confirm that it is simply not possible to assume that the unlimited toleration of any and all attempt to establish 'difference' might result in nothing more threatening than benign chaos. We know that is not so. Nor, it seems to me, is it politically acceptable to revel in all forms of difference for their own sake and tolerate the conflicts and contradictions which will inevitably emerge: a kind of 'free-market' attitude to identity and difference. Rather, it seems to me, it is necessary to recognise 'difference', though as always unachieved, but also to examine its conditions of production – the constantly changing power-relations through which identity/difference is established. And part of that examination, or so I am trying to argue here, will be an exploration of the conditions of production of the spatialities of identity – the spatial forms, negotiations and relations on which identities (in part) rest.

It has been argued here that both identities and spatiality are constructed out of interaction. On the one hand an essentialist concept of difference has been rejected. On the other hand spatiality has been conceptualised as that strong yet always provisional power-geometry which we confront, negotiate and construct/reconstruct in the living of our lives. We have seen this in the present restructuring of the global power-geometry of the world market and in the claimings and the closings of spaces on the estate. Moreover, it has been argued, the two terms are related. 'Objects', which in this discussion most significantly include personal and political identities, do not exist 'in' a pre-existent space. Both identities and their spatiality are constructed out of interaction, and they are constructed together. We make our spaces/spatialities in the process of constructing ourselves.

Furthermore, there is also a third term, linked to both of the others: power. Precisely because it is constituted out of social relations, spatiality is always and everywhere full of power. But power here is not seen as an external relation, linking already-formed identities inside a spatial container. Rather, it *constitutes* both identities and spatiality. Moreover, if power is inherently constitutive of the social and the spatial then the question for socialist/democratic politics is not how to *eliminate* power, but how to enable forms of power which are compatible with democratic/socialist values. And, conversely, how to challenge those which are not.

The implication is that what must be examined are the ways in which particular identities (relations of difference) and particular spatialities are jointly established. In and through what nets of power relations are they set, and how do they draw on them? All identities and spatialities, it has been argued, are relational. The question at issue is therefore the nature of those relations. Some identities and spatialities are established in and through relations of dominance and subordination.

It is not, therefore, particular forms of spatiality which are at issue. Mobility may be empowering in positive and egalitarian ways. Or it may be enforced (as free-trade agreements may enforce it upon peasant farmers). Or it may be empowering because established necessarily at the expense of others (the ability to *leave*, to leave *behind*, to be *more* mobile than others). Likewise a strategy of bounding spaces, of claiming some kind of spatial exclusivity, may be built on already-existing unequal power to reinforce a difference-in-domination (the case of Californians' political attacks on migrants from Latin America), or it may be a defensive move, to preserve a subordinate identity under threat (the Zapatistas' claims for indigenous spaces). Or again, closed spaces as bases for identity may be established through *means* which involve the exercise of domination (as the lads took over the square by the shopping centre at night, by the threat of

114

physical danger). It is the *relation* between identity, spatiality and power which is crucial. Just as with mobility, degrees of spatial enclosure and openness/porosity and their relation to the construction of identities may be established through a range of very different social relations. And it is these which must be evaluated. The identity of the TWOCcers and their spatiality were established together through the terms of certain forms of social power.

This is not to argue that making a distinction between these articulations of identity/spatiality/power is always simple. Multinational corporations versus indigenous peasants from Chiapas may seem a clear-cut case. The link between (a particular form of) masculinity, the threat of physical danger, and the exclusive use of a space may seem self-evidently politically questionable. And yet, *really* thinking through the integral relationship between identity, spatiality and power may raise more difficult questions too. The older men, in the first example, now feeling spatially trapped through the loss of their jobs, interpreted the spaces of home and estate as the world of women. As, presumably, a world which in some way excluded them. Were they right? And if so by what means were they excluded from these spaces? – as a result of their own requirements of identity-through-difference/domination, or through the construction of an identity/spatiality of home and estate which could not accommodate them in any immediately available form? In what ways might the spatiality of the estate have been made 'gender inclusive' and what might that have implied for both gender identities? Likewise, was the square-by-the-shops even in the daytime hours in fact equally open to all? From other such time-spaces that I know, I imagine that it, too, was peopled by some groups more than others. Older women and pensioners and young children perhaps. There were here too, quite possibly, notions of proper behaviour which would alienate some, even effectively refuse their presence. It is unlikely that even this time-space was not more claimed as 'theirs' by some groups than others, more welcoming to some, more affirming of their identity, while being for other groups more problematical to enter. A different set of relations of space/power/identity in the daytime square, then, and probably less oppressive than most, but nonetheless ones which bear examination.

To argue, therefore, that it is the conditions of production of, the joint operation of, space/power/identity which must be examined is not to say that distinguishing between such conditions and evaluating them politically will be simple. But it is to argue that it is possible.

NOTES

[1] The figures and information in this first point are based on research published by Population Concern (see, for instance, their *Annual Report*, 1993); I should like to thank them for their help.

[2] See T. Lang, and C. Hines, *The New Protectionism*, Earthscan, London 1993. Thanks to Tim Lang for discussions about these issues.

[3] Proposition 187, approved in California in 1994, denies to undocumented immigrants in that state access to all free public services except for emergency health care. Quite what its practical effect will be remains at the time of writing uncertain, as questions are being raised concerning its constitutionality.

[4] Lang & Hines, *op.cit.*

[5] See B. Campbell, *Goliath: Britain's Dangerous Places*, Methuen, London, 1993.

[6] See C. Mouffe, 'Post marxism, democracy and identity', paper presented at the Annual Conference of the Association of American Geographers, San Francisco, 1994.

[7] D. Massey, *Space, Place and Gender*, Polity, Cambridge, 1994.

Social Justice and the New American Urbanism: The Revanchist City

Neil Smith

In retrospect, we may come to see the period between the stock market crash of 1987 and a spate of attacks and uprisings in the early 1990s as initiating a new kind of urbanism in the United States. It is a new urbanism not in the world historical sense that the capitalist city has somehow been overthrown or that the patriarchal city has been erased. Rather it marks a more modest novelty but a significant one nevertheless. It largely follows the kinds of economic, cultural and symbolic transformations that are broadly identified with the 'post-Fordist' city (beginning between the upheavals of the late 1960s and the economic crises of the early 1970s), but represents a decidedly more *political* shift – a trenchant repoliticization of the city. It announces in the first place an internationalization of the US city in political terms and with it a dramatic questioning and remaking of highly local identities, and second a galvanization of global shifts and personal identities via a gathering and vengeful reaction that pervades an increasingly market-determined public policy – the advent of what I have come to call 'the revanchist city'.[1] Previously accepted notions of social justice and an explicit concern with injustice, so central to the progressive urban ambitions of the 1960s and 1970s, have been flushed away with the remains of liberalism. In the same period, the narrowest visions derived from Marxism have also proven bankrupt. The new urbanism results from the political and cultural rush to fill this vacuum.

Where David Harvey brilliantly fastened on the question of social

117

justice as a vital conveyance from liberal to radical formulations more than two decades ago, and thereby helped introduce a whole generation of urbanists to Marxist theory,[2] it has been suggested that today we may be in the situation of having to reinvent 'social justice', both as a political bulwark against the right and at the same time a response to critiques of Marxism. 'From multiple directions, then,' Harvey himself suggests, 'there emerges a strong concern to reinstate concern for social justice and to re-elaborate upon what it takes to create the values and institutions of a reasonably just society.'[3] Such a reinvention of social justice would galvanize a left political response, and it would help to overcome the embarrassed silence or outright hostility that has typically marked Marxist and revolutionary treatments of social justice.[4] And yet I am not entirely convinced. In the course of trying to write this essay, which I began in an obviously sympathetic embrace of this proposal, I began to have doubts. I will therefore try to do two things here. First, I want to present a brief portrait of this 'new urbanism' doubly inscribed by internationalization at one scale and by a deepening 'revanchism' on the other. Second, against this backdrop, I want to take on the question of social justice more directly.

FROM HEBRON TO OKLAHOMA CITY

When Dr Baruch Goldstein, an American Jewish settler from the West Bank, sprayed the Hebron Mosque with machine-gun fire on February 25th 1994, assassinating twenty-nine Palestinians who had been attending Ramadan prayers, *The New York Times* responded by exploring the emotional turmoil and embarrassment felt by many Israelis about the massacre.[5] Very little of a systemic nature was diagnosed from the event which was broadly laid to Goldstein's 'instability', his unfortunate psychology. For *The Times* and for most of their US audience, the murdered Palestinians, by contrast, remained unnamed. They were therefore also unknown, dead others, unimportant except as pre-ordained symbols of a 'sad intractable conflict'. Only as a belated afterthought were their names even reported in a few outlets of the US press. They were uncounted (literally: for days, reported estimates of casualties ran from twenty-two to forty-nine, and only after weeks did the US press desultorily settle on an official figure of twenty-nine; and in the most serious sense, they did not count).

When, less than a week later, a gunman in broad daylight shot at a van of orthodox Lubavitch Jews on the Brooklyn Bridge, killing one person, the pattern of response was astonishingly similar, despite the fact that the episode represented a diametrically opposed violence. The administration of Mayor Giuliani and the city's media again focused on the 'rage and pain' of New York's orthodox Jews. They speculated, or denied speculation, that 'the attack might have been only a hurried act of vengeance for the slaying of dozens of Muslims in Hebron'. Such speculation was increased when the NYPD arrested Rashad Baz, whom *The New York Times* identified as 'an alien'[6] – actually a Lebanese citizen whose visa had run out – and charged him with homicide. Subsequently no such connection was established, in fact, but the innuendo of Baz's supposed alien-ness made the link anyway: 'his possessions included Islamic prayer beads and other religious articles, as well as a newspaper clipping about a bombing in Lebanon', reported *The New York Times*. Lebanon, Hebron, what's the difference.

This case was immediately scripted as a *national atrocity*. Both words are important. Had it happened at night in the nearby Brooklyn neighbourhood of Bedford Stuyvesant it would most likely have been logged in police computers as just another *local* 'drive-by-shooting'. And if it had involved African Americans on both sides, it might not even have merited a mention in *The Times*, never mind the national attention as atrocity: one more ghetto murder. A little more coverage and angst would have been expended if the parties could have been passed off as assimilated white Americans, especially if the victim (or the shooter) was visiting the city from respectable upper middle-class suburbs. So what made the Brooklyn Bridge killing so symbolic? Apart from suggesting that international political struggles were at home on the streets of New York as much as Beirut, the shooting confirmed an already ubiquitous rescripting of internal 'enemies' – Arab immigrants – as really external. Second, this attack on Lubavitchers became an immediate means by which Jews more generally could be reinstated as victims, countering the discordant impact of the Hebron massacre.

Comparison was quickly and widely made between this case and the Crown Heights case two years ago when a young black child was killed by a Lubavitch youth who ran a red light and in an ensuing riot a young Australian Lubavitcher was killed. In that case, the local black population widely blamed the police for being more concerned to protect the car driver than to get the child to hospital, while Lubavitch sect members accused the police of deliberately not quelling the riot that ensued. The latter accusations were aimed at the mayor and the police chief, and became a central issue in the 1993 mayoral campaign. That campaign elected a new mayor, Rudy Giuliani, who happens to be white and who is the first Republican mayor since Robert Lindsay in the late-1960s, and who has spearheaded a particularly revanchist urban politics in the mid-1990s.

Several other recent events – in New York and elsewhere – equally coded by race and nationalism entwined with class and gender, express the extent to which international political ambition has begun to inscribe US urbanism in the 1990s. In Los Angeles, widely heralded in the 1980s as the new, raw, Pacific urbanism for a new century, the 1992 uprising following the acquittal of four police officers in the vicious beating of Rodney King, defied habitual media efforts to explain the 'riot' as a simple black assault on whites. The flood of racial stereotypes as a means to explain the uprising was deafening and in the end unsuccessful, for it was, as Mike Davis put it, 'an extremely hybrid uprising, possibly the first multi-ethnic rioting in modern American history'.[7] Likewise, the bombing less than a year later of New York City's World Trade Center – simultaneously a symbol of 1970s downtown renewal (and the massive displacement this involved) and the 1980s global urbanism – evoked vivid images of a real life 'Towering Inferno', and unleashed a xenophobic media hunt for 'foreign Arab terrorists'.[8] While the complete failure of the building's security systems led to its depiction as a 'sick building' in a 'sick city', the Trade Center bombing cemented the connection between American urban life and apparently arbitrary but brutal violence (terror) on the international scene. The xenophobic hysteria that followed engulfed even *The New York Times* whose language of blithe exaggeration passed for uncontested fact as they documented the search for foreign conspirators – 'a ring accused of plotting to blow up New York City'.[9] No mere Manhattan Project that.

No mere Manhattan Project indeed; and this was forcefully brought home in the bombing of the Oklahoma City Federal Building on April 19 the following year. The massive explosion, which killed 168 people, was quickly billed by CNN as 'Terror in the Heartland', as if to point out that it was not only in New York and Los Angeles that Americans were vulnerable to international terrorism. In the hours following the blast, the FBI organized a massive manhunt for 'two Middle-Eastern men' who were supposedly witnessed running from the scene. The media found various obliging 'experts' to declare that the bombing bore all the hallmarks of 'Middle Eastern terrorism' and used this testimony to spin a bewildering array of conspiratorial scenarios. Muslim Americans were harassed, the Nation of Islam was fingered as a possible perpetrator from within, and two men who had driven to Oklahoma in hopes of a quicker expedition of immigration documents from the Immigration and Nationalization Service (INS) were detained. A young man who had just got off a plane from London, and who was of Middle Eastern descent, was held for several days for being in the wrong place at the wrong time.

The anti-semitism and racism of this response were only outstripped by that of the stunned reaction to the news that Timothy McVeigh, a European American, right-wing extremist and sometime anti-government militia associate, had been detained as a suspect. A second suspect was apprehended, and despite desperate speculation that they had been used and that 'Middle Eastern terrorists' were still ultimately to blame, it was increasingly obvious that responsibility for the Oklahoma City bombing lay in the Middle West not the Middle East, and among white boys to boot; 'Terror in the Heartland' took on a momentarily more sinister meaning. For an instant, indeed, the meaning seemed inassimilable. To many, from Oklahoma to Washington DC, the idea that it was a 'homegrown American kid' who was responsible for what was widely billed as the worst act of terrorism in US history was, if anything, worse. That 'foreign Arabs' might hate America enough to commit a bombing was understandable, they seemed to be saying (in a moment of inadvertent revelation), but for it to be 'one of our own', as many officials, journalists and interviewees blurted out, was unfathomable. The discourse changed overnight to the psychology of militia members and the irrationality of anti-government attacks, even as the Republican majority in Congress, which was leading its own vicious attack on poor and working-class Americans, women, minorities, and immigrants, via a particularly nasty anti-government rhetoric, were peculiarly silent.

There are obvious questions about this pervasive framing of the Oklahoma City bombing. What gets to count as 'terrorism', and what is forgotten: did slavery and lynching not account for a more brutal and more protracted terrorism in US history? And who gets to count as 'our own': would the scripting of 'us' and 'them' have been different had the suspects been black instead of white? But beyond this, even the most cynical commentator probably could not have predicted the legislative course of a Congress suddenly galvanized against terrorism. The anti-terrorist legislation presented by the Clinton administration in response to Oklahoma City (and enthusiastically taken up by Congress) certainly included sweeping provisions restoring wide pre-1970s authority for FBI surveillance. But even more precious to the administration and legislators, were the widespread provisions against 'foreign terrorism'; among other provisions, the US government sought the power to designate (virtually at will) certain 'foreign' organizations as inherently terrorist, and to criminalize both membership in and financial support for any such organization by US citizens. The message was clear: sure, domestic terrorism may actually have been responsible for the murders in Oklahoma City, but that was an aberration; foreign terrorists are the real threat and they are therefore the appropriate target of new anti-terrorist legislation.

We might well be reminded of Menachem Begin who is reputed to have said, picking up on some anti-Jewish responses in the US to the sinking of the battleship USS *New Jersey* off the Lebanese coast in 1983: 'goyem kill goyem, and still they blame the Jews'. In Oklahoma City, Americans killed Americans, and still they blame the 'foreigners'.

A NEW URBANISM?

So why should we be tempted to see in these events, and the responses to them, some signs of an altered urbanism in the United States? At one level, after all, the official response to these events – Hebron to the Brooklyn Bridge, the LA uprising and the World Trade Centre, Oklahoma City – has been predictable: a lamentation and villainization of foreign terrorists and racial Others within, the more semitic (or, in the case of LA, the blacker) the better. And yet the response has also been more complicated, because the same foreign 'villains' are simultaneously present in US cities in large numbers, driving cabs, taking classes, repairing cars, doctoring to patients, renting apartments, running grocery stores, selling government bonds. In this respect, the language of American exceptionalism has been forced to co-exist with appeals for 'multicultural diversity' couched in terms of race, ethnicity, nationality and sexual preference. This in turn has contributed to an extraordinary rehardening – already broadly underway – of white middle-class identity as defensive crutch.

122

In the first place then, the internationalism of US urban formation is unprecedented. Urban politics and personal identities, social differences and geographical divisions are all being reshaped in a mélange of struggles that are intensely local, to be sure, but they are also increasingly refracted through international rather than more-narrowly defined 'national' events. Not since at least the 1920s, if indeed then, has US urbanism been so open to the tendrils of international influence. Then, it was first and foremost a question of record immigration changing the social and political demography of US cities; the internationalism-within was desperately contained in the white-heat of a self-replicating and self-patrolled nationalism forged variously through repression and ideology. The repression was widely and most prominently applied against working-class movements and especially 'foreign-speaking socialists', but its ideological counterpart came with theories of urban homogeneity and such academically inspired myths as the melting pot. The 'Chicago School' of urban research, explained how social differences, squeezed through a sieve of economic and geographical competition, were the hallmark of a distinctly holistic, American urbanism (and this model was quite successfully exported).

In this and many other ways, the inevitability of international differences has for much of the twentieth century been diluted into a supposedly hermetic American urbanity, a hermeticism that was dependent on a very real isolation (in terms of most people's everyday lives) from global events, if not, necessarily, from personal global connections.

This vision survived for decades as a central pillar of urban self-conception in the United States but is today increasingly unsustainable. On top of the more gradual internationalization of the economy, consumption practices and cultures, which have been proceeding gradually throughout much of the century, the spate of internationally inscribed urban dramas, from LA to the Brooklyn Bridge, has rendered that vision unrealistic. The Oklahoma City bombing, an act of purely domestic terrorism, is, paradoxically, the exception which dramatically confirms this proposition. The paramilitary militias that operate in an estimated forty states are organized on precisely the premise that this hermetic Americanism has been fundamentally eroded; much of their anti-government sentiment comes from the pervasive belief that the US government itself actually spearheads the 'international conspiracy' *against* the American people, and they offer as proof – and one militia leader so testified before a Senate subcommittee – that the government has abrogated the national sovereignty by inviting foreign troops (the UN) on to US soil. In the wake of the Oklahoma City bombing and the subsequent publicity they received, these paramilitary militias initially actually gained membership.[10]

Today there is again record foreign immigration to US cities, but now Europeans no longer dominate, the post-1989 emigration from Eastern Europe notwithstanding. Asians, Latin Americans and Middle Easterners especially have predominated among the new immigrants. Unlike the earlier period, however, today's immigration is combined with an unprecedented porosity of national economic and cultural boundaries thanks to the revolutionizing of transport and communications technology. But is this really so different from the 1920s? Was that not also a decade marked by significant internationalization of US capital? Indeed it was, but whereas it made sense in the context of the 1920s to conceive of national capitals expanding internationally in such a way that they ultimately strengthened the national base, in the last two decades or so the internationalization of capital has significantly eroded the national identification of a significant proportion of world capital. The scale of the organization of capital has, as it were, been turned inside out. And the political geography of internationalism – as witnessed, for example, by the North American Free Trade Agreement (NAFTA) – is comparatively slow to catch up.[11] A qualitatively different immigration experience, then, and a qualitatively different internationalization of capital are spawning a quite different political culture of urbanism premised on the reality that US urban areas are today dramatically more exposed to the political and cultural as well as economic dimensions of what is euphemistically referred to as globalization.

In many ways it might be argued that this incipient internationalized urbanism in the United States represents the local political culture that US foreign policy – political, military and economic – deserves. Most obviously, as conceded by the stunned response to the arrest of Timothy McVeigh for the Oklahoma bombing, it is not difficult to imagine why US cities might become targets for foreign terrorist attacks seeking revenge for US military and political actions abroad. More surprising, perhaps, is that the World Trade Center would appear to be the only such example, despite the paranoia of Congressional anti-terrorist legislation. But the connections go much deeper. Equally, in economic terms, increased access to 'foreign' products and imported cultural products may indeed respond to some kind of consumer demand, but it equally responds to the global strategies for profit maximization by US-based and other capital that provides these 'goods'.

But there are also less obvious connections. Saskia Sassen has argued forcefully that much of the new immigration from Asia, South and Central America and the Middle East to US cities since the 1960s cannot be explained simply in narrow economic terms, but rather that it represents a series of culturally filtered opportunities that emerge from US political, military and economic penetration of many national economies on those continents. If it happens in many different kinds of ways, immigration is the predictable result of the intensification of various kinds of ties, obligations and disruptions that resulted from the US wars in Korea and Indochina, for example, the exploitation of Mexico as a source of cheap labour, vigorous support of the military dictatorship in El Salvador, the establishment of a pro-US government in Iran prior to 1979, and so on.[12] Some of these interventions resulted in a migration stream which had a discernible effect in the LA uprising. Likewise, in a trend that dates most clearly to the oil embargo of 1974, older villainizations of Arabs have been dusted off and touched up as part of a larger US struggle for oil resources and geo-economic power. In other words, the target of officially sanctioned anti-semitism is increasingly displaced from Jews to Arabs, in consort with wider international shifts in US foreign policy.[13]

Let me make a couple of caveats about this argument. First, this 'new urbanism' at the behest of internationalization is a specifically US experience, and may even represent a certain catching up with the rest of the world. It is the US that has been out of step, for few other places had quite the luxury of global isolation that the US enjoyed. Alone except for Australia and Canada, the US was exceptional in never having its national territory attacked or even seriously threatened in World War Two; today, from London to Tunis, Paris to Baghdad, 'foreign' bombings are not by any stretch of the imagination the norm, but they are a known quantity; and nowhere else in the last half century, not even latter-day Japan, has been able to wield such economic, political and certainly cultural power for the purposes of restricting foreign imports of goods and ideas or forcing them to conform, and thus for realizing (with however limited success) such a hermetic nationalism.

Second, although it is sympathetic, this is a different argument from the emergence of so-called global cities. I am not simply arguing that a few cities have become crucial control nodes of international capitalism, although a convincing case can obviously be made for that, at least in the case (in the US) of New York and Los Angeles. But the new urbanism goes beyond global cities. The paramilitary militia movement is not only anti-government and anti-internationalist, but fanatically anti-urban too, and it is symbolic that a thoroughly non-world city in Oklahoma was chosen as a suitable target for this anti-internationalism.

A second dimension of the new urbanism takes us back more directly to the revanchist city, and here we begin at the opposite end of the continuum of geographical scales, with what Samira Kawash refers to as the 'homeless body'.[14] The explosion of homelessness in US cities since the early 1980s is surely .the most visible symbol of the bankruptcy of the liberal urban policy that emerged from the New Deal in the 1930s, blossomed in the postwar period, and that had a final flourish after 1968.

Until the uprisings of the late 1960s, the whole urban policy edifice was based on a loud liberal refusal of class, in the sense that class differences were acknowledged, to be lamented, only to be seen as resolvable via urban policy, and therefore an aberration *vis-à-vis* the principles of social justice. In the meantime the explicit inattention to other forms of social difference translated into an active and often deliberate perpetuation of racial discrimination in particular. But following the Kerner Commission Report, urban policy at least began to recognize race, if only by means of the same kind of refusal that had pertained to class.[15] Social movements more widely, especially feminism, environmentalism and the gay and lesbian movement, also forced changes in social legislation, from affirmative action to the legalization of abortion, and civil rights in the broadest sense. Liberal social policy, including urban policy, has obviously disintegrated since the early 1980s, and it is widely understood that this defeat resulted from a full frontal assault by conservative governments seeking to reinstate certain kinds of class, race and gender privileges. But it would be a dire mistake to forget too that the failure of liberal social policy was in part endemic, springing from its refusal of an analysis of the systematic causes of oppression and exploitation. The legalistic and individualistic assumptions of affirmative action, for example, are today coming home to roost, as opponents claim that this legislation is itself 'racist', i.e., anti-white. The implied symmetry of race (before it class, and more recently gender) is here built into liberal responses to oppression, and it has been only too easy for the right to use liberalism's own rhetoric of equality against it: 'why does our government not have affirmative action provisions for *us* too?'

The unprecedented expulsion of people from homes in the 1980s – at the behest of market forces, policy decisions, personal circumstances – has to be seen in this context. Homelessness is as much the result of an utter failure of liberal urban policy as it is of a vindictive reaction from the right in the 1980s. In the broadest sense this failure results from the unambiguous attachment of liberal policy to free market 'solutions' when of course it is the free market that is the source of the problem; as Harvey claimed from the beginning, in an argument that attracted considerable conservative ire but which now seems so obvious, in some respects, that we are in the process of forgetting it, the solution to the so-called housing problem will only come 'with a socially controlled urban land market and socialized control of the housing sector'.[16] In different places, however, the failure of liberal urban policy, the replacement of a public liberalism with the logic of the market, and the emergence of mass homelessness played out in different ways, and I would like to recount this particular path to the revanchist city in the context of New York.

In New York, it was various liberal Democratic administrations that presided haplessly, and apparently helplessly, over the meteoric increase in the homeless population from a few thousand in the late 1970s to an estimated 100,000 a decade later. At the same time, the City accumulated record numbers of dilapidated buildings that their owners had abandoned, yet even a mid-1980s $5 billion housing reconstruction programme, using many of these buildings, was unable to make serious inroads in solving homelessness. But it is not so much the dramatic increase in the numbers of homeless people in the 1980s as the equally dramatic shift in their treatment at the end of the decade that provides one of the most vivid markers of the advent of the revanchist city. As news stories began to appear in the context of economic recession of the early 1980s about the rapid increase in the numbers of homeless people, the most apparent response in New York, as in many other cities, was a vaguely patronizing compassion, from a distance. There were constant attacks on homeless people – sleeping homeless people set alight, to name the worst – but also a widespread enlistment of sympathy. The encampment of as many as 300 people in Tompkins

Square Park in the Lower East Side, and the periodic contest with police in the 'liberated' park between 1988 and 1991, became a symbol of both the desperation of homeless people and the significant level of qualified support they had in the city, vicious attacks notwithstanding.

By 1991, with a crippling economic depression underway – a recession that was felt most intensely on adjacent Wall Street, which had supplied many of the yuppies who gentrified the Lower East Side in the 1980s – the City launched a final attack against the homeless people and others who had squatted the park. The new squatter settlements, continually bulldozed by the City, came to be known, after the social democratic mayor, as Dinkinsvilles. If gentrification had been the administration's true policy, eviction was its housing policy. Even *The New York Times* understood the problem:

> Last June, police in riot gear tore down a shantytown in New York's Tompkins Square Park and evicted the homeless. Then they swept through vacant lots to tear down a new shantytown and evict the homeless again. Can't the city do better than chase the homeless from one block to another? Shades of Friedrich Engels.[17]

In retrospect – indeed we knew it at the time – the defeat of Tompkins Square Park marked the evaporation of even liberal sympathy for homeless people and the poor more generally, and the advent of a more brazenly cruel attack on the city's poor.[18] Liberal support for homeless people had exhausted its narrowly moralistic foundations as erstwhile sympathisers confronted their own increasingly tense economic predicaments. Mayor David Dinkins launched the first stage of a full scale homeless-removal campaign in 1991, but when in a funeral pyre to a failed liberalism, Dinkins subsequently lost the mayoral election to Rudy Giuliani, the vindictiveness against homeless people that had been a desperate act of a know-nothing-else liberalism fused with electoral expedience, became a systematic emblem of revanchist politics. At a press conference within weeks of being elected, Giuliani was asked what he intended to do about so many homeless people on the streets, given the record cold winter. 'Change the weather', came the Mayor's reply. But in truth the new mayor was targeting more than just the city's homeless population. Attacks by police on homeless people increased rapidly, and after a little more than a year in office, Giuliani revealed his broader agenda to a group of assembled newspaper editors. Faced with a budget deficit of between $3 billion and $4 billion, he was interested not only in cutting the supply of services but demand for them too. Service cuts and budget cuts achieved this two-pronged objective; he hoped thereby to encourage 'the poor population' who are so dependent on welfare and city services to 'move out of the city'. Shrinkage of the poor population would be a 'good thing' for the city. 'That's not an unspoken part of our strategy', the mayor summarized. 'That *is* our strategy'.[19]

The revanchist city is a city of occasionally vicious revenge wrought against many of the city's most dependent – unemployed and homeless people, racial and ethnic minorities, women and immigrants, gays and lesbians, the working class. It has everything to do with a defence and reconstruction of the lines of identity privilege (which came under attack after the 1960s) in the context of rising economic insecurity. If I have pointed to only a brief depiction of one aspect of the revanchist city – the generation, criminalization and dispersal of homelessness in New York City – it should be clear that this represents a much broader shift.[20] Indeed, if the specific internationalization of the city is very much a US affair, I think it is fair to suggest that the revanchist city, while perhaps baring its most malicious face in the US, can be identified in fainter tones in Europe. With anti-immigrant attacks, social service cutbacks and privatizations throughout the continent, a similar picture emerges. There too, the reworking of personal identities mingles with a defence of eroding national identities in the context of global change.

If I have highlighted two aspects of a new US urbanism – an internationalization from above, as it were, and a revanchism from below – it is worth pointing out that these seemingly different processes are already imbricated on with the other. The revanchist city is in many ways a direct response to the erosion of significant economic boundaries around the nation-state. Insofar as the globalization of the economy has swung economic power decisively away from nationally defined economies and political institutions toward international capitals and economic institutions such as the IMF, nationally defined states have become less useful and less convenient from the perspective of internationally mobile capital. Nation-states have therefore found themselves forced to compete since the 1970s in a variety of arenas that had previously been comfortably national and contained. Generally, they are less and less willing to expand regulations or even sustain existing regulations over capital. They have often encouraged the immigration of cheap labour, shrill xenophobic protests notwithstanding. And they have thereby found themselves less and less shackled to many traditional functions of the classical national state, including broad responsibility for ensuring a functional system of social reproduction. Ensuing economic competition between politically defined and territorially fixed nation-states therefore came precisely as the power of 'national capitals' waned, and necessity was quickly turned into a virtue. Privatization and the wholesale dismantling of many national systems of social welfare may have been (and was) an ideological ideal for conservatives, from the bottom up, but it was equally a response to the altered-scale geography of the global political economy. The dismantling and privatization of public functions represent rather desperate responses by national state governments to retain and redefine a political role for themselves at a time when their economic functions are increasingly subordinated to the global economy and even emerging aspects of a global state, especially the IMF. The 'trickle down' of this destruction of the public sphere – in reality a deluge – to the local level combined with sharpened economic and personal insecurity experienced by previously privileged or at least secure segments of the population are in many ways the progenitors of the revanchist city.

In the US, at least, a resurgent nationalism is in many ways the super glue that binds these international and local 'decentrings' together. If economic nationalism is, in practice, eroded, political and cultural nationalism are in many places fortified. American nationalism, as Lauren Berlant reminds us, is continually reinvented as a gendered identity,[21] and as the revanchist city suggests, much the same has to be said of race and class. As a response to the internationalism of everyday life, American nationalism is simultaneously reinvented today as a question of class imbricated most sharply with race.

SOCIAL JUSTICE

So where does this leave us with social justice? In the 1970s and early 1980s, a revolutionary geographical theory was indeed forged but increasingly at a distance from political practice. What this theory gained in terms of the sharpness of political analysis, focused largely but never exclusively on class, it lost in terms of the weakness of its theorization of cognate oppressions. On the other hand, the emergence of identity politics in the 1980s, to some extent at the expense of class analysis, presented a parallel, but alternative and much needed, political vision strongly linking justice and identity. But identity politics has too often given a left wing gloss to liberal visions of social justice – a sense of the automatic equivalence of different oppressions. The revanchist city has emerged very much in the interstices of these equivalences, exploiting the insecurities that emerge from the dramatic restructuring of identities that is currently afoot. This was never more evident than in the widespread political paralysis that greeted the spectre of Korean shopowners shooting at black and Latino looters and passers-by during the LA uprisings. 'How,' commentator after commentator asked, 'are we to decide between the contrasting claims of two sets of oppressed peoples?'

To the extent that the non-equivalence of oppressions is accepted, the temptation has been to hierarchialize oppressions in terms of superior claims for some moral high ground. This move is inevitably backed up by an appeal to history in which greater suffering confers greater virtue on the victims, and an archaeological arithmetic of different sufferings then ensues. Insofar as histories can be endlessly remade, this is what I like to think of as the Huttonian defense in the chess game of victimology: each oppression is endowed with no vestige of a beginning, no prospect of an end.

Friedrich Engels, more than once, indicted the idealist assumption that 'justice' represents the 'most abstract expression of right', and that the development of rights is therefore achieved via an 'ever closer' striving for 'the ideal of justice, *eternal* justice'. Rather, he contended, this justice which we discuss so abstractly 'is but the ideologized, glorified expression of existing economic relations'. And yet Engels also recognized that 'in everyday life ... expressions like right, wrong, justice, and sense of right are accepted without misunderstanding'. David Harvey uses this passage not just to critique traditional universalist treatments of justice but at the same time to reject an equally paralyzing 'relativism' *vis-à-vis* social justice, which has come in the wake of poststructuralism and postmodernism. Instead Harvey seeks an alternative vision of justice grounded in human practice:

> Justice and rationality take on different meanings across space and time and persons, yet the existence of everyday meanings to which people do attach importance and which to them appear unproblematic, gives the terms a political and mobilizing power that can never be neglected.[22]

In a sense we have no choice but to fight over that which, in its present form, we do not believe.

Recognizing the need to translate this intellectual perspective into political ammunition, Harvey draws on Iris Young's discussion of *Justice and the Politics of Difference*. Young proposes a 'democratic cultural pluralism' which simultaneously deflates the claims of traditional liberal universalism and is at the same time cognizant of the need to include 'unassimilated others' in a less than homogeneous system of justice. Building on this vision, Harvey enunciates six 'principles' of 'just planning and policy practices'. These deal with minimizing exploitation, militating against marginalization, self-empowerment of the oppressed, sensitivity to cultural imperialism, non-exclusionary and non-militarized containment of personal and institutional justice, and, Harvey adds, the creation of socially just ecologies. The activism of this vision emerges from the inevitable relationality of justice. At different places in different times for different people there will be different meanings of social justice, but the political task, Harvey seems to suggest with his six principles, is nonetheless to press for the establishment of certain 'temporary universals', as we might call them, which will be widely understood and will have the symbolic power to stir people to action. Social movements are about the solidification of particular ambitions for justice as social norms.

But for want of a better world, I am not sure that this resolves the dilemma of social justice for the left. It commits us to speaking in what will be taken outside the academy as still an unabashedly universalist language, more subtle claims to relationality and a grounding in human practice notwithstanding. In other words this vision and reiteration of principles lacks the motive force to shift the discussion from the liberal bedrock of ideals of justice – an admittedly tall order but a vital one. All the best principles of social justice were quite ineffectual in New York's homeless wars and in the battle for Tompkins Square Park after 1988, and as the reaction set in, they were eventually dismissed with ease as just so much liberal blather. Between bitter opponents there was a broad appeal to precisely the same principles of justice but utter conflict over what these principles meant in the here and now, and over whose 'injustices' got to count, or to count most.

In the context of a peculiar political quiescence and fragmentation, therefore, this project of rewriting principles of justice in a more inclusionary and more practically rooted way would, I think, have to be advanced and defended more on the grounds of intellectual than activitist politics. But here I suspect too that the proposal of alternatively slanted principles of justice remains too firmly on universalist terrain, and in fact I think that Harvey and Young share this discomfort. In a subsequent discussion, Harvey argues that while the application of any universal principle of justice may inevitably 'entail some injustice to someone', nevertheless it is not possible to sidestep the question of universality entirely without losing the ability even to talk of justice. He focuses on the search for an epistemology 'which helps us tell the difference between significant and non-significant others, differences and situatedness, and which will help promote alliance formation on the basis of similarity rather than sameness'. He includes as part of this epistemology, Young's redefinition of universality to give it a double meaning, implying not simply an imposed condition but a sense of active participation and inclusion by everyone in the practice and performance of justice.[23]

But this may not go far enough. It may be heretical, but I am almost inclined, in the face of the covetous and vengeful individualism that marks the revanchist city, and the similarly defensive nationalism of identity that has greeted the internationalization of the US city, to admit that the paralysis of the left concerning a well elaborated discourse of social justice actually expresses something of importance, something we should take seriously. Engels and Marx may have been right, then, to avoid the temptation to translate their critique of universal rights into an alternative list which, away from the heat of struggle, could be taken for a new and equally abstract philosophy of justice.

It is not, of course, that Marx and Engels had no commitment to justice. Clearly they were all about justice, but how was this political commitment expressed? 'Exploitation' was arguably Marx's most subversive concept, and it provides an excellent paradigm. The brilliance of Marx's redefinition of exploitation was that it combined two situated knowledges – that of the capitalist and the worker – in one vision; it was thereby simultaneously homogeneous and differentiated. Exploitation for Marx was *simultaneously* a judgment about social *in*justice *and* a measure of economic productivity; the calculation of the capitalist's rate of surplus value was simultaneously the calculation of the worker's rate of exploitation; a critique of liberal justice was always already inscribed in the analytical 'description' of capitalism, rather than asserted from the outside. The integrity of social justice *vis-à-vis* the social and economic structure which Engels diagnosed is here turned upside down as a weapon, and it seems to me that it is this kind of 'internal critique of ideology' that is urgently required today. How can we retheorize the non-homogeneousness of multiple oppressions and exploitations in such a way that also takes account of the imposed universalism of the capitalist system, itself the product and perpetuator of non-homogeneous social structures? At the very least, we need to devise a concept of justice that is, as with exploitation, simultaneously a description and a weapon? What would this subversive double meaning of justice look like.

From Locke, Hobbes and Adam Smith to the present day, liberal conceptions of social justice have traditionally centred on the language of *individual* rights, responsibilities and fortunes (in both senses), regardless of identity. It has of course been a centrepiece of radical critiques that *identity* always mediated this supposed universalism of individual rights. It may be a reasonable historical generalization that when questions of identity bubbled to the surface – especially questions of class or nationality, gender or race – this usually signalled a period of political upheaval, a challenge to identity-laden definitions of the individual. The revanchist city in many ways expresses the struggle to get the genie of identity back in the individualist bottle. Identity began as a subversive category that exposed the doubleness inherent in the system of abstract justice based on individual rights. Homeless people's rising demands for housing in the late 1980s and the liberation of Tompkins Square Park, translated abstract rights and principles into an identity politics that challenged the very basis of 'equal justice': why do we as homeless individuals have no right to housing? The defeat of that movement and the onset of the revanchist city was mobilized via a reassertion of individual rights mobilized through the medium of identity: 'don't I have a right to live without homeless people messing up the neighbourhood; don't men also have rights?' In the first move, identity translates justice over and against individualism, while in the second it becomes a vehicle for a reasserted individualism: a hallmark of the revanchist city, identitarianism (identity to the max) is identity exploded. The bubbling of identity cools.

Except, of course in relation to national identity. The danger of the new nationalism attendant on the internationalization of the US city is precisely that it will collude with the reaction to a progressive identity politics and collapse individualism and identity into a particularly revanchist mould.

Viewed this way we can see very clearly how an identity politics that equated individual political persuasion with gendered or raced identity became, however unwittingly, a leading edge of this reaction. For whatever else it will involve, the subversive doubleness of justice, is absolutely dependent on retaining and continually remaking the scale translation between individuality and identity. Whether a reworked theory of social justice is possible or even desirable remains a very open question. The *political* ability to reclaim the terrain of justice, however, and the ability to divert or redirect the 'new urbanism', will very much depend on keeping an open nexus between individual and identity, and resisting all attempts to police that freeway.

NOTES

[1] See my 'The Revanchist City: New York's Homeless Wars', *Polygraph*, (forthcoming); and 'After Tompkins Square Park: Degentrification and the Revanchist City', in Anthony King (ed) *Re-Presenting the City: Ethnicity, Capital and Culture in the 21st Century Metropolis*, Macmillan, London, 1996.

[2] David Harvey, *Social Justice and the City*, Edward Arnold, London, 1973.

[3] David Harvey, 'Class Relations, Social Justice and the Politics of Difference,' in M. Keith and S. Pile (eds), *Place and the Politics of Identity*, Routledge, London, 1993, p53.

[4] See also, Iris M. Young, *Justice and the Politics of Difference*, Princeton University Press, Princeton, NJ, 1990; R. Peffer, *Marxism, Morality and Social Justice*, Princeton University Press, Princeton, NJ, 1990; David Harvey, 'Social Justice, Postmodernism and the City', *International Journal of Urban and Regional Research* 16, 1992, pp588-601.

[5] *The New York Times*, February 27 1994.

[6] F.X. Clines, 'Suspect Arrested in Shooting of Hasidim', *The New York Times*, March 3 1994.

[7] Davis quoted in C. Katz and N. Smith, 'LA Intifada: Interview with Mike Davis', *Social Text* 33, 1992, p19; see also R. Gooding-Williams (ed), *Reading Rodney King/Reading Urban Uprising*, Routledge, New York, 1993.

[8] Andrew Ross, 'Bombing the Big Apple', in *The Chicago Gangster Theory of Life: Nature's Debt to Society*, Verso, London, 1994.

[9] R. Blumenthal, 'Tangled Ties and Tales of FBI Messenger', *The New York Times*, January 9 1994.

[10] Michael Janofsky, 'Groups Gain New Members Since Attack', *The New York Times*, June 18 1995.

[11] Just to be absolutely clear, this is in no way an argument that national capitals are no longer important or that the internationalization of capital dates only to the early 1970s. That would be absurd. It *is* to argue that the various revolutions in the organizational scale and structure of capital in the last two

decades or more have produced a dramatic *qualitative* shift in the geography of economic power. Nor is it intended to deny the very real resurgence in nationalism in many parts of the world, including the US. Rather, the old lines of internationalism-versus-nationalism no longer makes sense; both forces are operating together and are mutually implicated. For a more detailed discussion and example see my 'Remaking Scale: Competition and Cooperation in Pre/Postnational Europe'. In Heikki Eskelinen and Folke Snickars (eds), *Competitive European Peripheries*, 1995.

[12] Saskia Sassen, *The Mobility of Labour and Capital*, Cambridge University Press, Cambridge, 1988.

[13] For a broader treatment, see Edward Said, *Covering Islam*, Pantheon, New York, 1981.

[14] Samira Kawash, 'The Homeless Body', Unpublished manuscript, Rutgers University, 1995.

[15] *Report of the National Advisory Commission on Civil Disorders*, Bantam Books, New York, 1968.

[16] *Social Justice and the City, op.cit.*, p137.

[17] The quote comes from: 'Hide the Homeless?' *The New York Times* November 11 1991. c.f. Engels: 'The bourgeoisie has only one method of settling the housing question.... The breeding places of disease, the infamous holes and cellars in which the capitalist mode of production confines our workers night after night are not abolished; they are merely *shifted elsewhere*', (Engels, *The Housing Question*, Progress Publishers, Moscow, 1975 edn., pp71, 73-4).

[18] Sarah Ferguson, 'The Park is Gone', *Village Voice* June 18 1991.

[19] Quoted in Wayne Barrett, 'Rudy's Shrink Rap', *Village Voice*, May 9 1995, p11.

[20] For more detail on the question of homelessness and for a broader argument about the revanchist city, New York style, see my 'The Revanchist City: New York's Homeless Wars', *Polygraph*.

[21] Lauren Berlant, 'Live Sex Acts,' *Feminist Studies*, 'National Brands/ National Body: *Imitation of Life*, in Bruce Robbins (ed), *The Phantom Public Sphere*, University of Minnesota Press, Minneapolis, 1993, pp173-208.

[22] Engels quoted in Harvey, 'Social Justice, Postmodernism and the City,' *International Journal of Urban and Regional Research* 16, 1992, pp595-596.

[23] 'Class Relations, Social Justice ...' *op.cit.*, pp62, 57.

Street Sensibility? Negotiating the Political by Articulating the Spatial

Michael Keith

The street has for a long time occupied a cherished place in the lexicon of urbanism. Romanticised as the site of authentic political action, celebrated and reviled as the font of 'low' culture or feared as a signifier of dangerous territorialisation, the street is appropriated time and again in representations of the city.

This chapter takes as its empirical focus the racialised and racist mobilisations that occurred in the East End of London in the late summer of 1993. It was a summer of extreme right political success, racist violence and public disorder which resulted in confrontations between the forces of law and order and young British Bengalis. Disorder arose firstly from confrontations between the police and the crowd gathered in a vigil for Quddus Ali, victim of a horrific racist attack, outside the London Hospital. There was also further violence when raids on the shops and restaurants of Brick Lane by far right activists culminated in serious clashes between police and local Bengalis and a petrol bomb hit the local police station. It was in the week following these clashes that a mile or so away in the east of the borough Derek Beackon became the first successful local authority candidate from the British National Party (BNP) in a by-election in Millwall ward on the Isle of Dogs.

The chapter looks at some of the tensions in the notions of spatiality that are both masked and naturalised in our common understanding of 'the street'. It is a term that invokes a range of spatialities that are a constitutive feature in understanding not only the parochial specificities of Spitalfields and Stepney, Wapping and Whitechapel, but also the very nature of racist and anti-racist mobilisation. At times the vocabulary of resistance may appear similar or even identical to the language of the carceral and territorial imperatives that codify and institutionalise racist practices. On closer inspection subtle distinctions arise from particular articulations of street sensibilities, raising questions that are essential for a plausible and politically progressive reading of recent violent disorder and indispensable to an understanding of the constellation of contemporary debates around public space and the perennial discussion about 'insiders' and 'outsiders' in anti-racist mobilisations.

If we begin to unravel the problematic of authenticity we can begin to address the manner in which the grand scheme is linked to the multiple realities of the everyday, the global revealed in the local, even as the metonymic powers of the local can never alone render visible the nature of the whole.

POLITICS IN THE EAST END OF LONDON

At various times over the last few years living, working and carrying out research in the London Borough of Tower Hamlets I have sometimes thought that all politics in the East End of London is about authenticity. Veering between wanting none of the sectarian spectacle this creates and standing back in respect at the sincerity with which such claims are made, the garrulous rush to stake bids in the auction of authenticity can surely only be understood by reference both to outstanding expressions of communal solidarity and singularly frightening manifestations of mutual intolerance for which the area is famous.

Quite clearly on some levels this is nothing particular to a part of one city in the decaying metropolitan heartland of old capitalism. The right to make claims on behalf of one of many imagined communities, the right to articulate demands for jobs, for welfare and for houses, in short the representation of genuine political subjects, is the very stuff of social theory and political action. More often than not such claims to be heard contain within them, either explicitly or implicitly, reference to a place. And among these spatial reference points the street has historically occupied a privileged position in the cities of modernity.

There is a narrative structure through which the street itself may signify authenticity. Immersion in the street generates its own way of knowing the city, the politics of the street can connote both populism and transgression, whilst as the site of a celebrated vernacular aesthetic, street culture readily stands for the contemporary, truly 'where it's at'.

I want to work through three instances in which the street has been used as an organising trope in the fields of art, knowledge production and popular protest, to make sense of the multi-racial and multi-racist place that is the contemporary East End of London.[1]

In the last two years Tower Hamlets has witnessed the first election of a British National Party (fascist) councillor in Britain, an upsurge in popular protest, a mass mobilisation of young people, drawn in the main from second generation Bengali households, clashes between young people and the police and a savage 300% increase in racial attacks exemplified in the beating of Quddus Ali which was so severe that it left him in a coma and near death for three months.

In part I write from a strong personal belief that it is as obscene to divorce this grim and steady rise in brutal racist violence and populist racist culture from the mutating political economies which have produced the economic space of the East End as it is to reduce such racist cultural forms to the status of mere effects of these sea changes. I am trying to argue that it is through a sophisticated vocabulary of urbanism that we can link the contemporary cultural studies invocations of spatiality with political economies of the production of space in order to understand some of the most horrific forms of racism in the 1990s, something that is the object of endless popular interest and the subject of appalling institutional indifference and complicit political inaction. It is precisely this process of the production of urban spaces that lay at the heart of Harvey's *Social Justice and the City* and clearly tied his own work to that of Lefebvre. It is also through an understanding of these processes of production that it is possible to reconnect economy and culture, in part through the return to spatiality so salient to contemporary social theory, but also through a rejection of any simplistic opposition between 'real' and imagined or metaphoric spaces of identity.

STREET AESTHETICS AND STREET IDENTITY

The first case is that of an exhibition which took place at the

139

Whitechapel Gallery from 14 February to 29 March 1992.[2] The exhibition was of the work of the New York-based, Chilean photographer, Alfredo Jaar, as part of his broader project of 'a new cartography' examining the relationships 'between the developed and developing world'.[3] Jaar had worked with Gayatri Chakravorty Spivak to produce a site specific multi-media installation 'inspired by the Bangladeshi community living in east London'.[4]

At the ICA Jaar and Spivak talked about their work. Jaar's work has for a long time fascinatingly focused on the interplay of place, naming and the politics of identity using 'a spare honed aesthetic practice to provide visibility and spaces to sites and people in crisis'.[5] Together they wanted to make Whitechapel Gallery a truly public space open to all, a site specific installation that in the words of John Bird, the author of the exhibition guide, 'raise[d] the possibility of an aesthetic dimension that can contribute to change across the terrain of the social formation.'[6] Somebody asked them 'why do you want to come to London to do this work?' They replied that they do not find the question either interesting or relevant, it is just not an issue.

The installation was titled 'Two or three things I imagine about them', consciously drawing on Godard's *'Deux ou trois choses que je sais d'elle'* (Two or three things I know about her). It had three main elements and an introductory 'framing' of video and water.

The first element consisted of two neon lights, legible only in their reflection that is read in the mirrors placed alongside them. One says 'What is it to make the street visible', the other 'What is to make the visible visible'. The second element involved some images of young girls skipping, whilst on the floor nearby several speakers produce a hubbub of street noise, talking and shouting, many voices, mostly speaking Sylheti, Bengali and English. Thirdly a series of light boxes, with cropped fragmentary images of glamorous young Bengali women diagonally traversed the space of the gallery at ceiling level, with selective quotes from a sweat-shop manager placed across them. The quotes included comments such as 'They are all unskilled and illiterate', 'The £20 a week they earn just helps the family' and 'We are all a big family here'.

All of this was introduced by a large video screen with a looped film which partly features Spivak talking to 'local people' but consists mainly of an image of her in a soliloquy addressed to the camera. The Delphic image of the latter appears on screen as a talking head that is upside down, to see it the right way up it is necessary to look in the pool of water in front of the screen. Spivak intones:

> How to make the street visible. How to learn to see differently. To learn to see differently is to see with the back, to learn to see differently is to see well in front. To learn to see differently is to see broader....
>
> To learn to see differently. You are innocent, they are not? They are innocent, you are not? To see is to see differently. To learn to see differently. Seeing differently. Is it to make the street visible? To see and to make visible. What is it to see? What then is to make visible? Who are they? Who makes visible? Who sees? How do we see? How do we make the street visible?
>
> (IN A LOUDER VOICE) *How to make the street visible?*

The installation was clearly very clever, highlighting the practices of representation, the aesthetics of the gaze, the fragile play between representation and (in)visibility. It was exciting in the manner in which the standard conventions and protocols of the art gallery exhibition were transgressed. Deliberately enigmatic, the installation simultaneously tried to highlight the exploitation of the local rag trade, the absences and silences of practices of representation and also a more optimistic invocation of the possibility of the public spaces that find their exemplary form in the streets of the modern city.

But the exhibition itself prompted a considerable furore. A group of young women from a local school objected both to the way their images were cropped in the light boxes and the matching of them with the quotes from the sweat-shop owner, prompting protests at the gallery itself. They suggested that as successful sixth formers in the most successful school in Tower Hamlets they were ill served by the portrayals of themselves as victims of the exploitation of the rag trade. The installation had failed to capture the dynamics of the contemporary lives of young Bengali women, reproducing the stereotypes of victimhood. The length of time Spivak had dedicated to putting the piece together and finding out about the local streets was criticised in public, an exchange took place in the British press, and a well known black artist withdrew from a public talk about the exhibition at the gallery.

In one sense such a minor controversy might seem unremarkable. Yet even in its marginality the installation is in some important ways almost paradigmatic. Ultimately the representational space of the gallery was transgressed more symbolically than practically, failing to take along with it the audiences who came to see the installation, not to mention those whose images constituted it.[7]

Street walkers

The second case I want to reference is a particular instance of the spatial practice of walking and knowing the street, a specific invocation of the claims to knowledge that are made when 'botanising the apshalt'.[8] On September 10 1993, shortly after the attack on Quddus Ali and after clashes between police and a crowd that was mostly young, male and Bengali had broken out around a vigil outside the London Hospital, Brick Lane was attacked by a group of fascist sympathisers who ran down the street throwing bricks through the windows of restaurants, daubing racist graffiti and assaulting people on the street.[9] This occurred in spite of the fact that the area was saturated with police patrolling the area at the time. One van in particular had been on a small circuit that included Brick Lane itself for many hours and several young Bengali men had been picked up by the police. Into the early hours of the morning an impromptu march took place of between 50 and 200 which went straight to another main area of Bangladeshi settlement around Cannon Street Road, protesting at the outrage.[10] The following night several gatherings took place of local people, still furious at the previous night's events.

On Brick Lane groups of people, black and white, milled around palpably expectant and fractious. One meeting in a community hall I witnessed was particularly tense with a large crowd of extremely angry local people, mostly young, disgusted by the incursion that had been made on the symbolic heart of the Bengali community of Tower Hamlets, mad at the police for their perceived complicity. After the meeting I went with friends into one of the pubs just off Brick Lane, which itself had its windows bricked as part of the revenge actions on more than 15 public houses that had followed the Quddus Ali attack. And into the pub walked a man in a deerstalker and overcoat, his pipe making up the full Sherlock Holmes set, the simulacrum of an English eccentric; a walking guide with twenty American tourists in tow giving one of the many Ripper tours of Whitechapel; revealing the inscribed knowledges of the Victorian East End through the street walk; a performative flanneurie that re-enacted the serial murders and assaults.

On one level this appeared surreal, on another obscene. The place itself was staged as Jack's East End, the tour proceeded blithely unaware that there was anything beyond the ordinary going on; the American tourists were more concerned that they might be ripped off by the taxi drivers that arrived at the pub to pick them up than they

142

were by the hidden possibility that they could be caught in the middle of an urban uprising. And the authority of the guide remained, unquestioned and unquestionable, resting on identification with the street; an insider position that cast him as the font of local knowledge.

Seemingly only a single bizarre event, the incident is more typical than it might appear. The rich history of the Whitechapel area leads to a cluster of different tour guides working the area: Ripper tours, Jewish tours, Kray tours, Huguenot tours; the street walk on each occasion renders visible particular genres of spatialised knowledges. The tour itself becomes the medium through which the identity of the place is revealed, the knowledge production process replicated through the individuals making the tour. In this way the knowledge production process of the flâneur is mimed for the benefit of the contemporary tourist; but is it rendered inauthentic in doing so?

Paradoxically, it has always been the unknowability and the illegibility of the city that privileges the episteme of the street.[11] Knowing that nobody knows, or ever can know completely, places the spatial practice of the walk above the metanarrative certainties of the plan, the scheme, the totalising view of the panoramic view.[12] But such a valorisation can become the guarantee of parochialism – both a license to stroll and to gaze and a limit to the scientific value of botanised asphalt. It is also a privilege that is not open to all equally.

Yet the street is dangerous and desirable simultaneously, the site and material cause of inter-community violence and the condition of possibility of intercultural identification. The street is not a space which is necessarily signified but it is a medium through which particular cultural forms are expressed.

I think there is a point here where the project of Harvey's *Social Justice* meets the Sennett of *The Fall of Public Man*. A positively understood invocation of urbanism has to be about opening oneself up to difference.[13] The creation of a political space, a social space and a cultural space where the boundary stalking logics of identification are overturned, where uncertainty and unpredictability provide the conditions of possibility for the mutations, hybridity and combinations that define how newness comes into the world, are all definitive features of the lived city just as the roots of democracy and citizenship are part of the city's history.[14] But such spaces can never be assumed, we have always to answer Harvey's question 'in whose image is the city made?' The public sphere is always, almost self evidently, marked by traces of its historicity and spatiality.

In this context the relationship between flâneurie and epistemology is neither straightforward nor consistent. In most representations of the flâneur, the individual walks through the urban environment gaining self-knowledge as they read and tell their way through the great city. The frequently implicit masculinity of this subject position has prompted criticisms of the failure to acknowledge the gendering of both the right of the gaze and practices of visual pleasure itself.[15] Modernist cities were in part structured by gendering processes that defined the public/private distinction, whilst at times both the city generally and the streets specifically, represented as feminine, were eroticised through the process of exploration and capture of the soft city.[16] More recently the nuances of these gendering processes have been disputed in the assertion that the flâneur might be seen as androgynous[17] or else that a more historically inflected study reveals that spaces of the city were contested terrains open to selective appropriation by women.[18]

At other times it is the process of immersion that is celebrated as axiomatic of the constraints of knowledge production, the poets of the street contrasted to the will to power implicit in the aerial view of the urban plan.

It is against this background that it is interesting to think again about the will to know implicit in the practice of walking and the performative knowledge of the tour guide. The guide claims an insider status, a privileged position to narrate the secrets of the everyday. Yet even in its celebration, the episteme of the street is surely at its most powerful at the moment of recognition of its own limits, the act of making the streets legibile reinforces and reproduces the illegibility of the urban.[19]

Certainly the process of knowing the city through becoming lost in its streets, espoused by Walter Benjamin, is far more complicated than some celebrants of flâneurie have subsequently implied but we can still suggest that the links between walking, seeing, knowing and writing do create their own epistemic genealogy. It is a commonplace to note Benjamin's own notion of the flâneur prefiguring the popular fictional detective, a curio personified by the tour guide as Sherlock Holmes; the timely anachronisms of 1990s detective fiction as *film noir* navigation of the streets of Whitechapel.

Central to Benjamin's work was the politics of the manner in which reassuring narratives of historical progress are disrupted by alternative modes of temporality, the interruption of the normal and the taken for granted. Spatially, the order of things is likewise never more clearly revealed than through disruption, the striking juxtapositions of the street walk become pedestrian equivalents to the photographic montages of John Heartfield that so inspired him.

From Benjamin, for the purposes of this chapter, it is necessary only to stress that there is a misreading of his work, that is increasingly common in some forms of urban studies in which the ambivalence of his positioning becomes apparent. Whilst keen to stress the value of losing himself in the city, the process of street walking was for Benjamin a process of doubling; on the one hand the precariousness of the flâneur losing himself (sic) in the crowd led to an immersion in the street, but on the other hand this led to an identification with and fetishisation of the commodity so that the flâneur, once confronted with the department store, finds that 'he roamed through the labyrinth of merchandise as he had once roamed through the labyrinth of the city'.[20] Making contradictory sense of oneself in the street is about locating the body in the possibly incommensurable matrices of economy and culture.[21]

What Benjamin clearly never accepts is that the walk involves the sovereign subject moving through space. To understand the episteme of the flâneur it is essential to reject the notion of the individual body penetrating the spaces of the city. Mapping and walking instead prefigures and is prefigured by the process of identity formation. As an interior, the street is a constitutive feature of the walker, be it the flâneur as tour guide, detective, rebel or even white male academic.

What I want to reject is the dualism that is so central to Lewis Mumford's great work *The City in History*[22] through which he contrasts the urban as container with the urban as movement. The corporeal walker through urban space is always rhizomatically linked to the streets through which that body inscribes their route.[23] If we return to the scene just off Brick Lane, the relationship between the character who returns again and again to the Ripper and the resident who walks the same streets is one of degree rather than one of kind. The privileged 'inside' of the local is always contingent.

There are two points to be made here: first that the street is not the point at which immersion detaches the body from the matrices of political economy. It is, certainly for Benjamin, a point at which the flâneur and the commodity become subjects created by geography. Secondly, street knowledge is not hermetically sealed, in fact quite the opposite it is always part of the collapse of inside and outside.[24] Acknowledged as such, heterotopic public space is defined by and defines a street where it is possible to go out in publick[25] and meet strangers.

In this way the hermetically sealed inside of community politics is unlocked whilst at the same time the spatial practices through which particular places are inscribed differently by different spatialities and historicities are preserved. This sort of cognitive mapping is in part about the prioritisation of 'routes over roots',[26] partly about placing all people on the net of humanity but it is also valorising some claims to place over others, not a strategically essential moment of identification as much as a topography of authority claims which says, in a moment that this person's claim to this place at this time for these reasons is superior to that other person's. Such valorisation has to be of the moment, in a context. It is always precarious, invariably open to questioning; in short a form of synchronic authenticity.

In part I am answering Harvey's own rhetorical question 'in whose image is the city made?' with a call to focus on the process of making which is about both the inscriptions of both commodity flows and personal and collective agency. The street is just one modality through which these inscriptions are made visible. In such circumstances the bizarre spectacle of the guided tour has a place in the East End alongside the symbolic marches of protest that have been the first resort for communities besieged by the violent spectre of racism. We always have to map out where they are coming from and where they are going to.

Bluntly, it is on the street where it is possible to 'come to see with eyes of those who come from a special place', where emotional relations are based on actions shared rather than states of being and where public life can disrupt and transgress destructive *gemeinschaft*.[27] But it is never easy, never innocent of the inscriptions of time and space which the street itself represents and realises in the body of the individual flâneur.

Street politics: heroes and villains

Articulated as politics the street is 'where it's at', it is everything the ivory tower is not – which is why it is perhaps so much loved by academics. Here we find a generic narrative form that is not so much about making the street visible as about making the barricades visible, the intoxicating rush of ethical certainty, social justice in a spatially corporeal form.

But what kind of a vicarious experience is this? And who is to man these barricades, for let us make it clear that manning is the operative term here. The third case I want briefly to examine relates to the proliferation of political mobilisations that developed in Tower Hamlets from late 1993 onwards. These have been both national and local. Whilst the national anti-racist organisations have, once again, looked to make Tower Hamlets a battlefield for the fight against Nazism, there has also been a mushroom growth of movements amongst local people, both men and women, to combat the growth of racism. In particular there has been the clear politicisation and large scale mobilisation of local young Bengalis, demonstrated in vigils to show respect to victims of racist attacks, in marches through and laying symbolic claim to the area, in benefits to raise money and in the defence campaigns to protect those arrested in the struggle. Such mobilisations have become the subject of intense press and media attention; featuring on several documentary programmes, detailed journalistic essays and on the cover of a variety of journals, 'the youth' heralded as new political subjects of the East End.

I want to distinguish between two strands in this revolutionary story. The first is judgmental. There is no way in this chapter that I am attempting to evaluate, undermine or underestimate the remarkable patterns of politicisation that are taking place among second generation Bengalis in London. This is no ethnographic analysis of the experiences of young Bengali men and women. That is only one element of the mosaic that is East End life. I am, however, trying to comment on the racialised configuration of the whole mosaic. It is a configuration that reveals the East End as both lived and signified, an exemplary urbanism in which places are both the conditions of possibility and the expressive modality of identities.

But how are such identifications represented? I think it is important to understand the narrative tropes which make such stories comprehensible. There is a barely hidden genealogy here of place and identity, normatively construed. The black body interpellated through the street. It was after all Lord Scarman who so egregiously talked about 'West Indian' people as a people of the street. Here we have the corollary of Fanon's 'look a Negro', a successful racist placing of the body of the Other in the field of vision.[28]

The accompanying illustrations capture the sense of these stories of

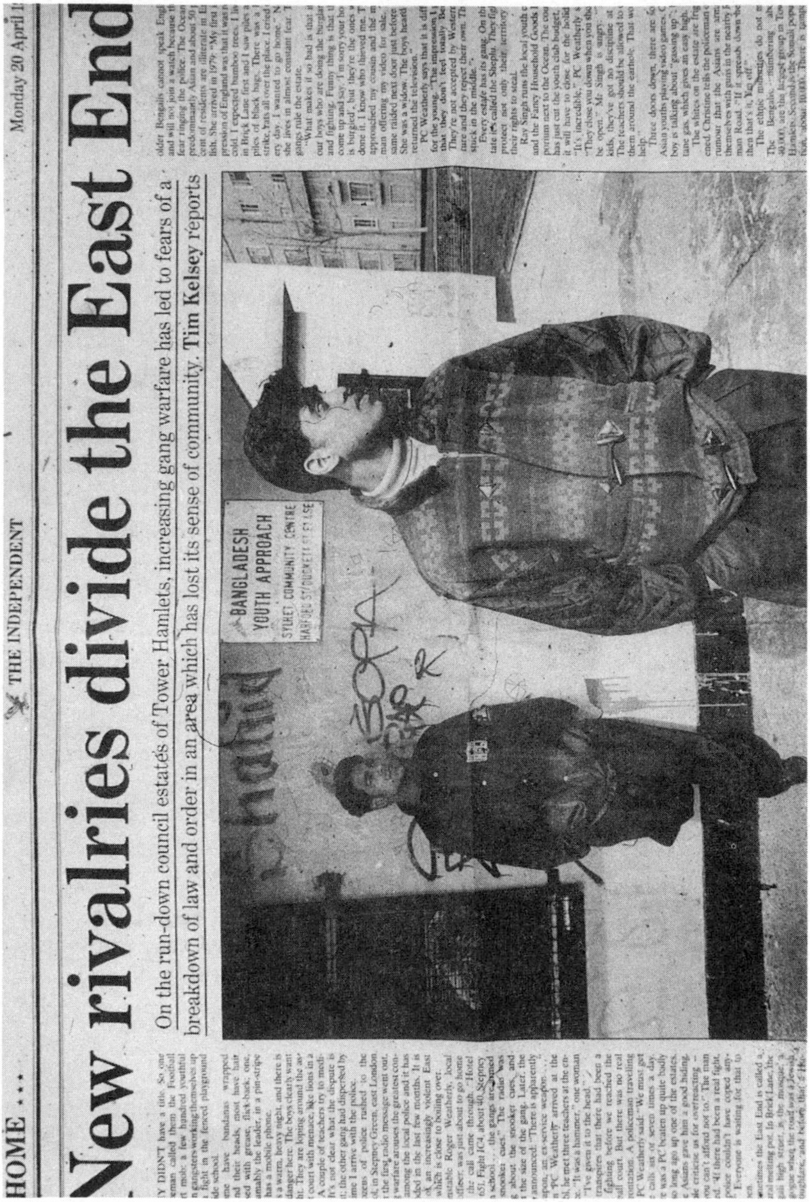

HOME . . .

THE INDEPENDENT

Monday 20 April 1993

New rivalries divide the East End

On the run-down council estates of Tower Hamlets, increasing gang warfare has led to fears of a breakdown of law and order in an area which has lost its sense of community. Tim Kelsey reports

FIGURE 1: *The Independent*, 20 April 1993.

FIGURE 2: *The Sunday Times*, 4 July 1982.

FIGURE 3: *Socialist Review*, April 1995.

the street. The first image is taken from *The Independent* newspaper in 1993. The second is from *The Sunday Times* in 1982, more than ten years earlier. Set side by side I believe there is a very real sense in which the two images merge one into the other. Set in time they are linked in a more complicit fashion, the earlier image not only prefiguring the later but also caught up in the intricate and complex processes of criminalisation[29] that renders *The Independent* photograph comprehensible.

We know these stories. They appeal to a knowledge that predates the moment the camera shutter closed. They place race in the field of vision in a way in which sense becomes self-evident. A young man looks directly into the camera, evoking a host of not only histories of black looks[30] but also common sense geographies of racism. These images work because we the viewer know what they mean, two or three things we know about the racialised masculinity of the dangerous street.[31]

But the carceral gaze that fixes the dangerous young men on the street in a placing of criminal otherness is not so easily confined to the invocations of delinquency that they may conjure up. In the wake of the events of late 1993 a series of anti-racist stories appeared with 'the youth' of the East End cast as the heroes of the struggles against the forces of oppression. Again there is not intention here to demean the mobilisations that did occur. But it is worth examining some of the images of these journals.

When we look at the cover of *Socialist Review* and the imagery of *The Independent* and *The Sunday Times* can we really say they are unrelated? Is it really coincidence that the lineaments of racist culture share so much in common with the rhetorics of revolutionary action?

This is undoubtedly a complex story. The subject positions of oppression are regularly taken on board as the vessels that secure movements of resistance – from pejorative black to politically black, from pejorative queer to queer politics – the categories are taken on board to be mocked and subverted in the mimesis of the mirror dance.[32]

But there is also a sense in which the liberal white left themselves, in desperate search for the transformative political subject will cast young Bengali men as the teleological delivery boys; and as Stuart Hall[33] pointed out in a not dissimilar context after the uprisings of 1981 the streets will not only stage glorious insurrection, they will also witness the fact that it is upon young male Bengali heads that the fully armed

151

apparatus of the state will fall; it is they who will be attacked on the streets at the vigil for Quddus Ali outside the London Hospital, and they who will be confronted by and confront the BNP gangs who increasingly conspire to roam the streets of Tower Hamlets to go Paki-bashing. Street politics is easy for the absent.

Three-way street

I think what the three examples share is the foregrounding of place and authenticity, which misleadingly conveys the authentic aesthetic, the authentic episteme, the authentic political subject. Place, specifically the street itself, serves as rhetorical backbone rather than as a medium of articulation through which beauty, truth and politics are mixed together and hybridised. It is possible to take the three examples in turn to see how this 'cross dressing' takes place.

In the Whitechapel Gallery accidentally orientalist fragments of eroticised glamour, boxed up and packaged, together with the disembodied murmuring of the chaotic public, are all framed by the arcane image of wisdom and insiderdom reflected in the pool of water. Narcissus lives.

In the pastiche detective figure of Sherlock Holmes, the walker who desires the otherness of difference, eroticising street life, is seduced by the aesthetically captivating nature of experience that allows them to read themselves into the illegibility of the great city and then rationalises this triumph of being over becoming by writing the street, by transforming the gaze into the script through a claim to knowledge – 'to have been there'.

And in the media coverage of 'youth movements' the subjectification of the transformative agent valorises street politics as ethical action and revels in the connotative dreams of Paris and the barricades. Through such connotative slippage a project is validated – the political is defined as the moment of contestation and action validates the epistemological frame through which such contestation is known.[34] And more than anything else there is the spectacle consumed – mass insurrection on the TV screens, heroes framed in the photographers' lenses nourishing the utopian romance in the eroticised imaginary.

In each case 'the street' is more than a stage on which authority claims are made; it is a constitutive feature of the authority itself; something that I want to go on to argue can only be addressed by unpacking the spatialities that such claims invariably invoke. These spatialities are themselves conditions of possibility which demand a more sophisticated and contingent notion of both politics and social justice than we are normally ready to develop; something that I believe can be addressed by a project of radical contextualisation.

RADICAL CONTEXTUALISATION

Is beauty truth, truth beauty? Are fact and value so distinct? The questions that are no more easily resolved now than two thousand years ago in part reveal the artifice of the moments of identity production, knowledge production and political judgement that I have just described. But they do share some important features. In each case the spatiality of the street is both the condition of possibility through which claims of authenticity are staked and also a sign of empirical specificity that is silenced as soon as it is voiced because geographical traces play to the audience as the stigmata of relativism.

Yet in each case the claims, mediated as they are by this silenced spatiality are all contingently valid just as they are contingently fraudulent. As Martin Luther King said 'the riot is the voice of the unheard' but equally when 'shouts in the street' turn into the brutal vocabulary of racial battering and ethnic cleansing then we find the moment when Rousseau turns into Robespierre.[35] Likewise, identifying with Otherness must surely depend upon both the representational spaces through which it occurs and also the mapping of such spaces into the political economy of the city, whilst the eroticisation of the street is surely on its own free of necessary morality.

In part this is no more than saying – *pace* Habermas – that the classic notions of public space filled by universals and individuals must be replaced with a more nuanced version that acknowledges both individual rights of humanity and communal or collective rights that reflect inscribed structures of power, a proposition outlined in Iris Marion Young's demands for an understanding of heterotopic public space. However, it is also a way of suggesting that an understanding of social justice and *fin de siècle* urbanism must always revolve around a politics of articulation, contingent epistemologies and situated aesthetics; a set of practices that has elsewhere been described as radical contextualisation.[36]

The project of radical contextualisation is at one and the same time straightforward and arcane. Many of the old binaries are subverted because neither abstraction nor empiricism (in knowledge production), neither theory nor practice (in political action), neither universalism nor relativism (in aesthetic judgements) can resolve any of Kant's three fundamental questions of philosophy – what do I know, what should I do, what do I want. The answers to all such questions depend on abolishing the *a priori* and spelling out of the grounds on which they are made, accepting that the traces of historicity and spatiality are always a constitutive feature of the processes of subject and object formation.

But the confusion between ethics, epistemology and identity is not just one of plurality. At one level I think it important to find a vocabulary that indicts the Jaar/Spivak installation as fascinating but fraudulent, that ties the revolutionary plaudits to their prefiguring of racism, and renders the walker as always problematic.

Through radical contextualisation it is possible to foreground both the dead ends of standpoint epistemology and the false promises of universalism. It is possible to cherish the public spaces of modernity without romanticising them. Third space, liminal space, the privileged margin – all open up the moment of identification as a moment of uncertainty. Reassuring narratives of time are dislocated by the uncertainties of the spatial. Acknowledged as such, heterotopic public space is defined by and defines a street where it is possible to go out in publick and meet strangers.

But the project of radical contextualisation is also about acknowledging the contingency of all identities, affirming that the traces of historicity and spatiality are inscribed not just by presence but also by absence, by a lack as much as a plenitude. Within this heterotopic public space claims of authenticity and redress are not just grounded, they are also constituted by their historicity and spatiality in what Homi Bhabha, drawing on Benjamin, describes as 'a dialectic of cultural negation as negotiation' in that

> Community is the antagonist supplement of modernity: in the metropolitan space it is the territory of the minority, threatening the claims of civility; in the transnational world it becomes the border-problem of the diasporic, the migrant, the refugee. Binary divisions of social space neglect the profound temporal disjunction – the translational time and space – through which minority communities negotiate their collective identifications. For what is at issue in the discourse of minorities is the creation of agency through incommensurable (not simply multiple) positions. Is there a poetics of the interstitial community? How does it name itself, author its agency?[37]

It is this incommensurability that arises from and constitutes the spatialities of subjectification that work through and on 'the street'. It is out of the incommensurability of different spatialities that both the spaces of resistance emerge as social practice and the moments of utopianism can insert themselves as political projects of discursive closure.

The spaces of the street are, in other words and a familiar language, contradictory. And a language of contradiction usefully returns us to the agenda of Harvey's *Social Justice and the City* not in search of Hegelian resolution but for bearings. For if, as Paul Gilroy has recently argued forcefully, 'the problem with the cultural left' is that they have never been cultural enough it is worth echoing this with the comment that cultural politics without political economy will be equally rudderless.

The power of a focus on the practices and processes of production of both culture and class, of moralities, identities and knowledges, is to place the stress on becoming rather than being, is to open up politics without reducing it to either economistic caricature or cultural self-indulgence. Invariably this must involve foregrounding the influences of time and space through either radical contextualisation or something that would look much like it. Moments of productive cultural syncretism, fusion and hybridity take place not just in any place nor in some rarefied, abstract liminal space or third space or marginal space. They are realised through particular articulations of spatiality just as those spatialities are a constitutive feature of their formation. The street is frequently one such articulation and it is as such that we can celebrate the 'shouts of the street'.[38] For where is the place at which 'communality is not based on a transcendent becoming'[39] if it is not the street, if it is not a celebration of the places where one can go out in publick and meet strangers.

The street is an organising frame through which the social is rendered visible, neither authentically real nor merely metaphoric, a moment of placing and a *mise en scène*. In this sense the street is both a state of consciousness and a locus of meaning, a way of thinking about the world and a semiotic source of dramaturgical keys and cues. As such it is an exemplary case of the sites of the urban. If, as Harvey said in the opening sentence of *Social Justice and the City*, 'The City is a manifestly complicated thing',[40] the complexity in part arises from the multiple spatialities by which it is constituted.

In one sense we clearly have to do away with authenticity, to understand the lie that is at the heart of the term. But in another it is equally the case that the rights of local people to speak out against property capital valorise a particular understanding of authenticity; the rights of British black communities to represent themselves in the anti-racist movement valorise a particular understanding of authenticity, the right of the Bengali community to defend themselves against racist attacks acknowledges a territorial authenticity and the political moment at which the democratic act is legitimated with a vote valorises a particular understanding of the authenticity of the 'real me'.

It is from such articulated speaking positions, in such explicit spaces of representation, and at particular historically contingent moments that a politics of authenticity will continue to find a place in progressive left politics. Diachronically, we know that authenticity has no place but if we freeze the moving film momentarily, in particular places at particular times, the authentic can be voiced synchronically, an appeal that is of the moment, directed to particular audiences and justified by specific ends. This is not so much an instance of the strategic essentialism favoured by Spivak and others as much as the 'true lies' described by Fanon.[41]

Authenticity is a true lie of political action, a strategy but not a goal. What we are currently seeing in the East End of London and in so many other places where authenticity underscores the very vocabulary of popular politics is what happens when such a strategy becomes mistaken for a goal in and of itself. In such situations the message is clear for both contemporary politics and *fin de siécle* urbanism, in the words of the Tower Hamlets 9 campaign 'No Justice, No Peace'.[42] It is a slogan in which the concerns of the local consciously and deliberately draw on a vocabulary of the global. The slogan of the Los Angeles campaigns that followed the uprisings inspired by miscarriages of social justice that defined the Rodney King beating echoes in London and resonates in a vocabulary of resistance. In so doing the street may be a reference point that crosses the globe and transcends localism just as it may be frighteningly parochial. To ignore both the possibilities and the dangers of either inflection is to deny geography.

Acknowledgement: Many thanks are due to Erik Swyngedouw and Andy Merrifield for organising the conference and for their responses to an earlier draft of this chapter. Thanks also to Les Back, David Goldberg and Gillian Rose for their helpful comments.

NOTES

[1] The area referenced in this paper is a small patch of East London in the London Borough of Tower Hamlets, bounded by the Highway in the South, Bethnal Green Road in the North, Spitalfields market in the West and by Burdett Road in the East. London's own Ellis Island, it is an area that has been inscribed with the presence of Huguenot, Jewish, African, Afro-Caribbean, Irish, Somali migrants along with countless other disposessed and displaced minorities, tracked, traced and explored by generations of urban explorers, spectators, philanthropists, walkers and academics.

[2] In the three cases I am trying to follow Stallybrass and White's contention that 'what is socially peripheral is so frequently symbolically central'. P. Stallybrass and A. White, 'The Politics and Poetics of Transgression', Methuen, London, 1986.

[3] Whitechapel Art Gallery flier, 1992.

[4] *Ibid*.

[5] Patricia C. Philips in exhibition catalogue 'Republica de Chile Pasaporte', n.p.

[6] J. Bird, 1992 n.p. in the guide to the exhibition. There was no conventional catalogue as such for the exhibition but instead a commentary by John Bird, three of Jaar's maps in his 'new cartography' and an essay on Jaar's work by Patricia C. Philips inside a replica Chilean passport. It is this 'package' that is referred to below as 'the catalogue'.

[7] Paradoxically the exhibition 'catalogue' closes with a quote from Spivak: 'It's all very well to theorise cultural practices and institutions as potential sites for discursive intervention into the construction of social meaning, but this has also to take account of discrepant audiences, different agendas and modalities of resistance – of the necessity of "doing our homework properly".' It is surely around. precisely this notion of doing 'one's homework' properly that the installation, provoking though it was, ultimately failed.

[8] Walter Benjamin's term, coined in *Charles Baudelaire: A Lyric Poet in the era of High Capitalism*, Harry Zohn, London, 1971, p36.

[9] Brick Lane lies at the heart of Spitalfields and is dominated by small Bengali businesses, particularly restaurants and shops. It is also the site of a mosque in an old Jewish synagogue. In many ways it is the symbolic heart of Bengali settlement in Britain.

[10] It is important to stress that in this and the subsequent example there is no attempt here to provide an authoritative account of these events or represent the perceptions or feelings of the Bengali community at this time. For such accounts see the bulletins produced by Tower Hamlets Against Racism, Tower Hamlets Anti Racist Committee and the interview with Kumar Murshid in *Regenerating Cities*, number 6, 1994.

[11] It is surely no coincidence that a postmodern displacement of metanarrative certainty by little narratives and local knowledges has found a narrative echo in the renewed fascination with the personal memoir, the wanderings of the contemporary flâneur – such as Patrick Wright, Iain Sinclair and Elizabeth Wilson in London.

[12] It is in this context that Frisby has argued for the relevance of the lessons of the flâneur to be taken on board in a reconsideration of the work of figures such as Robert Park and that the work of Walter Benjamin is reinstated in mainstream social science. D. Frisby, 'The Flâneur in Social Theory' in K. Tester (ed), *The Flâneur*, Routledge, London, 1994.

[13] Iris Marion Young, 'The Ideal of Community and the Politics of Difference' in L.J. Nicholson (ed), *Feminism/Postmodernism*, Routledge, London, 1990.

[14] This is not to say that these properties are necessary properties of an essential urban – only that vocabularies of urbanism are constitutive organising principles of them. M. Keith and M. Cross, *Racism, the City and the State*, Routledge, London, 1992.

[15] See, for example, L. Mulvey, *Visual and Other Pleasures: Language Discourse Society*, Macmillan, London, 1989; J. Wolff, 'The Invisible Flâneuse: Women and the Literature of Modernity' in A. Benjamin (ed), *The Problems of Modernity: Adorno and Benjamin*, Routledge, London, 1989.

[16] L. Davidoff and C. Hall, *'Family Fortunes: Men and Women of the English Middle Class, 1780-1850*, Hutchinson, London, 1987.

[17] E. Wilson, *The Sphinx in the City*, Virago, London, 1991.

[18] J. Walkowitz, *City of Dreadful Delight: Narratives of Sexual Danger in Late-Victorian London*, Virago, London, 1992.

[19] S. Marcus, 'Reading the Illegible' in H.J. Dyos and M. Wolff (eds), *The Victorian City: Images and Realities*, Routledge, London, 1973.

[20] W. Benjamin, *op.cit.*, p55

[21] In losing oneself on the streets only to find oneself and an identity within the matrices of contemporary capitalism Benjamin's uncertain flâneur predates Jameson's project of 'cognitive mapping' and in his doubt pre-empts Jameson's notion of 'incommensurability-vision'.

[22] See K. Robins, 'Prisoners of the City' in J. Squires, E. Carter and J. Donald (eds), *Space and Place: Theories of Identity and Location*, Lawrence & Wishart, London, 1993.

[23] G. Deleuze and F. Guattari, 'The Rhizome' in *A Thousand Plateaus: Capitalism and Schizophrenia*, Athlone Press, London, 1988.

[24] There is one caveat here. On the one hand the more optimistic characterisations of cross-cultural identification disrupt the metanarrative certainties of history with a spatially nuanced vocabulary – space subverts time, geography is the modality through which third space is articulated. On the other hand, celebrations of the city, be it the city as lived or the city as signed tend to slide towards an assessment of the immanent properties of the essential urban, something that is not suggested here.

[25] The reference here and later in the chapter is to Sennett's celebration of 'the publick' in *The Fall of Public Man*, Faber & Faber, London, 1977.

[26] I. Chambers, *Border Dialogues*, Routledge, London, 1990.

[27] These are the central values at the heart of Sennett's analysis of *The Fall of Public Man*, pp238-240.

[28] Fanon's opening of *Black Skin, White Masks* captures the subjectification of the black body through the white gaze. Taken together with his axiomatic notion that 'the black man's soul is a white man's artefact' and the memorably epigrammatic comment that 'The black man is not. Any more than the white

man', Fanon's work has become increasingly important in cultural studies projects that trace back the construction of processes of racialisation to the social context in which the formative experiences of identification and identity formation take place. It is this *taking place* element of this process that make an understanding of the spatialities of a sophisticated urbanism indispensable to anti-racist theory and practice. F. Fanon, *Black Skin, White Masks*, Grove Press, New York, 1967.

[29] See M. Keith, *Race, Riots and Policing: Lore and Disorder in a Multi-Racist Society*, UCL Press, London, 1993, especially chapter 12, for a fuller elaboration of the manner in which 'blackness' becomes a sign of criminal otherness in a manner that allows the tropes of criminalisation that have blighted the lives of British Afro-Caribbean communities to work across the 'Black/Asian' distinction of popular British racial discourse in a manner which narrates the experiences of young Bengali men and young Afro-Caribbean men through the same vocabulary.

[30] See bell hooks, *Black Looks: Race and Representation*, Turnaround, London, 1992.

[31] In discussing the framing of images of the beating of Rodney King, Judith Butler has made precisely this point forcefully with the comment that 'The visual field is not neutral to the question of race; it is itself a racialised formation, an episteme, hegemonic and forceful.' J. Butler, 'Endangered/ Endangering Schematic Racism and White Paranoia' in R. Gooding Williams (ed), *Reading Rodney King, Reading Urban Uprising*, Routledge, London, 1993, pp15-22.

[32] The most impressive exposition of this is surely to be found in Michael Taussig's *Shamanism, Colonialism and the 'Wild Man'*, University of Chicago Press, Chicago, 1987.

[33] See S. Hall, 'The Lessons of Lord Scarman', *CSP, Number 2*, 1982.

[34] See for instance how E. Laclau in *New Revolution for Our Times* defines the political in terms of contestable practices, Verso, London, 1990.

[35] It is precisely this sort of slippage that lies at the heart of Berman's *The Politics of Authenticity*, George Allen and Unwin, London 1971.

[36] In particular see E. Laclau but also Keith, M. and Pile, S. 'The Politics of Place' in Keith, M. and Pile, S. (1994). See E. Laclau, *op.cit.*, and M. Keith and S. Pile, 'The Politics of Place' in M. Keith and S. Pile (eds), *Place and the Politics of Identity*, Routledge, London, 1994.

[37] H. Bhabha, *The Location of Culture*, London 1994, 228 and 231. It is perhaps not insignificant that the demands to speak to the authenticity of territory is not equivalent across the range of the new cultural politics of difference. For example, the nuances of sexualised and gendered territorial authenticity contrast strikingly with those of race and class.

[38] See Marshall Berman, *All That Is Solid Melts Into Air*, Verso, London, 1982.

[39] H. Bhabha, *op.cit.*, p241.

[40] D. Harvey, *Social Justice and the City*, Edward Arnold, London, 1973, p22.

[41] Where representation necessarily misrepresents we find the political moment when the strategic nature of closure is revealed. Such closures are moments in a politics of articulation, an echo of something Fanon reflected on while listening to the radio in the midst of anti-colonial war: 'The Arabic

channel was of course jammed. But the scraps of sound had an exaggerated effect. Like rumours, they were constructively heard, and listening to them became an act of participation in revolutionary victories which might never have occurred. To quote Fanon, "the radio receiver guaranteed this true lie" ', S. Feuchtwang, 'Fanon's politics of culture: the colonial situation and its extension, *Economy and Society*, Volume 4, Number 14.

[42] The Tower Hamlets 9 are nine Asian youths arrested at the vigil outside London Hospital for Quddus Ali. The Tower Hamlets 9 Defence Campaign has been set up by local youth in Tower Hamlets to campaign on their behalf. Contributions to TH9, Defence Campaign, PO Box 273, London E7.

'Justice/Just Us': Rap and Social Justice in America

Marshall Berman

Thirty years ago, I was a graduate student at Oxford, first at Oriel College, then at St Antony's. I worked with Isaiah Berlin, James Joll, Anthony Quinton, John Plamenatz, Iris Murdoch. I wrote a thesis on 'Freedom and Individuality in the Thought of Karl Marx'. Intellectually, I had a great time, a far better time than I could have had at any American graduate school. But I didn't open up to Oxford as a place, I didn't let myself enjoy it. It was the first time I had ever been more than a couple of hours away from the Bronx, and Oxford felt so utterly *Other*. I know I loved the architecture, and I filled my letters home with sketches of Classic domes, Gothic towers, Romantic parks. But soon it got dark and cold, the gorgeous buildings cast long shadows, and I got lonely and paranoid. I came to feel that the place's very beauty was really there to crush the working class and the Jews and people like me. I traded stories of self-alienation with the two dearest friends I made, a boy from Montreal and a girl from Calcutta.

What made me feel most like an alien was *people*. In the Oxford of the early 1960s, feudalism lived. The first person I saw every morning was my servant – 'scout', he was called – whose job was to wake me up, lay out my clothes, bring me warm water to shave with, and remind me of my appointments for the day. I had a lot of trouble with this, and I never gave my scout a proper chance to do his job. I couldn't bear to be addressed as Sir, or treated as a 'gentleman'. And I couldn't stand the 'gentlemen' around me, who in those days still dominated Oxford's streets and quads: languid young men who looked like extras from *Brideshead Revisited*, who slouched around in tuxedos (which quite often looked like they'd been slept in), vegetating while their fathers owned the British Empire and the world. Or at least they *acted* like their fathers owned the world. I knew how much of it really was an act: the Empire was *kaput*; the children of its ruling class were living on trust funds that were worth less every year, and inheriting companies that were going broke. I knew that intellectually. So why did those silly kids, half asleep and putting on the ritz, intimidate the hell out of me? Those Evelyn Waugh extras were just as scared as I was, maybe even more, because at least I knew I was moving up in the world. (After awhile, I found out some of them were even scared of me!)

Over the years I came to see that the place I couldn't bear really wasn't there. Oxford in the 1960s was a Twilight Zone, an imperial capital of the mind whose Empire was extinct. If I had sensed the darkness just behind the twilight, I might not have felt so out of time. But twenty-year-old kids don't have much of a sense of time; historicity is one of the things we get as we grow up, and it's one of the reasons that growing up is nice. Anyway, thirty years later, Oxford seems to have found a solid place in a wider world, not imperial but multinational, and so have I.

In this chapter, I want to talk about rap music as a site of cultural conflict in American cities today. The conflict is taking place on three different planes: among rappers themselves, inside the serious rap audience, and within the large American public that doesn't know much about rap except that it is a powerful force in our cultural life. The conflict is not only about what rap is and what it should be, but about the nature of our shared *reality*, a reality in which rappers claim to be expert.

There are two themes I want you to keep in mind. The first is Antonio Gramsci's idea of an 'organic intellectual', an intellectual who belongs. Who is he or she supposed to belong to? Both to a place and to a people – sometimes, as Gramsci puts it, to '*the* people'. This idea is opposed to Karl Mannheim's idea of the intellectual as a being who is unconditioned and 'free-floating'. For the past twenty-five years or so, about half my life, I've been trying to become an organic intellectual of New York. New York was where I spent my childhood, and where I became an intellectual, and I always loved the place without thinking. It wasn't till I left – in fact, it wasn't till I came to Oxford – that I saw how much acute and chronic trouble my home town was in, how tempting and easy it was for its children to forget it, and how much it needed intellectuals who loved it.

My second theme is 'a shout in the street'. This phrase comes from James Joyce's *Ulysees*. It emerges in a conversation between one of Joyce's heroes, the young artist Stephen Dedalus, and Mr Deasy, the proto-fascist headmaster of the school where he teaches. Mr Deasy is saying that history embodies the will of God.

> —History, Stephen said, is a nightmare from which I am trying to awake.
> From the playfield the boys raised a shout. A whirring whistle: goal. What if the nightmare gave you a back kick.
> —The ways of the Creator are not our ways, Mr Deasy said. All history moves toward one goal, the manifestation of God.
> Stephen jerked his thumb toward the window, saying:
> —That is God.
> Hooray! ay! Whrrwhe!
> —What? Mr Deasy asked.
> —A shout in the street.

In my book about modernity and modernism, *All That Is Solid Melts Into Air*, this is a very important line. I show how much modernist writing and culture – from Baudelaire and Dostoevsky to Beat poetry, Pop Art and Rock and Roll – get their energy from the flow and the convulsions of the modern city streets. But I didn't produce much exciting street material from the years when I was finishing the book, the late 1970s and early 1980s, and my narrative trails off at the end. However, very soon after I put the book to bed, I began to hear rap seriously. I heard it, and saw it, in two places: in the college where I teach, in Harlem – City College of New York, which is something like an old London Polytechnic – and in the South Bronx, where I grew up. In those days the radio wouldn't play rap, and you had to go, to be where it was happening. Rap knocked me out: I thought, All right, here it is, my shout in the street, I can hear. Rap music was a primary energy source for me throughout the Reagan decade.

My title here, 'Justice/Just Us', comes from a rap called the 'Beat Street Breakdown', from a mid-1980s film called *Beat Street*. *Beat Street* was a low-budget movie that was made to showcase the Hip-Hop subculture, where inner city kids, mostly black, created rap music, subway graffiti and breakdance. The movie is made 'on location' in the South Bronx, with nonprofessional kids who play themselves, rapping and breaking and writing as they try to survive. In the mid-1980s, South Bronx 'location' meant sublime, spectacular, Piranesian ruins. (A German art critic I knew said that whenever her friends came to visit, and she offered to take them to her favourite New York scenes, Central Park, the Metropolitan Museum, the Brooklyn Bridge, her friends waved them all away, and said, instead, 'Take me to the burning buildings, I want to see the ruins.') Melle Mel, the rapper here, performs the 'Breakdown', with heartbreaking intensity, in memory of a friend who has just died: Ramon, a subway graffitist, was caught writing in the tunnels, chased by the Transit Police, and killed by an oncoming train. Here is the last verse:

> Search for justice, and what do you find?
> Just us on the unemployment line,
> Just us sweating from dawn to dusk,
> There's *no* justice, there's – *Huh!* – just us.

This is powerful protest writing, in the tradition of Broonzy and Guthrie, Ochs and Dylan, Springsteen, Bernice Reagon and Billy Bragg. It is also, like their best work, an essay in political theory. Its account of everyday reality is framed by an ideal aspiration: the search for justice. It contrasts this ideal with the fact that, per capita, American blacks are twice as likely as whites to hold menial jobs ('sweating'), and twice as likely to be unemployed or poor. To suggest these facts of life aren't just is clearly right.

But Melle Mel's brilliant quatrain also sounds like the work of a poor man who has never been out of his neighbourhood. He seems to think these things happen only to blacks: 'just us'. America's mass media, especially TV, would give him few clues that there are other people on that unemployment line. An important fact of life in the late-twentieth-century USA is that poverty and misery are multicultural. In fact, the great majority of the country's poor and oppressed people are white. But poverty today also means isolation, so that poor people of different ethnic groups are mostly ignorant of each other's existence. Our media sustain this ignorance: virtually the only time most Americans ever see poor whites is as part of racist mobs attacking blacks; as for poor Latins (by all statistical indices worse off than black, they don't appear at all. Latins are a lot closer than blacks to being 'invisible men'.) Maybe if the rapper could imagine other Americans who are poor and oppressed like him even though they don't look like him, maybe the fellow sufferers could become fellow-activists, and maybe then they might have at least a shot at justice. But so long as they don't see each other, they are bound to feel totally isolated and smashed by the whole structure of the world. Then their raps will be texts in what the historian Richard Hofstadter called 'The Paranoid Style in American Politics'.

What has this to do with justice? If black appears to be the only victims of injustice ('just us'), it makes the search sound pretty futile. The searchers find themselves running with Thrasymachus (from Book One of Plato's *The Republic*), who argues that justice is an empty scam, that it's impossible to criticize any ruling class for being unjust, because justice is simply whatever is in the interest of the ruling class. 'Search for justice, what do you find?' You find there's nothing there – unless you have *power*, and then you can shove your brand of justice down people's throats, and make them grovel and accept it, until someone else comes along who can do the same to you. Thus all life gets resolved into a clash of us and them. If the contending parties don't develop some common idea of justice that they can share, there will be no framework in which they can recognize each other. And then they will be running with Carl Schmitt, the Existentialist Nazi, who defined life as a fight to the death: it's *just us* or *just them*; no other outcomes are possible or even conceivable. We could easily be in post-cold war Bosnia, or in any other land where ethnic cleansing has swept the country.

America is not Bosnia; hate here isn't quite so lethal. But the idea that 'just us' are suffering is a familiar tribalist refrain of the 1980s. It's an idiom that the middle-aged folks can remember from the Black Power politics of the 1960s; though, ironically, its high point in American history was the 1860s, when it served as the official language of the slaveowners of the Confederacy. In the Reagan era, a wide range of social groups learned to speak the language of militant separatism. This foreclosed the growth of broad coalitions that could fight for justice together; meanwhile, our old ruling class, expert in its own separatism, stepped over the bodies, enriched itself immensely, and increased all the gulfs between itself and everybody else: 'just us' with a vengeance!

So there are problems with Melle Mel's argument, if it is an argument. But you know he hasn't given up searching for justice if you listen to his voice. If you listen, you feel like the Wedding Guest in Coleridge's 'Rime of the Ancient Mariner': this guy won't let go of you; you 'cannot choose but hear'. You hear a man stretching the English language to tell a desperate story, and making a call that cries out for your response.

I grew up in the South Bronx, rap's cradle, in the 1940s and 1950s.

My neighbourhood was mostly working-class and mostly Jewish (including many Holocaust survivors) then; life was mostly poor and hard. In the early 1960s, just as the shades of poverty were starting to lift, Robert Moses's Cross-Bronx Expressway chopped the neighbourhood in half, the job base crumbled, my family and thousands more moved out. By the mid-1970s, nearly all the Jews, Irish, Italians, Ukranians, had gone; so had the first waves of blacks and Latinos who came in. Poverty was deeper and more chronic. The deindustrialisation of American wiped out the blue-collar jobs that had kept generations of Bronxites alive. Drugs and arson are the biggest local industries now. The most striking visual feature, by the mid-1970s, was miles and miles of ruins. Dozens of blocks, blocks that for decades had been the densest and most crowded in the city, now were suddenly as open as deserts. Within a decade the South Bronx lost half its population, as hundreds of thousands of people fled the fires. (Population loss then became the pretext for closing the firehouses.) This was the decade when New York nearly went bankrupt, and *The Daily News* summed up very aptly the federal government's role in the story: FORD TO CITY: DROP DEAD.

At the very nadir of historical catastrophe, rap was born. In the beginning, it was a *musica povera*, made by kids who were too poor to afford instruments or lessons. Its primal form was a single black kid with a mike and a speaker that played a drum synthesizer track. Soon, as rapper's began to play in local clubs, it expanded into a bipolar form, in which an MC (master of ceremonies) held the foreground – he spoke, chanted, called, grunted, cried, and occasionally sang – while, behind him, a DJ (disc jockey) established a background, and created beats, rhythm, melody, harmony, and a total environment in which rap could take place. The DJ came equipped with two turntables, a drum track, and hundreds of records: on one turntable he would collage musical tracks, often at amazing speed, to make complex allusive melodies, while he scratched the other side to create percussion.

The invention of the digital sampler in the mid-1980s enabled DJs to create backgrounds as complex as any symphony orchestra. The best ones were even more complex: they appropriated every musical style in history, jazz, classical, folk, sacred, rock, soul, R & B, reggae, Broadway, Indian, African, along with background voices, street noises and machines. (Sometimes the production apparatus has become overloaded, as it did in white rock in the years after *Sgt Pepper*.) These spectacular backgrounds put more pressure on the MCs, who needed voices both strong and supple enough to scale the walls of sound. The tension between DJ and MC, between foreground and background, is what propels rap forward and gives it its moment-to-moment dramatic power.

But that isn't quite right. It makes rap sound too much like opera: we can get to love it – and in the last ten years, people all over the world have come to love it – without having to understand the rapper's words. To see rap as opera misses too much. Rappers confront us the way Wordsworth said a poet addresses his audience: as 'a man speaking to men'. They are using 'the language of men'. (And this means something a lot deeper than the language of males.) We have to listen to the *words*, and hear how they're being said, and imagine what they might mean, because a rapper's words have the power of life and death.

In rap's early days, as in the early days of sound film, language was mainly comic: words were juggled, caressed, turned inside out, twisted like snakes around the audience and the performers themselves. As a professor, I was glad to see how well these kids knew the power of words, and how they were staking their claim to the English language and using it to empower themselves. They denounced everything and everyone, including themselves, but their antic words and energy soared above it all so that none of it seemed to matter. They probably hadn't seen many Marx Brothers's films, but Groucho was their godfather. What, Groucho in the ghetto? Well, after all, didn't he come from the ghetto? Where else could he have come from?

There are still great comic raps coming out: 'OPP', Other People's Property, by Naughty by Nature (1991), is one of the sexiest and funniest raps ever made. But very soon a tragic crater opened up alongside the comedy. Considering where rap was coming from, how could it not? 'The Message', by Grandmaster Flash and the Furious Five, released in 1982, was rap's first international hit. It was a litany of dreadful things that could happen to a poor person in the South Bronx or someplace like it. You can imagine the details. The chorus, delivered with desperate intensity, went, 'So don't push me 'cause I'm close to the edge/trying not to lose my head. *Huh!*/It's like a jungle out there, sometimes it makes me wonder/how I keep from going under.' In the rap's second half, the narrator's perspective shifts, and he talks to somebody who is like himself, but dead: someone who had gone over the edge, 'lived so fast and died so young'.

'The Message', at once a cry for help and a snarl that no one can help, became an instant classic. Suddenly a lot of people wanted to hear rap, and thought it mattered. It opened up a genre that could channel the tidal flow of pain and rage that flooded American inner cities in the Reagan years of malign neglect. And, at a moment when American popular music was highly stylized and overblown, it sounded 'real', directly connected to a 'real life'. The life rap came from was distinctly marginal, but those early rap voices despaired of their marginality, rather than rejoicing in it (as postmod theorists of culture told them they should). At this point rap became important not just musically but culturally, and, moreover, not just in our ghettos, but all over our country, because it became an arena in which Americans contended and argued over the nature of the reality we share.

After 'The Message', many intellectuals started listening to rap. (A few had listened even before.) We admired its in-your-face intensity, its emotional authenticity, its unmediated desperation, but also its wits and ways with words, its power to be playful in the midst of death, its hope that words could have the power to pull the self through. Intellectuals and artists knew and cared about rap for years before big record companies or Hollywood producers would touch it. They wrote criticism that celebrated it, much as the young intellectuals of the *Cahiers du Cinema* a generation before had celebrated low-budget *film noir*. Here's a concluding sentence from one of those critical pieces, by me: 'They are saying, *We come from ruins, but we are not ruined.*' Here's another: 'From now on, nobody and nothing in the world is safe from rap.' Some intellectuals put together non-commercial films (*Wild Style, Beat Street, Style Wars*, and many shorts) that introduced the world to Hip-Hop, the subculture that had created rap, artistic graffiti, and breakdance. I got to know many of these intellectuals up in the Bronx, or on the #2 Subway line. It all reminded me of the Russian intellectuals of the 1880s, 'going to the people': we would teach them how to organize, they would regenerate us through their moral purity. Of course 'purity' meant something different for us. We never thought the poor people of the Bronx were saintly; what we thought is that they were authentic. But authentically what? the idea oozed ambiguity. Some people thought it would be better for rappers to stay in the Bronx forever; to move into the 'Downtown' world was bound to make them corrupt, like ourselves. I had the feeling that the rappers loved the Bronx, but now that the Bronx had taught them to talk, they wanted to talk to the whole world, and if we cared for them like we said we did, we would help them get as far into the world as they could.

I had just brought out a big book on modernism, and rap felt like proof that modernism still lived. It seemed like a bridge between my middle age and my childhood, between the middle-class I was now and the working-class where I'd started out, between smart people with education (like me) and smart people with none (the rappers, my parents), between Jews and blacks, between the stacks in the library and the signs on the street. This was when Gramsci's idea of the 'organic intellectual' came close to my heart; when an Italian newspaper asked me to describe myself, I said that I was trying to become an organic intellectual of New York, trying to carry the city's inner contradictions within myself. There were these three years or so in the middle of the 1980s – never before, never again – when I had this thrilling feeling that I *belonged*.

As the 1980s went by, more and more people, with a widening range of biographies, began to rap. Many came from the middle class and had serious education. Some of them could even use words like 'modernism'. Here's a sample from a group called Public Enemy, from suburban Queens:

> Lazer anesthesia, maze ya, ways to blaze your
> brain and train ya
> ... What I got, get on up, better get some,
> hustler of culture
> Snakebitten, been spit in the face but
> the rhymes keep fittin'....

'Hustler of culture': this rapper, Chuck D, knew something about modern poetry, as much as he knew about beats and rhymes. Public Enemy helped a lot to expand rap's vocabulary. They set a new standard in density and richness of sound, in lyrical brilliance, and in political seriousness and commitment. ('Fight the Power', incorporated into Spike Lee's movie, *Do the Right Thing*, and 'Welcome to the Terrordome', are their greatest hits.) Their politics were always vague, and sometimes seemed to verge into mere bad attitude, but the vagueness was probably artistically more fruitful than exact specificity would have been. The central imperative seemed to be that rappers should *think* and *care* about politics, that they should overcome the horizon of their street and think about the world. 'The ass is connected to the brain stem', rapped Chuck D. Before long, if you listened to rap radio, Machiavelli, Shakespeare and Nietzsche, Sartre and Camus began to appear in the mix, fighting for space with Reagan and Bush, Jesse James and Scarface Al Capone. More raps appeared that were not only smart but intellectual, reflective and complex.

Meanwhile, white kids began rapping, and some of them – the Beastie Boys, 3rd Bass – did it compellingly, and got respect on the street. The best white rappers tended to be Jewish kids, as marginal in their own way as blacks; they simultaneously flaunted their culture and parodied it, as the Marx Brothers had done in the 1930s, and as Bob Dylan did in the 1960s. (Dylan's 'Subterranean Homesick Blues' surely rates a place in rap's prehistory.)

I can remember the fall of 1989, that magic year when history seemed so wonderfully open. I was in Stockholm, rapping about rap, saying how it could create a universal language and a world culture. My Swedish audiences were a little mystified, but fascinated with this idea. So why do I feel so silly if I say it now? I still love rap, my body still moves and my heart soars when I hear it in a passing car or on a boombox in the street. I still hear raps and rappers that thrill me. And I still think rap *is* an archetype of 'world culture'. But that culture and that world both look a lot more problematic to me now than they did in 1989.

The post-Cold War world's troubles are being acted out in the starkest way right now in former Yugoslavia and the former USSR. Both those nations for generations tried to hold together very wide ranges of people and peoples. Their communist rulers, though at odds with each other, both offered their peoples an enlarged, inclusive and cosmopolitan vision of citizenship. I don't know just why it happened at the end of the 1980s, but finally they both collapsed. (One reason has to be that the visions were routinely betrayed in everyday life; on the other hand, they weren't betrayed any more in the 1980s than in the 1950s or 60s or 70s.) Both sides caved in to a wide array of centrifugal pressures, ethnic, national and religious: they could not overcome. In much of Eastern Europe, racist demagogues have come out of the woodwork and had tremendous popular success; thousands of people have been killed since those nations fell apart, maybe even hundreds of thousands; and it looks like Eastern Europe's civil wars are going to get worse before they play themselves out. One of the saddest things is what's not there: there's no idea of an inclusive citizenship based on a rule of law. What's replaced it is a bunch of exclusions, based on unstable mixtures of blood and soil and church and DNA and the gene pool and big guns, locked in a zero-sum war. Whoever wins here, humanism loses; it never even had a chance.

What happened in rap is a crude caricature of this reality. (Cf. Marx: 'the first time as tragedy, the second as farce'.) In the early 1990s, the overwhelming burst of energy in rap, emanating above all from LA, has been in a form that called itself 'gangsta rap'. If Public Enemy was special in its layered complexity, the gangstas – like an antithesis to their thesis – specialized in gestures of brutal simplification. Here is Eazy-E, of NWA, Niggers With Attitude, in *Straight Outta Compton*, the first breakthrough LA gangsta rap album:

> I'm the kind of nigger who's built to last.
> Fuck with me, I'll put my foot up your ass.

You could say this set the tone. Ironically, the persons that gangsta rappers most resemble – fluent in violence, free from guilt or pangs of conscience, able to rape and torture and murder and sleep well – is the cultural archetype that (in *Genealogy of Morals*) Nietzsche baptized as the Blond Beast.

Gangsta rap features stark explosive images of the rapper as predator, robber, rapist, murderer; guns and wounds are described in rich detail ('… and then I smoked him', 'and then I popped her', 'I'm gonna wet'cha' – you learn exactly where and with what); the MTV clips show you both the streets and the guns, which the rappers wave with flamboyant pride. Attitude ranges from surly defiance to willed stupidity to self-mockery and gallows humour. Both the narratives and sounds of gangsta rap show plenty of brains at work, but the genre calls for smart people to stupefy themselves. (This is nothing new in popular culture: think of early Marlon Brando, say, or the Rolling Stones. But they took pride in their theatricality, their ability to create *personae*: they never claimed authenticity.)

In virtually every gangsta rap, some act of explosive violence takes place. There are maybe four primal scenes:

1. Shoot-out between rival gangs, *à la West Side Story*; the fight is decided by who has the better guns; the rap features detailed description of the guns and emotional distancing from loved ones who die.

2. Shoot-out between two gangsters, same emotional complex as above; the survivor gets to tell the story.

3. Sexual encounter, which starts out with rape and gets worse: 'rape', because it is a convention of the genre that this is what women

want; 'worse', because rape doesn't give the narrator satisfaction, so he gets more frenzied and nastier. For anybody who loves rap, brutality towards women is the most disgusting thing in it, the hardest thing to listen to without turning off. Misogyny is a word often used, but it doesn't convey the paradox of a man's desperate need for, and total psychological dependence on, the person who is the object of his rage.

4. Here is the Mother of all Primal Scenes: cops stop the rapper on the highway. They strip-search him, beat and humiliate him *à la* Rodney King, but then somehow he gets a gun, and even as they scream for mercy he kills them all. Sometimes, while he is shooting, the narrator explains that he is doing this to avenge all black people (this theme has grown less easy as more black cops appear; they have to be shot separately). The primal road scene offers acid commentary on the American (and especially Californian) romance of mobility: these stories show how wheels don't make you free when you're black. Some versions add a slightly different spin: no one wants to stop you because no one cares, you're on a road to nowhere when you're poor, nobody knows you when you're down and out.

The visual flamboyance of the gangsta rappers's style gave Hollywood ideas for a new visual form, the Gangsta Rap Movie. *New Jack City* was the first, in 1990, featured Ice-T, an eminent gangsta rapper, playing the part of a nihilistic cop. These movies have created a new range of styles in youth culture, black and white. They have also created a new range of market tie-ins, and have helped to unify the film, video and music divisions of the few media conglomerates which, after a decade of frenetic mergers and acquisitions – remember, the history of rap is the history of Reaganism – now own it all.

Thanks to the market tie-ins, a few rappers have grown immensely rich while still in their early twenties, sometimes even in their teens. More striking, they have accumulated an immense moral authority among black youth today, which far surpasses any feelings their parents had for Stevie Wonder, Aretha Franklin or Sly Stone, let alone for Coltrane or Monk or Bird. When gangster rappers talk to the press, they are often very grave and solemn, as if they really believe in their moral authority, even when their raps themselves suggest they believe in nothing but the will to power. Teachers and other elders are dismayed, but we shouldn't be surprised, because our kids are Americans, and Americans have always treated spectacular wealth as a source of moral authority. (And some of those great jazz musicians died without ever getting rich at all.)

This creates some strange situations. KRS-1, one of the smartest and most volatile rappers, defends gangster rap by saying, 'Anything that terrifies whites, that makes them shake in their beds, is good for us.' Ice Cube says 'You [whites] need us [blacks] to look like rapists and murderers'. Well, there is plenty of classic literature (Faulkner) and social science (John Dollard) that shows how whites can project their own unspeakable desires on to blacks, and we have all seen the lynching photos (Rodney King's is only the latest) that show how they can act when they act those desires out. But given what rappers know about white racism, isn't it crazy to actively encourage it?

Not that any of this will hurt the stars. Today rap stars live in mansions in Beverly Hills and East Hampton, consult with public relations men and semioticians on the care and feeding of their images, and – like very rich people all over America – keep up their own private security forces. But at a time when black teenagers are dying of homicide at a rate something like *nine times* higher than American youth as a whole, it shouldn't be hard to imagine how the semiotics of gangster rap can make it easier and sexier for fourteen-year-olds to do what 'The Message' said a decade ago: 'you lived too fast and died too young'.

There's something to this moralism, but less than people in the media and in Congress think. Last fall the Reverend Calvin Butts, pastor of the Abyssinian Baptist Church in Harlem (Adam Clayton Powell's old church), ran over hundreds of rap tapes with a steamroller, in order, so he said, to destroy the destroyer of black youth. This was an impressive media event, as chilling as any gangster rap on MTV. (And here, too, the outcome was decided by superior hardware.) But we here, who know something about the history of culture, should be sceptical of the idea that culture causes human behaviour. We should think back to *the Iliad, the Mahabarata*, the bloody *Song of Deborah* (probably the oldest part of the Bible), and what must be the most highly publicized and sensationalized act of violence in history, the crucifixion of Jesus. We should remember that dramatic images of violence, more horrific than anything in rap, are at the roots of our most respectable and venerable traditions; and we should lighten up.

Of course, American culture is exceptionally rich in dramatic images of violence. Since our Second Amendment, which placed guns at the very centre of our political culture, images of violence have been among our prime exports to the world: our genocidal Indian warfare, our Indian fighters as murderous as any brave, Daniel Boone, Davy Crockett (first democratic politician to hire a publicist), the Alamo, Kit Carson, Custerism and its vocabulary of 'extermination to the last man', gunfights in the streets, the O.K. Corral, Billy the Kid, Jesse James and Buffalo Bill, Teddy Roosevelt's Rough Riders, the Klan, *Birth of a Nation*, lynchmobs – praised by Georges Sorel as the archetype of revolutionary justice – and, in the 20th century, for our Depression bank robbers and murderers, John Dillinger and Bonnie and Clyde, plus our mobs of urban immigrant gangs and gangsters, Public Enemy (since we're talking about rap), Scarface Al Capone (another rap hero), Meyer Lansky and Murder Inc., *Superfly* and *Miami Vice*. Western and gangster movies and TV police shows have not only flooded the world with these images, but consciously equated them with 'America', with myths about our national character, long before rap came along. Even people around the world who denounce America for its politics love us for our violent images: large crowds of leftists in Paris or Sao Paulo or Canberra get drenched in the rain for a chance to see *Gun Crazy* or *The Wild Bunch* or *Superfly*. And even our respectably academic field of American Studies features books with titles like *Gunfighter Nation* and *Regeneration Through Violence* (both by Richard Slotkin, both fine books). So the point to make about gangster rap is not how deviant it is, but how typically American; in Rap Brown's phrase, as American as apple pie.

Gangster rap carries on the great American tradition of the gangster film. The best thing ever written about this genre is Robert Warshow's 1948 essay. 'The Gangster as Tragic Hero'. As against the 'official optimism' of American culture, gangster films are part of 'a current of opposition, seeking to express by whatever means are available to it that sense of desperation and inevitable failure which optimism itself helps to create.' The gangster lives on a plane where 'the quality of irrational brutality and the quality of rational enterprise becomes one'.

> The whole meaning of the gangster's career is a drive for success: a steady upward progress, followed by a very precipitate fall. Thus brutality itself becomes at once the means to success and the content of success – a success that is defined in its most general terms, not as accomplishment or specific gain, but simply as the unlimited possibility of aggression.

The gangster's world is structurally opposed to the world of 'civil society', a sphere where people recognize each other's rights and settle conflict peacefully. But one of the subtexts of gangster film is always how much the cops are like the robbers, how thin is the line, how tenuous the claim of civil society to embody real human progress. Thus, in *New Jack City*, the first Gangster Rap film, Ice-T won fame and fortune playing a nihilistic cop who brings down a drug lord who is portrayed as *son semblable, son frère*.

The patron saint of the Congresspeople who would ban rap is Plato. (Of course, Plato would ban Congress, too.) In *The Republic* Book 2, he argues that people commit crimes (incest and murder are the ones that most worry him) because they get criminal desires from culture; if it were possible to wipe out not only dramatic poetry but the whole body of Greek mythology, then people wouldn't get any more bad desires, because they'd have no place to get them from, and then they'd be good. But Plato never finished thinking, he was always contradicting himself: in Book 9, he argued that everybody has incestuous and murderous desires, that desires like these were part of the human condition, and that we could tell that we had them by paying attention to our dreams – you can see why Freud loved to quote this; he also said that the difference between good men and bad men was that good men merely dream of what bad men actually do. This is the basis of Aristotle's idea (in *Poetics*) of *cartharsis*: tragedy should bring all our worst feelings to the surface, and help us work through them.

In the 1770s, Friedrich Schiller brought out a play called *The Robbers*, which put the gangster hero permanently on the map of modern culture. Riots broke out in several towns where *The Robbers* played, and even severer riots in towns where it was prohibited. When revolutionary movements erupted in Germany after 1789, many solid citizens predictably blamed the play. Kant may well have been defending it in the 1780s when he argued that if people can enjoy criminal images and visions, it will relieve them of the desire to commit criminal acts. Teachers among us can see a pattern like this in our best students (and parents can see it in our law-abiding children): for a little while they imagine themselves as marauders who terrify the world, then they re-enter real life and hit the books. Middle-aged people can discern a pattern like this in ourselves, if we can remember the Mickey Spillane books and horror comics we read in the dark, and the James Dean and Marlon Brando posters we put on our walls. The violent fantasies of gangster rap serve the same essentially conservative function that violent fantasies have always served, just as they did for Athenian citizens and for the audience at Shakespeare's Globe.

175

In the last few years, as some rappers have become very rich and famous, some of their audience and critics have come to feel that they've betrayed their people and become inauthentic. This is pretty silly: rap started in the neighbourhoods, but it soon became what it is, a world language, and people who love it should be glad the world has found out. It shouldn't bother us that the gangster *capos* are living in mansions. What should bother us is that they've surrounded their mansions with walls and moats of bad faith. The mystique of Afrocentrism provides good bricks for those walls. Rap in the 1990s is the most creatively impure music ever made. (And a late-20th-century audience, attuned to the 'impure' aesthetics of collage and montage, can 'get' it right away). But many rappers, the more impure their music gets, the more righteously they profess a cult of racial separateness and purity. The more they fast-break and slam-dunk the English language, the louder they protest they're only talking 'African'. The more their lives entwine with those of whites – producers, critics, managers, editors, film-makers, not to mention lovers and wives, and an audience that marketing surveys say is as much as four-fifths white – the more they insist they have no connection with whites at all, and speak to blacks alone. The better they thrive in the multinational markets that have turned their old neighbourhoods into ghost towns – and the Reaganite years of rap's history are years of radical social polarization, among blacks even more than whites – the more they insist they are nothing but homeboys, identical with all those they have left behind. Even as they raise rap into a universal language, they are fighting like an undertow against themselves to turn it back into a segregated men's room. Maybe it's all just schoolyard trash-talk and we should laugh. But it feels like authenticity, one of rap's deepest sources of strength, has turned into just another set of conventions and conformities, another chic new style, another big lie.

One more dread dynamic haunts gangster rap: guys who succeed are accused of going 'soft' (a typical interviewer's first question: 'people say you've gone soft'), so that they feel they have to prove they're 'hard'. But anything they do will be undermined by critics as a mere defensive manoeuvre. So no victory can ever be enough, and the stakes are always getting raised. In August 1993, the rapper Snoop Doggy Dogg, of Long Beach, California, whose album had just debuted at ← on the *Billboard* charts, visited his old neighbourhood and became implicated in the killing of a man. His involvement with the murder helped him to win great acclaim among young people, black and white, including many of my students, who had feared he was selling out. There seems to be nothing like homicide to keep a homeboy close to the streets. At what drive will the boys stop?

Gangster rap has provided such a 'high concept', and has so successfully conquered markets – record industry people say no earlier black music has made such a 'crossover' to whites – that it has often felt like a real gang, sweeping through a high school gym and blowing all its opponents away. This ambiance is satirized brilliantly in the 1992 film *CB4*, where a middle-class group of gangster rappers is terrified when real gangsters move in on them, and where a special Old Age Home for Rappers becomes the last stop for young men who are decrepit while still in their twenties.

The general American public seems unaware that there are any other forms of sensibilities in rap. But in fact there are plenty. Groups like De La Soul, MC Lyte, Arrested Development, PM Dawn, Salt-n-Pepa, Basehead, the Digable Planets, the Goats, the Disposable Heroes of Hiphoprisy, and many more, are all smart people and sophisticated musicians. They don't need to threaten their audience or each other to get attention, and they have enlarged rap's emotional repertory to include tenderness, irony, reflectiveness about the world, and questions about the subject's own identity. Their politics are various kinds of leftism, but they have managed to imagine militancies that aren't murderous.

You might think the gangster rappers, with all their wealth and power, would be able to share space, but it seems they can't. An ominous but fascinating incident last year dramatized the volatile politics of identity that pervade contemporary rap. The rapper KRS-1, who grew up in subways and South Bronx homeless shelters, considers himself the inventor of gangster rap (he may be right), and is mad that he isn't a millionaire. He is also a self-taught and serious intellectual who describes himself as 'the teacher of mankind'. (This enriches his creativity, but complicates his image, and bars him from the 'high concept' easy marketability of some of the gangsta rappers from LA.) About a third of his 'teaching' is brilliant and imaginative, a third is loopy and malevolent, and a third is utterly incomprehensible. Prince Be, the MC of PM Dawn, is rap's greatest ironist. He is also self-consciously effete and 'soft' (market label: *Psychedelic*), and he likes to laugh at machismo in rap. Late in 1991, he told an interviewer: 'KRS is the teacher, but the teacher of what?' The next time Prince Be played live in New York, early in 1992, KRS and his gang assaulted him, beat him up, knocked him off the stage, and announced that he, KRS, was the boss of rap. Some accounts of the episode treated it as a streetcorner brawl that KRS had won. Prince Be was shaken up, but he has refused to act like a loser. He has kept rapping and kept laughing and trying to show how rap can be a medium where the meaning of being a man can grow.

Sometime early in the 1990s, before the gangsters had taken over the gym, but at a time when rap sales were already up in the many millions, I remember a melancholy feeling coming over me. I felt: *Rap doesn't need me anymore*. I know this was a very self-dramatizing thing to feel – what, rap should need a Jewish professor? (Of course, Chuck D did say, back in 1988, that he wanted rap to be a 'seminar'.) It was mostly a feeling about me, how my bond with rap had made me feel like and 'organic intellectual' for a while, and how I was going to have to find new ways to feel whole. But the melancholy wasn't just about me; it was about a process that happens again and again in the history of modern culture. Some of our most creative cultural movements have been passionately promoted by small groups of intellectuals, long before any of our culture industries could see that there was something there. What I felt is linked to something that Harold Rosenberg and Clement Greenberg must have felt about Abstract Expressionism sometime in the 1950s, and that Charles Lamb and William Hazlitt must have felt about Romantic Poetry in the 1800s, and that Dr Johnson and Diderot must have felt about the novel in the 1750s: *the movement is getting over on its own*.

How do we frame this story? At the dawn of the Reagan era, intellectuals – mostly but not wholly white – found rap in the ruins. It was all the way out on the margins of America, and we helped it get its green card. Now it has made its way to the centre of American life, where big stars drive big cars, flash millions of bucks, shove the competition off the stage, and now and then kill people. Well, didn't we want them to get as far as they could go? So they're in the centre now, while we are still looking on from the sides. But wasn't there a moment when rap was about *justice*, – and justice meant more than 'just them'? I think there really was, and there will be again. But rappers are going to have to reinvent it from the inside, just as Karl Marx and his friends did, just as my generation of the New Left did for ourselves. As they figure it out, they'll have plenty to rap about. I hope we'll still be able to hear.

Meanwhile, my melancholy feeling made me see something about the place of cultural critics in history, about how we fit in. We open up new neighbourhoods of feeling and expression in scary, unfamiliar parts of the modern city. We harangue and seduce people to go, and we swear that once they get there, their whole being will be transformed – that's the point of the song, 'Take the A Train'. At last people do go, and they love it, and things happen just as we said they would, and we feel fulfilled. But then more people go than we intended, and stranger things happen than we imagined, and finally the whole neighbourhood looks overbuilt to us, though it feels fine to the people who went there on our word. Then we know we've got to go. We can still love it, but we've got to break our organic link. Our sadness is mixed with pride, because we know we've done our work well and helped the city grow. But now it's time to listen for new shouts in the street.

Margin/Alia: Social Justice and the New Cultural Politics

Edward W. Soja

Looking back over the last half of the twentieth century, it is difficult to find a book which has had a more definitive agenda-setting influence on so many disciplines than David Harvey's *Social Justice and the City* (henceforth *SJC*).[1] Published in the wake of a decade of urban uprising and social unrest and at the precise moment when the global economy was plunging into its worst crisis since the Great Depression, *SJC* would stimulate a profound change in the ways we think about each of the four intertwining themes Harvey chose to re-explore: the 'nature', as he called it, of Theory, Urbanism, Justice, and Space.

Using the achievements of *SJC* as a springboard, I will address these four themes again in the contemporary context where, I will argue, the rise of what is being called a 'new cultural politics' and the development of a transdisciplinary field of critical cultural studies, infused with a rich geographical imagination, may be stimulating another transformative rethinking of each of these four themes and their interconnections comparable to that which occurred in the aftermath of *SJC*.[2] This new agenda for rethinking social justice and the city both builds on Harvey's accomplishments and departs significantly from his most influential conclusions. To restate my argument in a different way, I paraphrase a passage from David Harvey's Introduction to *SJC* (p10), where he discusses the relation between the 'Liberal Formulations' that framed Part 1 of the book and the Marxist or 'Socialist Formulations' found in Part 2. What I have done in the following excerpt is to substitute the transition from one form of radical cultural politics to another for what Harvey describes as his own intellectual evolution from liberal to socialist interpretations of theory, urbanism, justice, and space.

The evolution which occurs between our approaches to the old and the new cultural politics (for Harvey, between Parts 1 and 2) naturally gives rise to contradictions and inconsistencies. The general approach to the new cultural politics is substantially different (and, I believe, substantially more enlightening) ... Yet the new approach takes on more meaning if it is understood how the viewpoints it espouses were arrived at ... It is also important to note that the material content and action strategies of the old cultural politics are not being rejected but incorporated and given new meaning by the evolving framework of the new.

THEORY-JUSTICE-URBANISM-SPACE: THE SPECIFIC GEOGRAPHIES OF CAPITALISM

One of the most memorable and lasting insights of *SJC* was Harvey's argument that the 'normal workings' of the urban system, the day-to-day practices of urbanism as a way of life, produced and reproduced a regressive redistribution of real income that benefitted the rich at the expense of the poor. Harvey described the capitalist city as an inequalities-generating machine *by its very nature*, thereby creating in the context of urban geographies and the interrelations of social processes and spatial form a fertile terrain for the cumulative aggravation of injustices. He specified this redistributive dynamic in three realms. One was the normal operations of the free market in land, labour, retailing, and finance, from the changing value of private property rights (especially when amplified or depleted by public investments) to the risk-avoiding redlining of banks and the location of supermarkets so that the 'poor pay more'. These free market-generated inequalities arose, Harvey argued, not through conspiracy or corruption so much as from standard market conventions and competition, from how the unfettered urban space economy worked toward achieving maximum organizational efficiency.

To this he added the everyday operations and practices of urban planning and public sector decision-making, providing a brilliant explanation for the familiar problem of why the 'good intentions' of liberal (and even some radical) planners so often result in those 'unexpected consequences' and 'great planning disasters' that urban critics like to write about. The urban public realm never acts as a free agent, but always within the dynamic economic and political fields shaped by market competition and profit-maximizing behaviour.

Without public control over these market forces, even the most innovative and progressive planning programmes are susceptible to co-optation by the invisible hands that generate, by their very nature, increasing inequality.

Finally, Harvey broadened his focus to what he would later call the 'urbanization process under capitalism', especially as it is manifested in the evolution of urban form and the production of the built environment. For these formulations alone, *SJC* became required reading in virtually every major urban planning department in the country. It also infused the largely descriptive field of urban geography with a new theoretical framework and a more practical and applied orientation.

Harvey added to his liberal formulations on the interplay of social process and spatial form an explicitly spatial conceptualization of social justice based on these endemic redistributive effects of urbanization. Pushing the liberal discourse and its universalized principles of social justice to its limits, he creatively extended the concept of 'territorial redistributive justice' and grounded it in a set of achievable goals based on need, contribution to the common good, and 'merit', which he defined primarily in terms of maximizing the prospects of the 'least advantaged territory' and its poorest residents. In this search for the means to achieve a just distribution of real income and resources justly arrived at, Harvey reached the end of his universalizing liberal formulations with a growing frustration that these laudable goals might never be achievable given the persistent power of the 'normal workings' of the capitalist city.

In a philosophical transformation that would resonate throughout the field of urban studies and beyond, Harvey at this point vaulted into a Marxist critique that radically shifted the terrain defined by his four themes of theory, urbanism, justice, and space. Rather than in liberal formulations, he rooted the origins of redistributive injustice in the matrix of the social relations of production and, more generally, in what came to be called the class-structured 'specific geography' of capitalism. For the next twenty years, the effort to make practical and theoretical sense of the specific geography of the capitalist city attracted the attention of progressive urban scholars from many different disciplines. A new critical discourse on urban political economy emerged, tying together what were formerly separate debates on social justice, urbanism, the social production of space, and the nature of social theory.

SJC also contained another new twist that would have a long lasting effect. Without being overly explicit, Harvey opened up his neo-Marxist critique to what I will call radical modernist cultural politics. More than just an appreciation for the superstructural elements that impinge upon the economic base, this attention to culture and community, to race and ethnicity, to struggles over issues of collective consumption and reproduction, arose most emphatically in his liberal formulations, but were also given room in the construction of radical socialist subjectivity and in the struggles to overcome the exploitative class dynamics of urbanization.[3] Influenced by Henri Lefebvre's spatial critique of everyday life in the modern world and Manuel Castells's theorization of urban social movements, Harvey, from the very beginning, recognized the need to give more substantive attention to cultural issues in the new urban political economy and the Marxist geography that was developing around it. For the next twenty years, this challenge would be raised again and again by almost everyone involved in studying the capitalist city and the political economy of urbanization. And it would provide the context and conjuncture for another transformative rethinking of social justice and the city as significant as that expressed in Harvey's shift from liberal to socialist formulations.

THEORY-JUSTICE-URBANISM-SPACE: TOWARDS A NEW CULTURAL POLITICS

Reflecting on the efforts over the past two decades to inject a critical and substantive cultural dimension to the urban political economy and Marxist geography that developed under the impetus of *SJC*, two summative observations come to mind. The first is that attempts simply and with the best of intentions to *add* culture to political economy will lead almost inevitably to a subordination (and degradation) of the former by the latter. What this suggests is that the exciting new field of critical cultural studies, which has been developing its own creative conceptualizations of the four themes of theory-justice-urbanism-space, may be fundamentally inaccessible within the still prevailing epistemological framework of radical political economy and in the strategic contexts of what I described earlier as modernist cultural politics. The second observation is a corollary of the first: that an appropriate theoretical and practical understanding of cultural politics today requires not just the addition of a cultural dimension, but also a deep cultural and epistemological critique and restructuring of both radical political economy and Marxist geography as they are presently constituted. Implied in these two observations is the profound difference between what I have chosen to call the old (modernist) and the new (increasingly postmodernist) cultural politics. Some further elaboration on this difference is necessary, for it is central to the argument being presented here.

Both the old and the new cultural politics are built around particular conceptualizations of radical subjectivity and significantly different strategies for collective action in response to the urban intersections of space, power, and social justice. In the most radical brands of modernist cultural politics – including not only class struggle but also the array of radical social movements built around race, gender, ethnic community, sexual preference, locality, region, and nation – the political logic of radical subjectivity tends to emanate from a similar framework of mobilization, consciousness, and action.[4] At the source of virtually all radical modernist political movements is a presumption of the binarization of power and an almost ontological belief that subordination, exploitation, and other forms of oppression and inequality (and hence injustice) arise from this fundamental binarization, whether it be bourgeoisie vs proletariat, capital vs labour, man vs woman, white vs black, core vs periphery, the colonizer vs the colonized. One of the most telling illustrations of this imposing binary logic of modernist radical subjectivity is the board game 'Class Struggle', invented by Bertell Ollman, a Marxist political scientist and former colleague of David Harvey. Although players can choose several different roles – peasant, student, shopkeeper – only two players can either win or lose the game, those representing the essentially determinitive structural dualism of capitalist vs worker.[5]

Critical modernist thinking about this all-encompassing bifurcation of power, and the political strategies that derive from it, have typically been grounded in a process of demystification, an attempt to strip away all the veils that obscure the fundamental material operations of binarized power relations. As a starting point, all appearances that the binary is 'natural' or primordially given must be rejected in order to recognize that the inequalities and injustices derived from the binary division of power are socially produced and therefore subject to social transformation. Marx was one of the great masters in this process of demystification, using the commodity form and a materialist interpretation of history to expose the reifications and fetishisms that shroud working-class consciousness 'for itself'. *SJC* was just the beginning of a much longer project in which David Harvey would restlessly expose, layer by layer, the hidden bifurcations of class power embedded in the space economy of urbanism, in those 'normal workings' and 'specific geographies' of the capitalist city; and later, in what he would describe as the 'limits to capital', 'the urbanization of consciousness', and, most recently, 'the conditions of postmodernity'.[6]

Typically flowing from this demystification is a condensation and focusing – some would say reduction – of radical subjectivity and political strategy around an awareness of the subordination and oppression that are built deeply into the specific power binary chosen to mobilize collective consciousness. In Marxist urban political economy, for example, radical urban social movements are seen as arising from their roots in the social (class) relations of production as they are expressed in everyday urban life and the evolving spatial organization, built environment, and uneven deployment of the capitalist city. Afrocentric black nationalisms and certain forms of radical feminism similarly build their politics around their own Big Dichotomy, expressed, respectively, in the bifurcated social relations of racism (white vs black) and patriarchy (male vs female). In all these cases, social struggle is aimed either at a radical inversion of these binarized power relations (a dictatorship of the proletariat, for example); or, more commonly, at the erasure or equalization of the power differentials that define the binary in the first place.

Radical subjectivity that is rooted outside the chosen primary dualism tends to be seen within the movement as 'false consciousness' or, at best, a secondary source of possible mobilization absorbable under the primary umbrella. One modernist social movement rarely intersects with another on equal terms; most are channelled in parallel streams of consciousness and action that are essentialized along a singular overarching axis. Within each social movement, many genuinely believe in cross-cutting complementarity, promote open-ness, and deny any totalizing essentialism, but the practice of modernist cultural politics has been characteristically exclusive and the relations between different radical movements have all too frequently been filled with friction and competitive rancour. Because the critical theories associated with radical modernism have never succeeded in developing a political logic or epistemology that can override the exclusive power of those Big Dichotomies, modernist cultural politics is often sidetracked into scurrilous debates over whose binary is the biggest, whose cause is ultimately the most empowering.

Aggravating the divisiveness that still characterizes radical modernist cultural politics, even among those, like Harvey, who are most creatively adapting to the particular circumstances of the contemporary world, is the fear of fragmentation, a belief that politically cooking in many different channels will spoil the broth of radical transformation. The fragmentation of political struggles continues to be seen almost exclusively in a negative light, as a sign of debilitating weakness rather than potential strength, as the product of well-intentioned but nevertheless 'false' consciousness. This is not surprising given the fixation on one or another Big Dichotomy and the failure to theorize adequately the political logic of combining channels, of finding ways to overcome the essentializing either/or logic of the binary to open up a more politically flexible and inclusive logic of the and/also, a recombinative logic of coalition formation among all those subjected to oppression, whatever the source.

Accelerating in the 1990s, a new, radical, and increasingly postmodern cultural politics has been developing from the critical deconstruction and reconstitution of these radical (as well as liberal) modernist traditions, in much the same way I suggested earlier that Harvey's Marxist formulations selectively restructured and absorbed, without entirely rejecting, his liberal positioning in Part I of *SJC*. There is both continuity with the old and significant redirection into new and, I would say, more enlightening paths that are built around what the African-American philosopher, Cornel West, describes as 'creative responses to the precise circumstances of our present moment', a 'new cultural politics of difference' aimed at empowering and enabling radical social action.[7] The leading edge of this transformative rethinking of modernist cultural politics has been centred in a group of scholars and activists committed to the power and potential of a radical postmodernist cultural politics: a diverse group of cultural critics who, in contrast to the modernist left, do not consider 'radical postmodernism' to be an impossible oxymoron.

As I hope has been made clear, this new, explicitly postmodern cultural politics does not represent a complete break with radical modernism. Its theoretical and political practices continue to draw (selectively, to be sure) on modernist principles, theoretical formulations, and action strategies. Recalling David Harvey's dramatic shift from his earlier liberal formulations in *SJC*, the material content and action strategies of radical modernism are not being rejected *tout ensemble*. Rather, they are being incorporated and given new meaning through the evolving framework of radical postmodernisms (pluralized here to stress their non-totalizing multiplicity and openness). The discovery of modernist residuals in the work of avowedly radical postmodernists – often the source of skittish delight among radical modernist (and many not-so-radical postmodernist) critics – is therefore not so much a sign of contradiction, weakness, and confusion as, more often than is recognized, an indication of strategic intention and strength: part of the normal workings of radical postmodernism.

It is also important to note that radical postmodernism is not entirely uncritical of the prevailing postmodern discourse. In her essay on 'Postmodern Blackness', for example, the African-American scholar-activist bell hooks presents a powerful critique of the dominant postmodern discourse for its tendencies toward white male exclusivity and its persistent separation/abstraction of a generalized 'politics of difference' from the more materially specified, contextualized, and lived 'politics of racism'. From her grounded perspective, she writes:

> The overall impact of postmodernism is that many other groups now share with black folks a sense of deep alienation, despair, uncertainty, loss of a sense of grounding even if it is not informed by shared circumstance. Radical postmodernism calls attention to these shared sensibilities which cross the boundaries of class, race, gender, etc., and could be fertile ground for the construction of empathy – ties that would promote recognition of common commitments, and serve as a base for solidarity and coalition ... To change the exclusionary practice of postmodern critical discourse is to enact a postmodernism of resistance.[8]

Thus, while there are significant continuities between modernism and postmodernism and between the old and the new cultural politics, there is also as profound a shift of critical attention and political positioning as occurred between Parts 1 and 2 in *SJC*. And the parallel can be extended further, for the 'evolving framework' of radical postmodernism is being constructed through another transformative re-exploration of the nature of theory, justice, urbanism, and space.

THEORY-JUSTICE-URBANISM-SPACE: RECENT ELABORATIONS

One of the most important deconstructive and reconstitutive acts taken by the postmodern feminist, postcolonial, poststructuralist,and post Marxist cultural critics has been a head-on attack on the binary logic that has so often straightjacketed modernist cultural politics. Through a critical strategy that might usefully be described as *thirding-as-othering*, the binarization of power and thus all the Big Dichotomies are cracked open and disordered, initially by the assertion of at least a third alternative, an Other choice. This critical thirding selectively draws on both sides of the binary yet leads to a reformulation significantly different from each alone as well as from some additive combination or dialectical synthesis of the two opposing positions. The assertion of the Other term disrupts the logical and epistemological foundations of the binary, promoting a more open, flexible, and eclectic 'both/and also ...' search for new possibilities, different ways of (re)constituting the nature and meaning of the multitude of binary relations that have so powerfully shaped western philosophical and political thought: subject-object, material-mental, individual-societal, real-imagined; and, with regard to the cultural politics of class, race, and gender: capital-labour, white-black, male-female.

Such a critical disordering (often phrased simply as decentring) brings with it a rejection of epistemological formalism and rigidity, especially when rooted in essentialist assumptions and totalizing metanarratives, to use another term that has achieved prominence in the postmodern discourse. These rejections are often seen by radical modernists and many other critics of postmodernism as setting loose an irresponsible anarchy of 'anything goes' eclecticism and relativism that signals the end of all of modernism's progressive projects. And indeed, there are many elements in the postmodern debate which easily lend themselves to such an interpretation, feeding the very active fires of contemporary 'pomo-bashing', especially on the left.[9] But there are other critical developments which signal not the end of the radical project but a different beginning, the creation of a new approach to contemporary politics and radical subjectivity that builds upon a constructive rethinking of precisely those four themes which were threaded through *Social Justice and the City*.

A new and different approach to critical social *theory* has been at the core of the development of radical postmodernism. The critique of binary thinking has been the point of departure for a far-reaching epistemological deconstruction that has moved theory formation in two different directions. The first has re-emphasized the importance in theory construction of praxis, the transformation of knowledge into action, and the tactical epistemology that is provided by radical subjectivity/identity and one's specific political project. Of particular relevance to this movement has been the pronounced cultural turn in postmodern critical theory, built around the recognition that the political power of the economic is now increasingly cultural in its real and imagined, material and ideological, manifestations. Rather than simply adding a cultural dimension to radical political economy – the preferred amendment of radical modernists – culture, and postmodern culture in particular, is being used to restructure the foundations of radical political economy in both theory and practice. Again, a brief quote from bell hooks is illustrative.

> Postmodern culture with its decentred subject can be the space where ties are severed or it can provide the occasion for new and varied forms of bonding. To some extent, ruptures, surfaces, contextuality, and a host of other happenings create gaps that make space for oppositional practices which no longer require intellectuals to be confined to narrow separate spheres with no meaningful connection to the world of the everyday... [A] space is there for critical exchange ... [and] this may very well be 'the' central future location of resistance struggle, a meeting place where new and radical happenings can occur.[10]

The move forward from epistemological debate to the promotion of radical subjectivity in practice has been closely associated with the new cultural politics of identity, difference, and otherness, a politics that is polyvocal, radically open, and openly radical in its active promotion of social transformation. This continued insistence on a political project of transformation is the primary guiding force of radical praxis in a contemporary world where there are no longer any unquestioned epistemologies, master narratives, or totalizing theories to rely on. Postmodern racial subjectivity is not only motivated by the force of a political project, it is this project that helps to protect against the dangers of 'anything goes' relativism and to create a politics of multiplicity that can gain strength rather than weakness from the fragmentation and disorder that is so much part of the postmodern condition. Empowerment from multiplicity, fragmentation, and disorder is no easy matter, but the prospects for achieving it are much greater in the new cultural politics than in the old.

Moving from epistemology in another direction, there has also been a significant rethinking of modernist ontologies of being and becoming, a revisioning of what the world must be like in order for us to obtain knowledge of it, that is, for epistemology to be possible. A new social ontology is being created that reasserts what has been left out, silenced, or simply binarized in the traditional philosophical privileging of epistemology. Drawing on the writings of such (modernist? postmodernist? both/and also) scholars as Henri Lefebvre, Michel Foucault, Anthony Giddens, and Roy Bhaskar, this new social ontology is also arising from another critical thirding, one that is breaking down the long dominant existential binary that has for centuries grounded being and becoming, as well as the fundamental subject-object relation, almost exclusively in temporal and social dimensions, in the tightly interwoven historicality and sociality of human life. More than ever before, ontological arguments are being critically thirded to include an existential spatiality on equal terms with historicality and sociality. This ontological restructuring is having a notable effect on contemporary theory, contributing significantly to a growing spatial turn to the interpretation of postmodern culture and, more generally, to what I once described as 'the reassertion of space in critical social theory'.[11]

A rethinking of the nature of *justice*, and especially the conceptualization of spatial or territorial justice that featured so prominently in Harvey's *SJC*, is also taking place in the development of radical postmodernism. This rethinking hinges on an alternative approach to conceptualizing two key aspects of the new cultural politics, *difference* and *identity*. Rather than the 'equality politics' espoused by universalizing liberalism, with its call for the homogenization of difference and unification of identity; or the 'revolutionary politics' of modernist Marxism, which in another way ultimately seeks similar goals; the new cultural politics seeks social justice through the assertion and preservation of difference and the maintenance of strategically chosen and non-exclusive individual and collective identities. The critique of traditional liberal and socialist approaches to social and spatial justice is pushed further by a reconceptualization of the workings of power in society that is no longer bound by the binarisms of the past.

The struggle for justice is thus redirected to what Lefebvre called not

190

just *le droit à la ville*, the right to the city, but also *le droit à la difference*, the right to difference, to be different in an increasingly homogenizing world.[12] The assertion of the right to difference foregrounds the multiplicity and recombinatorial nature of radical consciousness, and the potential advantages to be gained from the fragmented and shifting cultural and political identities that are a material part of contemporary existence. It also relocates the search for social justice in a radical praxis that actively seeks community and coalition among all those marginalized and peripheralized by the workings of power, whatever the sources of their subjection, domination, or exploitation.[13] There is no one path to achieving social and territorial justice, and no one class, gender, race, or nation to lead the way. Neither the liberal strategy of redistribution and equality of opportunity, nor the socialist strategy of class struggle is entirely rejected. Instead, both are recast and tactically combined in a more open cultural politics of justice that is relational, contextualized, situationally specific, and achievable primarily through strategic coalitions that confront and redirect the social, spatial, and historical workings of power.

Margin/Alia, the title phrase of this essay, is meant to capture the radical core of this postmodern reconceptualization of the struggle for social justice. It serves both to illustrate the rethinking of theory and justice that has just been (too briefly) discussed, and to introduce again the themes of urbanism and space which I will re-explore in the remainder of the chapter. To help bring all four of these themes together, I will explain the meaning of Margin/Alia through what bell hooks so creatively described in Chapter 15 of *Yearning* (1990) as 'choosing the margin as a space of radical openness'. hooks's last paragraph summarizes her position.

> I am located in the margin. I make a definite distinction between that marginality which is imposed by oppressive structures and that marginality one chooses as site of resistance – as location of radical openness and possibility. This site of resistance is continually formed in that segregated culture of opposition that is our critical response to domination. We come to this space through suffering and pain, through struggle ... We are transformed, individually, collectively, as we make radical creative space which affirms and sustains our subjectivity, which gives us a new location from which to articulate our sense of the world.[14]

For hooks, the political project that impels radical postmodernism involves occupying the real-and-imagined spaces on the margins of hegemonic power, reclaiming these lived spaces as locations of radical openness and possibility. These strategic spaces enable one's radical subjectivity to be activated, and practised in conjunction with the radical subjectivities of others. They are spaces of inclusion rather than exclusion, sites where radical subjectivities can multiply, connect, and combine in multi-centred communities of identity and resistance, locations where the more narrowly channelled movements mobilized around class, race, gender, empire, ethnicity, sexual orientation, age, nation, environment, region, etc. can come together to challenge the workings of power. This does not mean one abandons the primary identities associated with radical modernism, but rather that these identities are kept radically open by a chosen positioning on the margins, a postmodern politics of location that is motivated by the search for new connections, a search for, paraphrasing hooks, 'who we can be and still be black, or feminist, or working class, or heterosexual' and so on.

> As a radical standpoint, perspective, position, the 'politics of location' necessarily calls those of us who would participate in the formation of counter-hegemonic cultural practice to identify the spaces where we begin this re-vision … For many of us, that movement required pushing against repressive boundaries set by race, sex, and class domination … it is a defiant political gesture. Moving, we confront the realities of choice and location … [We] stand in political resistance with the oppressed, ready to offer our ways of seeing and theorizing, of making culture, towards that revolutionary effort which seeks to create space where there is unlimited access to the pleasure and power of knowing, where transformation is possible.[15]

To move from theory and justice more directly to urbanism and space, here is a final message from bell hooks:

> This is an intervention. A message from that space in the margin that is a site of creativity and power, that inclusive space where we recover ourselves, where we move in solidarity to erase the category colonizer/colonized. Marginality is the space of resistance. Enter that space. Let us meet there.[16]

Making theoretical and practical sense of *urbanism* and the contemporary capitalist city has been deeply influenced by the radical postmodernist critiques. For the most part, the accomplishments of David Harvey and others in unravelling the structured foundations of the urban geographies specific to modern capitalism have been taken as given but treated as seriously limited in scope and flexibility. A new terrain of critical urban studies has been opened up to explore other forms of marginalization and peripheralization, subjection and domination, as well as a wider range of strategic spaces of resistance than those immediately contained in the exploitative political economies and economic alienation of urbanization under capitalism. This reflects in part the extraordinary urban restructuring that has been taking place over the past three decades, a restructuring that has been closely associated with an increasing postmodernization of urbanism as a way of life.

In many ways, the capitalist city that was so brilliantly analysed by David Harvey, Manuel Castells, and so many others in the 1960s and 1970s is no longer what it used to be. Post-Fordist political economies have radically altered and disordered the space economies of post-war urbanism; globalization has packed into the postmodern metropolis the most culturally heterogenous concentrations of capital and labour the world has ever known; and the form of the city has exploded to an unprecedented scale, scope, and complexity. The dualized cities of capitalist vs working class as well as white vs black and man vs woman, have similarly exploded into much greater complexity and disorder, increasing not just the levels of inequality and injustice but also the parameters through which inequality and injustice are defined. And at the same time, everyday life in the contemporary city has become increasingly 'carceral' and 'hyperreal', the first exemplified in the intensification of social surveillance and the multiplication of fortressed turfs within the security-obsessed urban fabric; and the second by a dramatic change in what might be called the 'urban imaginary' brought about by what Jean Baudrillard once called the 'precession of simulacra', the increasing intervention of a hyperreality of simulations into the real and imagined spaces of urban life.[17]

To continue to approach the postmodern metropolis with the same analytical frameworks and confident epistemologies that were applied to understand the capitalist city in the 1970s is now highly unlikely to provide the same powerful insights. Recognizing this, the new critical urban studies has itself become radically expanded in scope, involving in the study of urbanism not just the mixture of political economy, sociology, and geography that dominated radical modernist approaches but a much wider range of disciplines and critical perspectives. This has sparked an extraordinary revival of interest in and attention to the contemporary city and urbanism among literary critics, novelists, poets, artists, anthropologists, feminists, philosophers, photographers, film theorists, and others loosely affiliated in the hybrid field of critical cultural studies. It maybe that never before has there been such an intense and transdisciplinary interest in the specific nature of urbanism and urban life.

With that bold assertion, I turn now to *space*, the last of the four themes posited by David Harvey in *SJC* and one that has already infiltrated deeply into the discussions of theory, justice, and urbanism. Here too, as with urban studies, it can be argued that much of the most interesting and innovative work re-exploring the nature of space is being done outside the traditionally spatial disciplines, by which I mean geography, architecture, and urban and regional planning; and that the best of these contemporary writings is coming from scholars, especially radical women of colour, who, like bell hooks, are comfortable with being labelled postmodern in their theory and practice. With significant exceptions, the spatial disciplines have largely ignored the insightful new perspectives on space and spatiality being developed by these usually post-prefixed 'outsiders'. Some are occasionally tapped for their insights on the spatial conditions of postmodernity or their greater flare in the use of spatial metaphors, but the critical challenges these insights represent for the still stubbornly modernist disciplinary traditions are most often kept at a distance.

This postmodern retheorization of space, however, is of extraordinary importance not just to the study of social justice and the city or to the spatial disciplines, but to every effort to make practical and theoretical sense of the contemporary world. Another kind of critical thirding is taking place that builds upon the rebalancing of the ontological 'trialectic' of sociality-historicality-spatiality mentioned earlier, to expand radically what David Harvey so vividly portrayed in 1973 as the geographical imagination. For at least the past century the geographical imagination, the ways in which we think about the spatiality of human life, has been persistently bicameral, that is, organized around only two general modes of interpretive thought.

Spatiality has either been approached as concrete material forms, patternings, and practices, 'things in space' susceptible to more or less objective empirical analysis and explanation; or else has been seen in primarily rational, mental, or ideational terms, 'thoughts about space' that are more or less subjectively or epistemologically interpretable or understood. The first of these modes of spatial thinking concentrates on what Henri Lefebvre described as Spatial Practices or *espace perçu*, empirically perceived space. The second mode concentrates on what Lefebvre called Representations of Space, *espace conçu*, or conceived space.[18] In their extreme forms, these modes are reduced to either pure materialism or pure idealism, but in practice most spatial thinkers work in between the two extremes in a presumed middleground that partakes of both. Theorizing space through these bifocal lenses has created a rich accumulation of knowledge and critical insight into the significance of space in society, in history, and in human behaviour.

But that is not all there is to spatiality. There is more to be encompassed than can be seen through the conventional bifocals, a radically different way of thinking about spatiality that stretches the geographical imagination well beyond its traditional scope, an Other Space of almost limitless proportions that is simultaneously real and imagined, material and metaphorical, ordered and disordered, phenomenal and existential, empirical and intuitive, knowable and unknowable, and much more. Lefebvre called this all-encompassing 'Other Space' the Space of Representations and described it as *espace vécu*, lived space, the space in which we actually live, in which we struggle, in which we perceive and conceive. It is the space Foucault tried to get at in his notion of 'heterotopology' and Baudrillard blundered into with his notions of hyperreality and the precession of simulacra.[19] It is reflected in the magically real space of Jorge Luis Borges's short story, 'The Aleph.'[20] And it is also the space and spatiality that is being opened up by radical cultural critics such as bell hooks, Gloria Anzaldua, Arjun Appadurai, Trinh T. Minh-ha, Edward Said, Homi Bhabha, and many others who are today redefining the boundaries of the spatial disciplines.[21] It is what I have chosen to call real-and-imagined *Thirdspace*. It is not possible here to explain in detail this still evolving new mode of looking at, interpreting, and acting to change the embracing spatiality of human life. But a return to the ontological restructuring discussed earlier can help to clarify its substance, meaning, and scope. What has been happening in this postmodern retheorization of space is a kind of rebalancing that is comparable, and significantly related, to the reassertion of spatiality against the longstanding privileging of historicality and sociality in ontological and, more broadly, philosophical and political thought. Limited to its bicameral perspective, the geographical imagination has always been theoretically and practically constrained with respect to the rich and all-encompassing historical and sociological imaginations that have developed with respect to the existential historicality and sociality of our lives. In this new thinking about space, the social production of space becomes equivalent in substance, meaning, and scope to the making of history and the construction of social relations and practices.

We have long been comfortable with the recognition that everything about human life has a significant historical and social dimension, that thinking historically and socially will help us understand the worlds we live in. We also recognize, when we think about it, that we cannot know everything about this historicality and sociality, whether it be expressed in a momentous event or the biography of any given human individual. Some things will always remain unknowable, mysterious, hidden, incomprehensible in the broadest meaning of the word. But we nevertheless turn to our historical and sociological imaginations to make sense of our lives and lifeworlds, events both mundane and revolutionary, relations both intimate and routine. In the reconceptualization of spatiality that springs from the writings of Lefebvre and Foucault and has been so imaginatively extended by postmodern feminist, postcolonial, and poststructuralist scholars over the past decade, the spatial or geographical imagination is engaged, both theoretically and practically, at the same level as (and in intricate and often problematic relations with) the historical and sociological imaginations. Everything in human life, knowable and unknowable, is thus simultaneously historical, social, *and spatial*. And this new positioning of spatiality makes a difference: it matters in all aspects of life and in all modes of thinking about the world.

The meaning and substance of these arguments are not likely to be comprehensible if seen through the bifocalized modernist lenses of an older and more constrained geographical imagination; or if the assertions about the significance of spatiality in all discussions of social justice and the city are ignored or misunderstood in an effort to confine debate to such traditional binary choices as liberalism vs socialism or, for that matter, modernism vs postmodernism. But if there is just one conclusion to be carried away from this essay it is that, more than ever before, making practical sense of the contemporary world requires a new mode of thinking about space-theory-urbanism-justice, a more inclusive terrain where, in bell hooks' words, we can recover ourselves and move in solidarity to erase the category colonizer/colonized and the injustices and oppression that emanates from it. I end this intervention with my version of hooks's provocative invitation: Enter that (third)space. Let us meet there.

NOTES

[1] David Harvey, *Social Justice and the City*, Edward Arnold, London, and Johns Hopkins University Press, Baltimore, 1973.

[2] In the first chapter of *SJC*, 'Social Processes and Spatial Form: The Conceptual Problems of Urban Planning', Harvey introduced the concept of the 'geographical imagination' (or, alternatively, 'spatial consciousness') and creatively explored its similarities and differences with respect to the 'sociological imagination' (with its more vivid temporal or historical consciousness) that, drawing on C. Wright Mills, has been described as 'the common bond of all disciplines in the social sciences.' (p23) Harvey's critical conceptualization of 'the geographical versus the sociological imagination' opened a new debate not just on the interrelations of social processes and spatial form but also, more broadly, on the complex relations between geography, history, and social theory. My own work (see *Postmodern Geographies: The Reassertion of Space in Critical Social Theory*, Verso, London, 1989) has been deeply influenced by Harvey's original conceptualization. See also, Derek Gregory, *Geographical Imaginations*, Blackwell, Oxford, 1994.

[3] Significantly perhaps, especially given the developments that would occur over the years after 1973, there is almost no mention of gender issues or feminism in *SJC*, and very little attention is given to the writings of women on the themes of social theory, justice, urbanism, and space. Of the 144 authors cited in the Author Index, for example, only four are women; and while 'Man-Nature Relationship' appears in the Subject Index, there is little in the listings or the text to suggest that women are involved too.

[4] The discussion presented here and in much of the remainder of this essay is drawn from my forthcoming book, *Thirdspace: Journeys to Los Angeles and Other Real-and-Imagined Places*, Blackwell, Oxford, 1996. See also Edward Soja and Barbara Hooper, 'The Spaces That Difference Makes: Some Notes on the Geographical Margins of the New Cultural Politics', in Michael Keith and Steve Pile (eds), *Place and the Politics of Identity*, Routledge, London, 1993, pp183-205.

[5] As Erik Swyngedouw has reminded me, there is a third possible outcome to 'Class Struggle': total nuclear destruction.

[6] David Harvey, 'The Geography of Capitalist Accumulation: A Reconstruction of Marxist Theory', *Antipode*, Volume 7, 1975, pp9-21; 'The Urban Process Under Capitalism', *International Journal of Urban and Regional Research*, Volume 2, 1978, pp101-31; *The Limits to Capital*, Blackwell, Oxford, 1982; *The Urbanization of Capital* and *Consciousness and the Urban Experience*, Blackwell, Oxford, 1985; and *The Condition of Postmodernity: An Enquiry into the Origins of Cultural Change*, Blackwell, Oxford, 1989.

[7] Cornel West, 'The New Cultural Politics of Difference', in R. Ferguson, M. Gever, T.T. Minh-ha and C. West (eds), *Out There: Marginalization and*

Contemporary Cultures, MIT Press, Cambridge MA, and The New Museum of Contemporary Art, New York, 1990, p20.

[8] bell hooks, 'Postmodern Blackness', in *Yearning: Race, Gender, and Cultural Politics*, South End Press, Boston MA, 1990, pp27 and 30.

[9] There are, of course, many other reasons for the left's rampant anti-postmodernism. Perhaps the most important has been the successful political manipulation of the postmodern critique of radical modernism for reactionary or neo-conservative/neo-liberal causes. For many on the left, postmodern politics is virtually equated with the increasing empowerment of anti-progressive forces and governments, symbolized most vividly in Reaganism and Thatcherism. As a result, the epistemological 'break' proclaimed in postmodern critiques is too easily interpreted as a termination and abandonment of progressive political projects rather than as a formidable challenge to shift the terrain of radical politics. Anti-postmodernists thus work hard to make the newness and challenges of postmodernism disappear by making postmodernization appear as more of the same thing, pure historical continuity, a frenetic 'hypermodernism' that can continue to be theoretically and practically understood with only patchwork adjustments to established frameworks of radical modernist thought. See, for example, David Harvey's *The Condition of Postmodernity, op.cit.* What actually disappears in all this is the possibility, if not the necessity, of radical postmodern theory and practice.

[10] hooks, *Yearning, op.cit.*, p31.

[11] This last reference is from the subtitle of my *Postmodern Geographies, op.cit.* Rather than elaborating further on this ontological restructuring and its evolving framework (which I describe as a triple dialectics or trialectics), I refer the reader again to my forthcoming book, *Thirdspace*.

[12] Lefebvre locates the struggle for the right to be different at many levels, beginning significantly with the body and sexuality and extending through built forms and architectural design to the spaces of the household and monumental building, the urban neighbourhood, the city, the cultural region, and national liberation movements, to more global responses to geographically uneven development and underdevelopment. His critically spatial conceptualization of difference can be traced through at least three of his books: *Le Droit à la ville*, Anthropos, Paris, 1968; *Le Manifeste differentialiste*, Gallimard, Paris, 1971; and *La Production de l'espace*, Anthropos, 1974 (English translation by Donald Nicholson-Smith, *The Production of Space,* Blackwell, Oxford, 1991).

[13] Here I refer the three primary arenas of counter-hegemonic struggle defined by Michel Foucault. Subjection involves subjectivity and submission, a struggle over who defines the subject, individually and collectively. Foucault argues that 'nowadays, the struggle against all forms of subjection – against the submission of subjectivity – is becoming more and more important.' But he is quick to add that struggles against domination (ethnic, social, religious) and exploitation (against alienation, the social and spatial relations that separate individuals from what they produce) are of equal significance. See Foucault, 'Afterword: The Subject and Power,' in M.C. Dreyfus and P. Rabinow (eds), *Michel Foucault: Beyond Structuralism and Hermeneutics*, University of Chicago Press, Chicago, 1982, pp208-26.

[14] *Yearning, op.cit.*, p153.

[15] *Ibid.*, p145.

[16] Ibid., p152. To this intervention, hooks adds: 'Spaces can be real and imagined. Spaces can tell stories and unfold histories. Spaces can be interrupted, appropriated, and transformed through artistic and literary practice. As Pratibha Parma notes, "The appropriation and use of space are political acts." '

[17] For a fuller elaboration of these changes, see Soja, *Thirdspace, op.cit.* They are also briefly described in 'Postmodern Urbanization: The Six Restructurings of Los Angeles', in S. Watson and K. Gibson (eds), *Postmodern Cities and Spaces*, Blackwell, Oxford, 1995, pp125-37.

[18] Lefebvre, *The Production of Space, op.cit.*

[19] Michel Foucault, 'Of Other Spaces', *Diacritics*, Spring 1986, trans. Jay Miskowiec; Jean Baudrillard, 'The Precession of Simulacra', in *Simulations*, Semiotext(e) Inc., New York, 1983, trans. Paul Foss, Paul Patton and Philip Beitchman.

[20] Jose Luis Borges, 'The Aleph', in *The Aleph and Other Stories: 1933 1968*, Bantam Books, New York, 1971, pp3-17.

[21] bell hooks, *op.cit.*; Gloria Anzaldua, *Borderlands/La Frontera: The New Mestiza*, Spinsters/Aunt Lute Book Company, San Francisco, 1987; Arjun Appadurai, 'Disjuncture and Difference in the Global Cultural Economy', *Public Culture*, Volume 2, 1990; Trinh T. Minh-ha, *Woman, Native, Other: Writing Postcoloniality and Feminism*, Indiana University Press, Bloomington, 1989; Edward Said, *Orientalism*, Vintage, New York, 1979; Homi Bhabha, *The Location of Culture*, Routledge, London, 1994.

Social Justice and Communities of Difference: A Snapshot from Liverpool

Andy Merrifield

> In a Liverpool me see a colourful people/Forget about de Beatles/Treat everyone as equal/I was observing a people who can win/They're made of bone and blood/and skin
>
> Benjamin Zephaniah, 'Liverpool'[1]

PROLOGUE

This chapter explores the complex interrelationship between social justice, cultural difference and the ideal of community. The argument will be formulated theoretically first of all, though flesh will be added to these abstract insights when I look at how the dynamics of this trinity unfolds in a concrete urban setting: namely, in Toxteth, Liverpool. This 'snapshot' from Liverpool will be set against a backdrop of three recent discussions of justice, notably those propounded by Marshall Berman, Iris Marion Young and John Rawls.

My central point is to acknowledge the inspirational nature of heterogeneity in the city and to affirm the liberational qualities of diverse urban activism. At the same time, however, I want to suggest that unless expressions of difference also speak some language of *commonality* they can be threatened by a process of 'inclusivity' that engenders separatism and isolation, and which ultimately perpetuates the unjust status quo that is sought to counteract in the first place. Meanwhile, I also explore the contention that grappling with the dialectic of particularity and universality, of exclusivity and inclusivity, and of fission and fusion in social life is tremendously pertinent for the development of socially just urban strategies.

'JUSTICE/JUST US' AND THE POLITICS OF DIFFERENCE

Let me begin by outlining two ideas I want to keep close to hand in what follows. The first comes from Marshall Berman's essay in this volume. Berman explores the relationship between rap music and the militant tribalism of African-American youth as they graphically speak the injustices of urban poverty and misery. Given the current status of black youth and the litany of horrors afflicting minority populations in American cities, Berman recognizes that the brusque reaction exemplified by gangsta rap is understandable. Equally, he acknowledges that this is not only a powerful account of everyday urban survival; it is also a clever essay in political theory that is reaching out for an ideal aspiration: the quest for social justice. As Berman observes, and contrary to prevailing postmodernist rhetoric, these kids don't dig marginality: they want an education, a job, and a future in mainstream American society.

But Berman quickly pounces on the potential shortcomings of this 'just us' sentiment. For if, he asks, blacks appear as the only victims of injustice and there isn't recognition of a commonality of oppression with fellow sufferers and fellow activists, it surely renders the pursuit of a broader inclusive concept of justice pretty futile. In other words, if there's no justice to be had and all that's left is 'just us', the search for a common ideal of justice soon disappears under the welter of separatist hate. Under such circumstances, the reification of difference forecloses potential commonality and kinship, and thus precludes the formation of progressive coalitions to challenge the unjust status quo. The upshot is that it's politically disenfranchising to reject completely some form of common (universal?) ideal. This ideal would strive to bind people together, but in a togetherness *in difference*. This ideal would express more what we have in common as well as affirm how we are different, would ask us to reach out to pull people in – exploring and negotiating what is common to us all and what we can share – rather than push them away because they are different and 'other'. Besides, denying commonality, doesn't actually abolish it without ultimately leading to an intractable 'us versus them' zero-sum antagonism – contemporary Bosnia, as Berman also reminds us, immediately springs to mind.

This precarious divide between the difference of militant separatism and a difference celebrated and negotiated within a common frame of reference has been chronicled by Iris Young. Therein lies my second conceptual beacon. In *Justice and the Politics of Difference*, Young tries to maximize cultural heterogeneity and social group difference while minimizing its potential separatist pathologies.[2] Her concept of justice now challenges institutionalized domination and oppression through embracing a 'politics of difference'. It redefines the notion of justice away from the Rawlsian ideal, which Young upbraids for its exclusive prioritization of distribution, for its hollow pursuit for abstract universality, for its *a priori* assumption of a homogeneous public, and for its lack of historical and geographical embeddedness.[3]

In point of fact, John Rawls has actually changed tack somewhat from *A Theory of Justice*, his classic liberal disquisition on the basic features of a fair society. In his recent *Political Liberalism*, Rawls now redefines a 'well ordered society' to the extent that a relatively homogeneous society which is united in its basic moral beliefs is no longer recognized as viable.[4] Instead, Rawls views a democratic society as 'a plurality of reasonable yet incompatible comprehensive doctrines' (ppxvi-xvii). 'Reasonable pluralism,' Rawls admits, 'shows that, as used in *Theory*, the idea of a well-ordered society of justice as fairness is unrealistic.' Still, Perry Anderson has taken Rawls to task, arguing that the 'contradiction between the postulates of consensus, to which Rawls continually subscribes, and the reality of dissensus, to which his best impulses belong, is incurable.'[5] While this symptomatic silence with respect to particularity and context clearly weakens Rawls's thesis, his appeal for a 'reasonable pluralism' in public life isn't, in the short term anyway, quite as woolly as it maybe sounds, nor is it entirely incompatible with Young's own normative politics of difference. Moreover, when people are utterly excluded from active political participation in city affairs, distributional issues, of the sorts Rawls pinpoints, are often all that's left for communities and groups to organize around and to seek substantive representation. And it's within such a political context that dialogue and conflict doubtless ensues, but where a platform for a progressive 'politics of difference' can perhaps begin to be constructed. Here, too, questions of what are 'reasonable' and 'fair' surely enter the fold and become negotiated.[6]

Yet what's reasonable is never fixed and is necessarily contested over time and space. As a concept, 'reasonableness' covers the 'major religious, philosophical, and moral aspects of human life ... and organizes and characterizes recognized values so that they are compatible with one another and express an intelligible view of the world.'[7] 'Reasonable persons,' Rawls avers, 'see that the burdens of judgment set limits on what can be reasonably justified to others, and so they endorse some form of liberty of conscience and freedom of thought.' Meantime, it's 'unreasonable for us to use political power, should we possess it, or share it with others, to repress comprehensive views that are not unreasonable.'[8]

Young would probably concede that 'reasonableness' has to be a factor in a politics of difference, though with certain reservations. Firstly, Rawls's thesis seeks to extend the liberal moral doctrines of Kant and Mill, specifically Kantian moral constructivism and his ideal of 'kingdom of ends'. In *The Moral Law*, Kant claimed the latter was founded upon 'a systematic union of different rational beings under common laws.'[9] Young's 'politics of difference', conversely, seeks to destabilize such reasoning, and questions the degree to which human beings can be wholesome, coherent and rational subjects, fully present to themselves. Secondly, Young's radical normative ideal pushes much further than Rawls's, who ultimately rests his case on the humanizing and 'democratic' powers of the liberal bourgeois state. As he notes, 'a plurality of reasonable yet incompatible comprehensive doctrines is the normal result of the exercise of human reason *within a framework of the free institutions of a constitutional democratic regime*' (pxvi) (emphasis added). Arguably, it's precisely the failings of representative democracy and the constraints imposed upon the modern democratic state by a fully blown capitalism *that has created a bottleneck in the realization of justice and equality in the first place.*[10] Young is acutely sensitive to this and hus challenges all fo ms of institutional domination and bureaucratic oppression; she struggles against the capitalist states's 'tendency to suppress difference by conceiving the polity as universal and unified.'[11] Moreover, Young suggests that the liberal notion of impartiality' means all moral situations are treated according to the same rules, hence denying difference and generating a dichotomy between reason and feeling.

Young, then, affirms a heterogeneous public and group difference, but underwrites this with contextual sensitivity. She argues that to evaluate and counteract exploitative and oppressive practices, each face of oppression must be thoroughly embedded in an actual historical, social and institutional context. Therein a 'multi-dimensional' conception of justice is posited, one that confronts 'five faces of oppression', (none of which are mutually exclusive): exploitation (in the workplace as delineated by Marx, as well as the injustices arising from the 'social processes that bring about the transfer of energies from one group to another to produce unequal distributions'); marginalization; powerlessness; cultural imperialism; and violence. Young's thesis meanwhile raises a number of critical questions about the ideal of community: the 'classical' nostalgic concept of community, characterized by face-to-face *Gemeinschaft* encounter and shared experience of those alike, often excludes those that aren't alike. More sinister implications here are certain forms of reactionary spatial and temporal distancing, like xenophobia and racism. To uphold the community's integrity of a traditional community, Young maintains, minority groups are strictly locked out. Features that make cities so exciting and potentially empowering – cultural diversity, sexual and political freedom – are henceforth crushed. Young concludes that the politics of difference in an unoppressive city would counteract different forms of oppression, give political representation to minority group interests, and celebrate the richness of diverse cultures and communities in what she excitingly terms an 'openness to unassimilated otherness': an inspirating paean to the fullness of urban life.

Here Young offers a rich alternative to the hazards of the 'just us' logic spelt out by Berman. Still, these two insights cut both ways. For the 'inclusivity' implied in a just us sensibility threatens Young's ideal too, especially when one inserts the latter into the cauldron of the contemporary urban environment. Of course, celebrating difference, plurality and multiculturalism is luminous stuff, as all leftists would doubtless concur. But a dialectical twist might equally loom large: it's possible to see how an 'openness to unassimilated otherness' might, on occasion, be subverted and lurch towards the celebration of an exclusionary difference, namely 'there's just us in our difference' (an otherness closed to unassimilated openness?). This isn't what Young has in mind. Nonetheless, prioritization over whose is the more important difference amongst differences is, when the going gets rough, perhaps always just a step away. And this might spark intolerance to other differences when some groups claim monopoly over oppression and victimhood: victims themselves turn into obdurate chauvinists, and show disdain to anybody who tries to empathize or share their pain and grief. In the end, the struggle to rebuild the shared social space of the city with its citizens at the helm becomes frustrated within a sea of different separatist agendas. Therein lie the prospective threats brooding over a concretized politics of difference.

Let me now be more specific. For I want to shift trajectory somewhat by bringing these theoretical and hypothetical insights to bear on recent occurrences in Liverpool's notoriously impoverished district of Toxteth. Focus here, though, will be sharpened even more through an examination of one of its most deprived wards, Granby. In what follows, I hope to demonstrate how urban reform can in fact be numbed when the celebration of difference becomes defined without commonality *between* particularity. This situation raises a philosophical and theoretical conundrum of translating what are multiple particular standpoints into a standard of objective validity to which a legitimately negotiated common value can be conferred. For me, Young tends to understate the dilemma of fusion amongst fissions; though I don't have any delusions about the enormity of this task. Salman Rushdie wonderfully captures the ambivalence implied here. In an essay called 'Outside the Whale', he writes that we are 'obliged to accept that ... [we are] part of the crowd, part of the ocean, part of the storm, so that objectivity becomes a great dream, like perfection, an unattainable goal for which one must struggle in spite of the impossibility of success.'[12]

COMMUNITY AND DIFFERENCE IN TOXTETH, LIVERPOOL

The plight of Liverpool in general, and Toxteth in particular, is widely known by now, usually for all the wrong reasons. So it seems hardly necessary to belabour its dismal details. Yet a couple of comments are maybe necessary in order to contextualize the Granby experience. Liverpool is without doubt one of Europe's most ravaged urban areas, and since the crisis-ridden 1960s and 1970s has suffered immeasurable capital flight, disinvestment, job and population loss, to say nothing of domestic political and social traumas.[13] The city has suffered economic devastation, and experiences increasing local demoralization over the failure of successive Conservative government nostrums.[14] That Liverpool has an image problem is clear enough.

Toxteth itself – which forms part of the larger postal code district of 'South Central' Liverpool 8 – succeeds in accentuating this situation and is a battleground for a whole gamut of urban ills. Inner city poverty is palpable in Toxteth, as various studies evince. A recent Liverpool City Council report on 'Quality of Life' in Liverpool showed 40% of Liverpool's population live in poverty and 15% in 'intense' poverty'.[15] In the city's four inner city wards, 6 out of 10 households lived in poverty and 3 out of 10 were intensely deprived. The July 1981 Toxteth insurgency provided a grim caveat of the fragility of public consent when excluded citizens face deepening impoverishment and suffering. Then, the 'voice of the voiceless' was momentarily heard, but quickly quelled by the unprecedented police usage of CS gas on the British mainland.

The 'mini-riots' of 1985 and 1990 similarly highlighted the immanent volatility of a city life forged out of racism and one that is forced to react to the shoves, pokes and cajoles of the invisible hand. Today, Toxteth mixes dusty wind swept streets and derelict buildings with rich ethnic vitality and cultural difference. This is foregrounded by a series of rehabilitated Georgian terraces which bestows the area a piquant twilight grandeur. Meanwhile, ubiquitous police riot vans, dispatched from a ring of five nearby police stations, assume an ominous presence. Toxteth, then, like many inner city areas in Britain, blends hatred, squalor and violence with grass roots organizing, hope and dynamic cultural creativity – much of which remains uncommodified, though consequently faces perennial funding crises. The annual Merseyside Caribbean Carnival (organized by Toxteth-based textile and training company 'World Promotions') is one of the largest multi-cultural events in the north-west of England. The festival celebrates the city's Afro-Caribbean culture and numerous community floats parade through the streets of Liverpool for two days each August.

To speak in terms of black community in Toxteth is, however, something of a misnomer, since its denizens are distinctively polyglot. Aside from vernacular English, at least six other languages are spoken: Arabic, Bengali, Chinese, Hindi, Somali and Urdu. And of course this diversity is cross-cut by differing religious creeds. Presently, all Liverpool City Council communiques to Toxteth residents come translated in six languages. Notwithstanding, confusion, isolation and alienation abounds, especially for newly arrived immigrants (like Somalis escaping their war-torn homeland). In certain cases, as I'll show later, communication breakdown together with the poverty, frustration and anxiety of inner city living, can equate to misunderstanding, intolerance and victimization within as well as without black groups.

But these different minority groups are united in the sense that they all experience racism. The oft-cited Gifford Report candidly laid bare the city's horrific legacy of racism. The Inquiry team and ensuing report forcibly indicted Merseyside Police for its insensitive and invidious law enforcement practices in Toxteth, as well as the Militant-controlled City Council between 1983-7 for its virulently colour-blind stance.[16] Militant, a Trotskyist faction of the Labour Party, came to dominate Liverpool City Council after its dramatic electoral victory in May 1983. Militant councillors reigned supreme in Liverpool up until 1987, during which time they imposed their own brand of local socialism. They also came into direct conflict with the Conservative central government over budgeting and collective consumption funding. Militant favoured a hard-edged class stance, and achieved notable successes (like its large-scale public housing strategy). Notwithstanding, they also isolated potential allies, too, like the voluntary sector, and, especially, the city's black community.

The Gifford Report revealed that Liverpool's black populations were denied access to jobs, experienced different forms of institutional discrimination, and were exposed to taunts, threats and violence if they ventured outside of a clearly demarcated sector of the city. Black people in Liverpool were, therefore, dramatically geographically circumscribed. Those blacks who have dared to go to outlying districts, quickly return to Liverpool 8 (or adjacent Liverpool 17), and speak of 'Walton Alabama' where Liverpool's own Jim Crow laws seem to prevail. So Toxteth has assumed the status of a relatively safe haven that straddles the 'choice-constraint' dialectic. Within Toxteth itself, the vast bulk of black residents live in three census wards: Abercromby, Arundel and Granby, with the latter having a similar number of black and minority groups as the other two combined. The trials and tribulations of Liverpool 8 consequently reach a critical point in Granby, and I want to amplify experiences there by looking at recent renewal initiatives. Later, I will try to glean more general insights about justice, community and difference on the basis of earlier theoretical postulations.

RUINS, RENEWAL AND SOCIAL JUSTICE IN GRANBY, TOXTETH

In recent years, Granby has sadly become synonymous with drug dealing and crime. It has also become the frequent terminus for high-speed stolen cars, apparently thieved elsewhere in the city. This has resulted in immense nuisance for local residents: intolerable noise, danger (cars have been set alight) and dreadful heartache (several young children have been killed by speeding cars, causing acrimony between residents and police, as the former demand tough action against the culprits). In a bid to ameliorate these disturbances, Granby Street was opened up in 1993 at the junction with Princes Avenue. Until then, the street had been blocked off, and social isolation was arguably exacerbated by its *de facto* physical isolation and fortress-like quality. For any keen urbanist, of course, such a ploy will be instantly recognized as the tonic Jane Jacobs prescribed some time ago: '[a] well-used street,' Jacobs presciently observed, 'is apt to be a safe street.'[17] And it is safe, or at least safer, because it's busy, and its users can, Jacobs reminded us, effectively engage in a voluntary and casual form of 'self-policing'. On the face of it, this tactic looks to have helped Granby Street. Tensions over speeding cars do appear to have quelled somewhat and the street, while bereft of any discernible 'street ballet', is now certainly less threatening to pedestrians.

Meantime, more stubborn problems linger. Unemployment in the ward, although notoriously difficult to ascertain with great accuracy, is thought to be running at around 80-90% for black teenagers. Predictably, some have withdrawn into their own communities and reverted to 'informal' practices to counteract the growing alienation, despair and disillusionment. Ray Quarless, Director of Steve Biko Housing Association, claims that opting out of 'the system' invariably proves advantageous and rational as an alternative survival mechanism for the youth: from an unemployment statistic subjected to often humiliating institutional scrutiny, they're given the opportunity to tap into the burgeoning informal sector of hustling, wheeling and dealing, and maybe petty crime.[18] The proliferating drugs scene is, of course, added temptation for further urban entrepreneurship and market expansion. More worrisome, this area of vulnerability and desperation is now a proving ground for sales and trafficking of heroin and, more latterly, of crack – one of Britain's first crack factories was in fact discovered at Kelvin Grove, Toxteth in 1987.[19]

But such a lurid situation has seemingly given police justification for employing a para-military style of community policing in Granby. As the black-run Liverpool 8 Law Centre contest, blame for 'conflictual stances' between police and local communities is 'squarely on the tactics of Merseyside Police.'[20] With numerous drugs-related raids, and the continued assertion that all stolen cars and 'joy riding' on Granby Street is perpetrated by or is linked to local youth, Merseyside Police have adopted ever more sophisticated modes of surveillance and repression – reaching Orwellian proportions with ubiquitous 'chopper squad' patrols.[21] This has fanned the flames of conspiracy theories, which, fanciful or not, are rife in the area: the police, some locals opine, allow stolen cars into Granby Street as an excuse to move in.

Lately these tense circumstances provide the backdrop for a broad sweeping redevelopment plan that has been proposed for the Granby Triangle, a space of acute social and physical deprivation delimited by Princes Avenue, Kingsley Road and Upper Parliament Street. During the summer of 1994, Liverpool City Council assumed responsibility for regeneration of Granby Triangle, for overseeing a sort of Granby Marshall Plan. Over the course of that summer, consultation exercises between the council and relevant housing associations (Liverpool Housing Trust, Co-operative Development Services and Merseyside Improved Houses) took place. In an effort to broaden this consultation process, the council set up liaison exercises with local residents, inviting them to exhibitions and asking them to complete questionnaires with respect to their views about the way forward.

Primarily, the programme is designed either to rehabilitate or renew the Triangle's crumbling and abandoned housing. But the implications of the redevelopment go beyond the area's physical fabric and impact upon its future social and cultural texture: any prospective transformation affects directly or indirectly various community and resident associations, schools, small businesses and shops. Local retailing along Granby is always particularly hard pressed economically with its limited market catchment and generally poor clientele. What's more, those businesses resilient enough to survive so far are now in further danger due to the closure of Granby Street's Post Office early in 1994 because of successive hold-ups.

Undoubtedly, improvement of the area's housing, infrastructure and local enterprise is desperately needed. For example, a Granby Housing Condition Survey undertaken by the City Council in 1992 suggested that 25% of properties were now vacant. A further 5% were derelict and 50% were either unfit or seriously unfit for human habitation. In response to this stubborn poverty and decay, in 1992 the City Council received £9.4 million to implement a programme of rebuilding. This funding is made up of £0.4 million from the council's own capital programme with the remainder representing a central government alms (initiated via the Housing Corporation) as part of the Merseyside Special Allocation (MSA). This money is infuriatingly trivial when one considers the extent of Granby's devastation. And it tends to pale into insignificance when matched with the colossal patronage the Merseyside Development Corporation (MDC) has received from central government since 1981 to subsidize the predictable enclave of expensive apartments and consumption sites at the Albert Dock.[22] That said, this £9 million somewhat paradoxically has yet to be mobilized. To understand the reasoning behind this two year inaction over Granby we have to probe beneath the surface a little more. Consider the following turn of events.

The City Council suggested that failure to get things moving was due to the 'absence of an agreed strategy for the area' (Report of Joint Meeting of Policy and Resources and Housing Committee, November 1994). The council and local housing associations were keen to reach consent over the constitutive nature of the strategy because 'if no clear programme is put in place for the whole area this resource will be lost'. The report maintained that it was 'felt that the loss of MSA funding would be disastrous for the area without which any solution would be impossible ... Grant aid and private borrowing necessary to meet development costs will only be available for a scheme which brings about comprehensive regeneration of the area ... The options are clear: do nothing or find a common sense compromise that allows a meaningful regeneration plan to go ahead'.

So the Labour City Council appealed for a *common sense compromise for meaningful regeneration*. 'Common sense compromise' suggests that a negotiated and commonally accepted concept of what was deemed 'reasonable' was required. Clearly, though, certain doctrines might be reasonable to some people yet unreasonable to others. This bodes the question of how, when a multiple of different reasonable groups and people confront one another, are we to arbitrate as to what is a unanimous and fair notion of reasonableness? And who would do the arbitrating? Is it possible, moreover, for us to derive a politics of difference in city life which is reasonable to all? At the end of the day, it seems, some form of compromise is unavoidable. And not everybody, I fear, will think it fair nor reasonable. And so it goes in Granby, where no conception of legitimate compromise has so far been established, hence the current inaction over redevelopment proposals.

The prospective plan for Granby is at loggerheads because diverse demands and vested interests seem to have prevented local groups working together to devise an integrated neighbourhood programme. As such, they have failed to pinpoint commonality within their own community differences; nor are these groups willing to be forced by the council and housing associations into a commonality that some locals see as 'reasonable' but others as 'unreasonable'. In the absence of common ground, then, many local groups, residents and community organizations, and the City Council and housing associations, have locked horns in a stubborn stalemate.

To what extent, though, can the City Council's appeal for a common sense compromise be considered reasonable? Given its perennial budget problems, the council's parameters for manoeuvre and response to competing demands are relatively narrow. (Budget restraints are one of the unfortunate legacies of the Militant years: its house building programme came at great cost, and their Japanese and Swiss bank loans have reputedly left the city with a £750 million debt.) At a deeper level, of course, we here encounter the limitations of the redistributive paradigm.[23] Insofar as once the institutional and bureaucratic decision-making process (itself defective and riddled with its own place-specific ineptitudes) is placed within a broader political-economic context, we recognize how the local state budget becomes constrained by central government's powers to redistribute national-level revenue. And the latter, too, is embedded in a European and global capitalist system conditioned by, and constitutive of, market vissicitudes, and interest rate and exchange fluctuations; all of which takes place, as it were, 'behind the backs' of residents in Granby and is so abstract that it's immediately out of reach within their daily life practices, even though it weighs down terrifically upon it. What's left in the here and now, accordingly, is for the latter to get the most reasonable deal from a patently unreasonable system. Unsurprisingly, Young adduces that 'social justice involving equality among groups who recognize and affirm one another in their specificity can best be realized in our society through large regional governments with mechanisms for representing immediate neighbourhoods and towns.'[24] Plainly, over the last 15 years or so in Britain at least, this logic has been greeted with the obverse ideal: the political power of invariably Labour municipal councils has been eroded by an ever more centralized and unaccountable Conservative central government, which in many instances has actively sought to deter local participation.

In Granby there's been major disagreement over whether redevelopment should centre on building afresh or rehabilitate existing housing stock within the Triangle. The council is keen to push for the former: it's neater, more efficient and cheaper in the long run, though the policy more generally is pejoratively viewed by some locals as 'well-intentioned liberalism.' The plans to tear down around 700 properties are unpopular, but opinion seems divided. Despite the colossal deprivation – or maybe because of this deprivation – people feel bonded to their homes and to their neighbourhood, and some are unwilling to move out of both. Nevertheless, a recent ballot initiated by the council indicated that 80% of residents favoured demolition and new build redevelopment. But the ballot has been impugned by Anna Minter, Secretary of the Granby Residents' Association, who suggests that residents feel strongly that they are being harassed and intimidated by the City Council and housing associations into agreeing to the proposed plans for demolition. She says that 'the majority of people making this type of complaint are elderly, disabled or non-English speaking.'[25]

Some residents feel neglect in Granby has been deliberately deployed to force people to leave. Acts of gentrification and ethnic cleansing are other accusations that have been made. The City Council has been attacked for its appalling maintenance and street cleaning standards which has meant many bins stand unemptied for weeks. Street lighting is also notoriously poor, leaving the darkened pavements even more threatening for local residents. City Council officials appear, however, aware of their own shortcomings. Alistair McDonald at the council claimed that the Granby scheme has been 'hanging there for two or three years. There's a need to clear the air. [The issue] hasn't been brilliantly handled ... [But] there's a deep discontent within the community ...'[26]

Apparently compromise over how to proceed has been hampered, in the first instance, by conflict between different tenure groups each of whom appear to have mutually exclusive interests at stake. Such a state of affairs is itself a kind of 'politics of difference' since tenure group, presumably, expresses a particular partial standpoint, and throws up thorny questions about redistributive justice and fairness in the city. And it has been divisive within local residents' associations in Granby. One story, for example, tells of 'selfish owner occupiers who want to spoil it for everyone else'. The Granby Residents Association, which is probably the most vocal community group in the area and was established back in 1992 at the time of the initial consultation exercise in Granby, largely voices the opinions of many owner occupiers. Thus it isn't, according to Elaine Stewart, Senior Officer, City Council's Housing & Consumer Services Directorate, representative of popular opinion in Granby (Interview, 1995). Still, Anna Minter of Granby Residents Association, herself a homeowner, is adamant that the council and housing associations have employed 'under-handed tactics' that are 'hell-bent' on destroying the neighbourhood. Should the proposed block-by-block demolition take place, then it's obvious that prevailing market rates for houses in Granby mean minimal compensation, hence problems with re-purchasing. Many houses are only worth between £8,000 and £20,000, and obviously compensation would hardly cover the cost of buying a house elsewhere in the city. The Residents Association has spearheaded the GRAD (Granby Residents Against Demolition) campaign. Hearsay, however, suggests that many people are afraid to speak their frank opinions in street meetings, and have reluctantly supported anti-demolition motions. Furthermore, the South Granby Residents Associations, which is slightly older than Granby Residents Association and comprises a mixture of tenants and owner occupiers, is apparently pro-development on the basis of gradual demolition of some properties.

Meanwhile, writ large in Granby is sentiment like: 'this does not concern you as a white man, we're doing this for the black community.'[27] This last remark implies that the issues in Granby are solvable only by local blacks themselves; all of which suggests that complications here go beyond merely vested housing interests. Certainly, tenure itself is embroiled in issues like length of residence, ethnic status, and unevenness in power relations between particular local groups, both black and white. Figures show that blacks in Toxteth are nearly three times as likely to be housing association tenants as whites (21.4% compared with 8.2%). As for council tenant representation, numbers are comparable: around 22.3% and 28.8% for blacks and whites respectively. By the same token, to speak simply in terms of an exclusively black issue in Granby – or that there's 'just us' – isn't likely to be empowering for anybody. Two immediate caveats should be stressed here.

First of all, there have been antagonisms between Liverpool-born/ older-established blacks and newly arrived non-English speaking immigrants over housing allocation. The Somalian population especially, which runs into a couple of thousand in Liverpool, find themselves targets of abuse here. Although the city has a long established Somali population, over the last few years this has grown with the influx of newer immigrants fleeing their country's civil war. These people have gained fast-track entry into the area's housing and social services, which has sparked resentment from the indigenous blacks who now feel that Somalis are receiving preferential treatment. So local *black* interests are certainly not unified: they are heterogeneous and frequently internally acrimonious. This is maybe what makes Toxteth cultural life so vibrant and rich, yet makes its politics so frustratingly elusive and piecemeal. Indeed, antagonism does exist between different black groups in Toxteth, as Ray Quarless of Biko Housing Association makes clear, particularly when competing community agendas struggle for limited redistributive transfer payments from central government coffers (Interview, 1993). In this light, to speak of the Community in Liverpool 8 is a misleading concept. These experiences, too, underscore how economic pressures inevitably wedge into, and constrain and reshape, expressions of identity and single-issue politics.

The second point to heed is the 1991 Census for Liverpool. Even allowing for the plausible belief that official census figures understate the city's black population (and that its long standing mixed-race quality makes ethnic categorization notoriously difficult), it's nonetheless clear that the bulk of Granby's 13,000 or so residents are poor whites. The Census records ethnic minorities (ie 'Black Caribbean', 'Black African', 'Black Other', 'Chinese', 'Other Asian', and 'Other') as forming 27.7% of the overall ward population. (For Liverpool overall, 3.7% are officially classified as black or ethnic minority, around 17,000 people, of which 7,000 or so reside in Abercromby, Arundel and Granby.) So many of the 70%-odd indigent whites in Granby are fellow-sufferers and hence potential allies for blacks and other oppressed groups in their fight for justice. True, black poverty is often generated by a whole set of different structural and ideological forces than white poverty. At the same time, blacks and whites surely have common demands to decent housing, schooling, and quality of life, and a shot at a future that goes beyond mere survival.

Over recent years, Toxteth's heterogeneous social landscape has engendered diversified forms of activism. Ironically, this might be as much a stumbling block as a gloriously inspiring virtue. There's no doubt that the 1980s represented a great political awakening for black and minority groups in Toxteth. And community groups there have flourished remarkably. By my reckoning there are presently around 60 community groups/ethnic societies and associations with listed addresses in Liverpool 8. These various groups are frequently single-issue and speak many different 'discourses' that range from nationalism and identity politics, to gender, residency issues, and religious affiliation. The only discourse here that is perhaps muted and garbled is that of social class. Admittedly some of the area's co-operatives and housing groups are broadly class-based. But these usually exhibit an 'inward' sort of class consciousness rather than one that reaches out beyond the neighbourhood's immediate low-income housing concerns.

In the past, class interests in Liverpool have almost unfailingly been conducted through the medium of the local Labour Party and its councillors and cadre. Today, though, many working-class and unemployed blacks reach out for representation via some other means, invariably racial, national or gender-based forms of solidarity and kindred support. The mid-1980s experiences with Militant, as recounted earlier, enter the fray here. The wounds inflicted by Militant's antagonism to special treatment of black groups during its reign have yet to heal and are still painful for the city's black population. The upshot is that explicit questions of class have tended to disappear from local black and ethnic organizational agendas.

All the same, there's been some attempt to co-ordinate the myriad different and frequently disparate community groups in Toxteth, many of whom disband almost as quickly as they come about, especially when they have to struggle to eke out funding. For example, the Princes Park Community Council is basically an umbrella organization that is now one of the only two remaining Community Councils left in Liverpool. Partly funded by the City Council, it meets once a month and is made up of those delegates from area-wide community organizations. Not all Toxteth community groups are, however, members. This leads to dislocation and inevitable prioritization of the affairs raised by the more vocal and established community groups. But the dilemma here more generally is how, when these groups are forced to confront structures of power in their neighbourhoods, can single issue agendas be affirmed at the same time as they are negotiated within more commonally agreed district strategies? How, in other words, can single issue groups make connections with other groups within an openly unified organization? And this, too, without their own particular agendas being either depoliticized or subsumed under broader 'universalist' Party political agendas (like under Militant, which forced a vulgar class-based manifesto). Failing that, in the absence of any effective forum for debate and negotiation to establish some kind of commonality or to promote empathy, fragmentation of these different marginal voices – affirmed by those who are probably ignorant of each other or who often see little need for interaction – ushers in the possibility that different particulars might hermetically seal themselves off from a potentially progressive and reasonable accord. This, in turn, militates against their chances of survival as a locally active and recognized community group.

It's not too implausible to infer that there are hints of some of this compartmentalization occurring in Toxteth, even with the Community Council, which presently has limited efficacy anyway. And such a situation is surely apparent in Granby, where the proposed redevelopment plan has accentuated the need for an agreed notion of 'reasonable commonality' between variegated particulars so as to push ahead for a 'more reasonable' politics, maybe even for the politics of difference that Young invokes. Granted, within contemporary urban theory appeals for commonality are unfashionable in the light of the postmodern celebrations of boundless difference. But when assorted ruling classes force people to consume themselves in the visceral wreckage of inner city life, where they are subordinated and often placed in zero-sum situations, if any meaningful minority politics is to be devised, this has to be a prerequisite.

It can't, though, be achieved by identifying oneself in purely separatist terms. This is a 'just us' discourse, and it would be particularly unfortunate in Liverpool 8 for a number of reasons. First, it would fail to recognize the ambiguity and rich hybridity of the area's heritage – what Paul Gilroy (following Du Bois) elsewhere calls 'double consciousness' – with its long-standing immigrant population and culture.[28] Second, it would create a factitious border around the contact zones of different communities in Toxteth in a way that seals a potentially creative porosity: that is, a porosity between people who might look different, act different, and who maybe don't understand each other, but who nevertheless share a commingling of culture and experience. All community activists and anti-racists in the area desperately need to promulgate and mobilize around this reasoning. Besides, digging out 'city trenches', to use Katznelson's telling phrase, around strictly racial or single issue contour-lines in Liverpool 8 makes it tough to forge a transformative politics that gets to the heart of local job creation, racism, crime, drug addiction, decrepit housing, and rundown schools and parks.

Clearly, the pursuit for common agreement involves negotiation within local communities themselves, before they can pit their wits against external forces. And in the daily routine of real life urban politics this is frequently a messy and tedious business. In Toxteth, this is vital as the first tentative step towards the formulation of any robust longer term regeneration, not just of housing but also of establishing economic and cultural development, and local political empowerment. In the meantime, unless communities recognize each other's plight within some common standard of justice, then disagreement and internal conflict translates itself into inaction and perpetuation of the unjust status quo. Maybe the lesson that the impasse of Granby's redevelopment can teach those concerned about struggling for social justice in the city is that difference has to be affirmed while holding on to some mutually agreed definition of commonality. Otherwise there's no practical way forward.

CONCLUSION: FROM A POLITICS OF DIFFERENCE TO DIFFERENT POLITICS (AND BACK AGAIN?)

I have tried in this chaper to explore the dynamics of community, justice and difference by bringing them to bear on a contemporary situation in Liverpool. The argument has been loosely framed around Iris Young's invocations for a 'politics of difference', Marshall Berman's explication on the ambivalence of certain tribal particularist ideals of justice, and John Rawls's redefinition of a 'well-ordered society'. The politics of difference that Young envisions is a lofty abstract ideal that has to be the benchmark of any emancipatory urban politics. At the same time, dangers of 'exclusive inclusivity' haunt this vision, which can undermine 'openness to unassimilated otherness'. The Granby sketch suggests that the politics of difference can take on an entirely different meaning when it's taken from a standpoint *within* different groups. Then, it can so easily be hijacked and degenerate into the sort of 'just us' sentiment that Berman problematizes.

Yet this isn't to imply that sometimes 'just us' may be the only immediate line to take to radicalize and demand for just deserts. Minorities are, of course, the stuff of radical politics; and the experience of inferiority does indeed prompt feelings of isolation, of a recognition that maybe there's 'just us' against the powerful structures of injustice and domination. Similarly, it's extremely difficult to see how anything positive can be won for dispossessed groups in a society based upon oppression, inequality and unreasonableness that doesn't require standing on somebody else's toes: preferably those who hold the reigns of power and who are unlikely to surrender their vested interests without a battle. On the other hand, a discourse of 'just us' which prioritizes an 'ontological essentialism' rather than a 'strategic' one, is always destined to lead to isolation and ostracism in the long run. For it's not a politics of difference, but a different politics: it's a different politics because it sees no one, embraces no one, empathizes with no one. Meanwhile, no one listens, least of all the ruling classes, who are adept at creating separatism, and who prosper from it.

Battling against this limited and limiting politics, however, requires some forum for listening to different voices so that the terrain of debate and negotiation can be broadened and where competing voices can be 'reasonably judged'. Social policy and urban planning, as initiated through state institutions, must be pressured and sensitized to such a requirement. Inevitably, this will focus upon distributive issues, but it will have to be so much more too, as the deadlock at Granby betokened. Then, the ground can be cleared for an imaginative alternative that isn't either perpetual 'just us' strife, nor tyrannical imposition, where reasonable becomes simply what is reasonable to the powerful and is then shoved in the faces of the powerless in an unreasonable manner (à la Thrasymachus from Book One of Plato's *The Republic*). The different politics affirmed by oppressed people can therefore be incorporated into a politics of difference that is galvanized within a form of democratic citizenship. But this will involve patient and tolerant compromise – what Freud in *Civilization and Its Discontents* called 'expedient accommodation' – between groups so that a practical coalition politics can be bashed out to inform action. Whatever the outcome, we can follow Walzer's reasoning that 'tumult is better than passivity, shared purposes (even when we don't approve) are better than private listlessness.'[29]

But let's get real too. As we have witnessed, even getting people who are different to talk about compromise proved a veritable stumbling block in Toxteth. The inaction over regenerating Granby seems not only a missed opportunity in material terms, it equally misses a great chance to radicalize and yoke different communities by bringing people together to combat injustice and racism in the area. This affects the future trajectory of Toxteth more generally: there's such a vast array of activism and activists there, in the shape of various community groups and resident associations and ethnic, identity and lifestyle support networks, that a pretty hefty alliance might one day be in the offing *if these groups can be brought together.*

The quest of bringing oppressed people together has more general currency. For it's nigh impossible to achieve a democratic, non-exclusionary urbanism without having recourse to some standard of universality, a value that is non-reducible and applies to all. But, as Salman Rushdie movingly reminds us here,

> human beings do not perceive things whole; we are not gods but wounded creatures, cracked lenses, capable only of fractured perceptions. Partial beings, in all the senses of the phrase. Meaning is a shaky edifice we build out of scraps, dogmas, childhood injuries, newspaper articles, chance remarks, old films, small victories, people hated, people loved; perhaps it is because our sense of what is the case is constructed from such inadequate materials that we defend it so fiercely, even to the death.[30]

That we are wounded creatures suggests that finding ideas which do bind us together is all the more vital. And this is especially so in our cities where meaning is indeed a 'shaky edifice'. This is what makes city life so wonderfully exciting, yet at the same time so precarious. In the end, negotiating the fusions and fissions of a *fin de millenaire* city life is a particularly daunting prospect. The big question is how we can celebrate fission in our cities while becoming solid citizens.

NOTES

[1] B. Zephaniah in R. Tameen (ed), *Undercurrents: An Illustrated Anthology from the Inner City*, Strange Publications, Liverpool, 1990.
[2] I.M. Young, *Justice and the Politics of Difference*, Princeton University Press, Princeton, 1990.
[3] Michael Walzer's perceptive essay, *Interpretation and Social Criticism*, Harvard University Press, Cambridge, Mass., 1987, had similarly reproached

the tendency of political philosophers, especially since John Rawls's *A Theory of Justice*, to conceptualize justice in a temporal and spatial vacuum.

[4] J. Rawls, *Political Liberalism*, Columbia University Press, New York, 1993.

[5] P. Anderson, 'On John Rawls', *Dissent*, Winter, 1994, pp139-144.

[6] Interestingly, Susan Fainstein in the present volume argues that David Harvey's ethical propositions in his work on social justice and the city implicitly accepts the Rawlsian justice as fairness principle. According to Fainstein, this poses difficulties because it affirms a moral standpoint which is generally treated with suspicion by Marxists. If Fainstein is correct, it suggests that Harvey is unable to supplant so unequivocally the liberal formulations, expressed in Part I of *Social Justice and the City*, with any Marxist counterpart (Part II). In any event, given the relative retreat of the Marxist left, a step back to reconsider the distributive justice paradigm in Part I is probably unavoidable for the time being. Maybe the toughest challenge, both theoretically and practically, is how the above project can be redefined from the left standpoint espoused by Young's politics of difference? Put differently: how is it possible to link up race, ethnicity, and identity (questions revolving around themes of cultural imperialism, oppression and domination) with political-economic and class issues over redistributive justice, *without* the latter erasing the constitutive qualities of the former?

[7] Rawls, 1993, *op.cit.*, 59.

[8] *Ibid.*, p61.

[9] I. Kant, *The Moral Law – Groundwork of the Metaphysic of Morals*, Hutchinson, London, 1948, edited and translated by H.J. Paton. Quotation from pp100-1.

[10] Perhaps the most damaging case to be made against Rawls is, consequently, the argument that, if the modern liberal state is 'democratic', as Rawls believes, one could ask why is there the need for *any* normative theory of justice at all? Presumably, by his own logic, to fulfil this definition *all* decisions made by the state would be considered reasonable and fair, which patently they're not. Of course, this then means that Rawls's assumption about the state is incorrect, and hence, in turn, the underlying premise of his theory of a well-ordered society is undermined irrevocably.

[11] Young, *op.cit.*, p11.

[12] S. Rushdie, *Imaginary Homelands*, Granta Books, London, 1991, pp100-1.

[13] M. Parkinson, *Liverpool on the Brink*, Policy Journals, Hermitage, 1985; see also 'Liverpool's Fiscal Crisis: An Anatomy of Failure', in M. Parkinson, B. Foley and D. Judd (eds), *Regenerating the Cities*, Manchester University Press, Manchester, 1988.

[14] As Ray Quarless, Director of Steve Biko Housing Association, once put it: government officials parachute into Toxteth like 'excited missionaries' and make little difference by the time they leave (Interview, May 1993). The most infamous 'excited missionary' was former Environment Minister, Michael Heseltine, who in the early 1980s became known as Minister for Merseyside. But despite his much fabled open top bus peregrinations of Toxteth with prospective private investors in the aftermath of the riots, local residents quickly discovered that 'all we got from Mr Heseltine was trees in Princes Avenue, and even they were planted by contractors from outside' (cited in

Gifford *et al.*, *Loosen the Shackles: First Report of Liverpool 8 Inquiry into Race Relations in Liverpool*, Karia Press, London, 1989, p51).

[15] Liverpool City Council, *The Liverpool Quality of Life Survey*, Chief Executive's Dept., Liverpool City Council, Liverpool, 1991.

[16] A. Gifford *et al, op.cit.*

[17] J. Jacobs, *The Death and Life of Great American Cities*, Penguin, Harmondsworth, 1961, p44.

[18] My knowledge of Toxteth has been greatly enhanced through numerous conversations with Ray Quarless who has been active in community politics and housing issues there for several years now. The Biko Housing Association, specifically, has made impressive gains in Liverpool 8 since its 1982 inception. Biko currently owns 100 homes in and around Liverpool 8, and has just completed a new development within the Granby Triangle. It has further plans for a new housing and small business scheme on the prominent site at the Upper Parliament Street/Princes Road junction. Quarless, who became Director in 1989, claims that Biko 'are trying to develop a strategy that will encompass business development for black people, employment for black people, training for black people, and also training for equal opportunities for organizations dealing with the developments' (Interview, 1993).

[19] The escalating problems of crack have, however, been met with a novel grassroots response. Local Granby barber, Ken Drysdale, has established a drugs awareness project in a back room of his barber's shop. Provoked out of frustration over the city's ineffectual formal drug services, Drysdale decided to act for himself. The project aims to reduce drug-related problems and enhance understanding of them; to encourage members of the community to live a drug-free life; and to encourage those unable or unwilling to abstain from drugs to move away from drug-use patterns that harm themselves or the community. But, as Drysdale poignantly remarks: 'what kind of world is it when it takes me, a barber, to start something like this?' (See 'Crack and the Cropper', *The Guardian*, June 17 1992).

[20] Merseyside Community Relations Council, 'When the Finger Points on Granby Street', *Newsletter*, No.12, 1990.

[21] This £1 million helicopter is armed with a powerful searchlight and highly sensitive night vision equipment, and with low-flying manoeuvres can pinpoint suspects from the air. Yet the helicopter is controversial, and has been the target of an unsuccessful petrol bomb attack at Liverpool Airport by a masked gang of raiders (see 'The Crime Busters from Out of the Sky', *Liverpool Echo*, January 5 1989).

[22] Whereas MDC's central government cash contribution increased from £10 million in 1981/2 to about £35 million in 1986/7, the City Council's housing capital allocation over the same period declined from £40 million to £27.5 million (Liverpool City Planning Department, 1987). Since 1987, MDC's budget has been:

Year	Amount (£ m)
1987/88	28.65
1988/9	21
1989/90	27
1990/1	25

1991/2   27 (estimated)
1992/3   26 (estimated)
(*Source*: Merseyside Development Corporation, Corporate Plan: 1989/90–1993-4, 1989).

Bizarrely, the MDC squandered more than £1 million in 1992 on a Tall Ships Regatta and concert on the River Mersey to celebrate the 500th anniversary of Columbus's voyage to America.

[23] See Young, *op.cit.*, Chapter One; David Harvey, *Social Justice and the City*, Edward Arnold, London, 1973, Part 2.

[24] Young, *op.cit.*, p248.

[25] 'Focus on Liverpool', in *Black Housing*, Volume 10, Number 4, July/September, 1994, p29.

[26] Cited in Charles Wootton Newsletter, *The Granby Triangle*, Charles Wootton Centre, Upper Parliament Street, Liverpool 8 (undated).

[27] Cited in *Black Housing*, p29.

[28] P. Gilroy, *The Black Atlantic: Modernity and Double Consciousness*, Verso, London, 1993.

[29] M. Walzer, 'Multiculturalism and Individualism', *Dissent*, Spring, 1994, pp185-191. Quotation is from p180.

[30] S. Rushdie, *op.cit.*, p12.

Cultural Strategies of Economic Development and the Hegemony of Vision

Sharon Zukin

When David Harvey published *Social Justice and the City* he greatly expanded our abilities to criticise cities for their continuous production of inequality. Over time, his analysis broadened as he confronted the 'cultural turn' in social critique, as well as the growing importance of cultural consumption for indicating the acquisition of social capital. His central empirical interest lay in applying a cultural analysis to the material construction of the built environment. In addition to changes in capital flows, Harvey was intrigued by how symbolic orderings of time and space – embodied in all kinds of narrative myths, including those that surround monumental buildings – represent the collective interest of dominant social groups. Perhaps his finest essay of this type examines how the building of the Basilica of Sacre Coeur on its site in Montmartre effaced bloody traces of the Paris Commune of 1871.[1] Later, in his descriptions of postmodern architecture and of shopping centres that are intended as keystones of upscale urban renewal, Harvey connected the polymorphous perversity – the seeming transgressions – of contemporary design to carefully calculated strategies of financial speculation.[2] Reading such writers as Pierre Bourdieu and Michel De Certeau, Harvey began to write about culture in the built environment as a crucial area of social practice where the inequalities of capitalism are reproduced.

But much of the writing in critical cultural studies has taught us to ask more, and assume less, about the production of inequalities. The primary contribution of most post-Marxist theorizing in recent years, including both feminist critiques of Marxist work and post-structura-

223

lism in general, has been to emphasize the indeterminacy of both viewpoints on, and outcomes of, social processes. While no social critic has rejected the idea that there are dominant structures of inequality, most contemporary criticism rejects the assumption that dominance is first and foremost rooted in the economy. Post-Marxist critique de-emphasizes the notion of 'structures' and substitutes a cultural Otherness for an economically inflected 'social class'. Overarching status differences affecting women, problems of resisting historical hierarchies of colonial and postcolonial power, and the social construction of group identities have emerged as paradigmatic fields of both theory and empirical inquiry.

Focusing attention on cultural practices and cultural categories has had the great virtue of enriching an experiential understanding of social justice. But these concepts cannot stand alone. No one has yet produced empirical research on injustice and identity without connecting experience in some way to material inequality. A subordinate 'position' is not endowed with material resources. People in different positions do, however, control differential access to money, respect, and jobs.

Nevertheless, post-Marxist critique asserts the relative autonomy of culture from economic organization. At its most interesting, such an approach emphasizes the potency of signs and symbols, including language and visual artifacts, for maintaining both domination and resistance. In a less viable formulation, it may isolate cultural factors – such as the ever-appealing concept of identity – from their material context. If we really want to work on the relative autonomy of culture, however, we must understand empirically how cultural strategies isolate, denigrate, mitigate, or compensate: we must understand how culture creates its own material structures. It may be that symbolic cultural practices do not just 'represent' material interests; mediated by material resources, they may produce, perpetuate, or diminish inequalities. Empirical research on social justice and the city can take this as inspiration on a far broader range of studies than in the past. Not only is it important to study processes of deriving representations,[3] but it is also important to study the inequitable results of struggles over aesthetic strategies such as historic preservation,[4] over visual images of urban public spaces, and over the development of cultural consumption such as tourism.[5]

A third contribution of post-Marxist critique has been to dramatize the always-present interest of social research in agency as well as in structures. Contemporary critics have attracted readers across a political spectrum by emphasizing the fluidity of social identities and acknowledging the choice, rather than the predetermination, of collective interests. Together with the rejection of economic determinism, this interest in agency has disenfranchised the language of social class and directed attention toward the micro-politics of gender, ethnicity, and race. Yet an emphasis on agency and the acknowledgement of multiple viewpoints might make us amoral about goals and consequences. If all expressions of agency are equally valid, and we don't trust 'structures', by which criteria can we evaluate social justice?

Provocatively, in writing about Otherness and cultural innovation, literary critics have developed the idea that social products – not least, culture itself – are hybrids and fusions.[6] Given the racial and ethnic complexity of nearly all contemporary societies, the idea of fusion replaces some of the older collectivistic concepts of social justice (e.g. egalitarianism, integration, community). Rejecting binary differentiations (such as white or black, female or male) implies accepting a somewhat different set of 'progressive' criteria: fighting racism, promoting tolerance, protecting freedom of choice. Thinking in terms of cultural 'hybrids' rather than binary differentiations gives rise to a more complex understanding of ideology and behaviour. It also challenges the implied schism between powerful and powerless groups – as well as the power of traditional concepts of power. Yet the notion that culture is always a hybrid says nothing about either justice or equality. While urban cultures may be interpreted as a dialogue between the 'Gold Coast' and the 'Slum' (as in the works of the Chicago sociologists of the 1920s), there is no doubt which trope represents the better conditions.

So far, however, so good: post-Marxist critique has broadened the range of both relevant theories and empirical observations without giving up the goal of making a critical analysis of inequality and injustice. But how do we proceed with actual cities? In taking the cultural turn, we have risked throwing out the baby of materialism with the determinism of Marx. Few critical social theorists would really propose that we ignore material inequalities, or that we give up materialism as a key to perceiving the world. What theorists have not done is to figure out how to use materialism without negating the fluidity, the fusions, the indeterminacies, and the general democratization of critique itself. How do we combine the insights of contemporary critical theory – on representations, fusions, and the

225

multiple powers of domination – with the forceful dynamic of materialist critique? How do we do empirical research on postmodern societies that have turned away from social class mobilization and toward increasingly mobile publics and attachments? How do we pose issues of inequality outside the rubric of production systems and the language of social class?

This is an especially interesting problem because so much of the dominant capitalist economy has also undergone a cultural turn. In the rich old countries of the world, the most dynamic areas of capital investment include the media and entertainment. Growth in employment is concentrated in those sectors previously understood, by definition, as cultural production, including the arts, tourism, and restaurants. In any major city, particularly the so-called global cities such as London, New York, Los Angeles, and Tokyo, culture is a significant and growing economic sector. Whether it is related to the information revolution in new technologies or to the social status of media stars, culture provides a symbolic rallying point for claims of urban hegemony. We in the older capitalist countries live, in short, in a symbolic economy, where the production of symbols is intimately connected both to the production of jobs and the production of space.[7]

From this point of view, we can think of power in cities as the power to impose a vision on space. Those who impose the vision 'frame' space much as museums frame art historical canons by favouring some representations over others. We cannot take it for granted that powerful people and institutions have an absolute power to frame space – but most times, the building of cities favours their interests over others. Interesting questions arise when the built environment of urban spaces either *fails* to favour the framing proposed by dominant groups, or when political or cultural strategies slowly *alter* an existing landscape of power.[8]

Living in New York City, which presents itself as the 'culture capital of the world', may give me a jaundiced view of the material significance of cultural strategies. Nevertheless, I believe the trends toward aestheticization and commercialization that begin in large centres of the worldwide symbolic economy are only the most transparent expressions of general conditions. While such cities as New York (and Los Angeles, London, and Frankfurt ...) have large numbers of immigrants and artists who can translate into material products cultural strategies of globalization, competition, and social control, other places are following their lead. Thus in the 1980s and 1990s, smaller cities all over the world have elaborated cultural strategies of economic development, designed public spaces for social control, and designated large numbers of buildings for historic preservation. As these policies multiply, it is vital to examine how strategies that originate in cultural practices affect material inequalities and speculate on how they might democratize the hegemony of urban visions.

CULTURAL STRATEGIES OF ECONOMIC DEVELOPMENT

There are many different 'cultural' strategies of economic development. Some focus on museums and other large cultural institutions, or on the preservation of architectural landmarks in a city or regional centre. Others call attention to the work of artists, actors, dancers and even chefs who give credence to the claim that an area is a centre of cultural production. Some strategies emphasize the aesthetic or historic value of imprints on a landscape, pointing to old battleground, natural 'wonders', and collective representations of social groups: houses of worship, workplaces of archaic technology, and housing. While some cultural strategies, like most projects of adaptive re-use of old buildings, create panoramas for visual contemplation, others, like Disney World and various 'historic' villages, establish living dioramas in which contemporary men and women dress in costumes and act out imagined communities of family, work, and play. The common element in all these strategies is that they reduce the multiple dimensions and conflicts of culture to a coherent visual representation. Thus culture as a 'way of life' is incorporated into 'cultural products', i.e. ecological, historical, or architectural materials that can be displayed, interpreted, reproduced, and sold in a putatively universal repertoire of visual consumption.

It has been apparent since the 1980s that the organization of consumption, no less than the organization of production, has real economic and political consequences. Cultural 'attractions' are truly multidimensional, for they have an impact on the circulation of capital, the creation of jobs, and the relative fortunes of specific places. The unexpected commercial success of gentrified neighbourhoods and artists' quarters, and the catalyst to urban and regional development provided by such greenfield entertainment complexes as Disneyland and Disney World, give credibility to using self-conscious cultural representations as engines of growth. True, the jobs they create are not 'productive' in the traditional sense, and often pay low wages, but they are connected to the larger transformation to a service economy in several ways. They shift people and spaces to service uses from other economic activities. They offer a 'clean' image of place that attracts new businesses, especially in the services. Both materially and symbolically, they create a new landscape that diverts attention from old political battles. In the process, and with occasional lasting recriminations, alliances are forged over the less contentious area of 'culture' than over the more exasperating area of the economy.

I minimize the conflicts involved. I do not intend to ignore the struggles over particular pieces of real estate, and over who might be displaced by their cultural appropriation, as well as over whose representations of whose culture are going to be enshrined by which institutions. In the United States, however, where localities are responsible for their own economic development, and in Great Britain, where localities are increasingly cut off from the traditional governmental welfare policies that cushion unemployment, cultural strategies emerged by the mid-1980s as a relatively consensual means of managing economic decline and envisioning possibilities of economic growth. Whether this is a realistic strategy in the long term is another question. But in the aftershocks of deindustrialization and economic recession, an increasing number of local business and political elites look toward cultural strategies to re-make their cities.

The headline on the lead article in the *Wall Street Journal* of February 1, 1985 is a bell-wether in this regard: 'Old New England City Heals Itself; Can One in Midwest Do So Too/Local Consensus That Helps Lowell, Mass., Lure Jobs Is Missing in Akron, Ohio/From Old Mills, New Park.' The story contrasts the apparent resurgence of Lowell, whose textile industry declined in the 1920s, with Akron's continued decline, following losses in the rubber industry in the 1970s. It locates the key to Lowell's success in the creation of a National Historical Park, financed by the federal National Park Service, in 1984. Not only did the Park Service clean up the derelict and polluted industrial sites of abandoned textile mills, but local bankers and politicians formed a 'formidable consensus' that financed redevelopment oriented toward small-scale, 'technically innovative' businesses. The park also attracts tourists who want to view the nineteenth century industrial past, generating new service jobs and a more detached view of industry. Akron is not so detached from its industrial history. There is no political consensus surrounding the new recreational park, which is sited on land that could be used for suburban housing development for nearby Cleveland. Moreover, since the park prohibits hunting, some local residents oppose it for limiting their recreational opportunities. Most important of all, local industrialists are still in place and do not favour subsidizing new strategies of economic development that exclude them. It would be interesting to compare the relative fortunes of Lowell and Akron in the year 2000, long after the 'Massachusetts Miracle' of high-tech and service-led growth abated and the southern tier of the Middle West, favoured by Japanese implants, regained auto industry jobs. The general point, however, is the perception – even at the *Wall Street Journal* – that cultural strategies of development are significant.[9]

And why not? We know that tourism (or the hotel and tourist industry, including restaurants) is the biggest employer, after the auto industry, in the United States. Tourism engenders new work, sexual, and other social relations;[10] it fits as 'social regulation' with the general development of a service economy based on mass media and telecommunications. On a local level, developing tourism works well with real estate interests and absorbs, at least ideologically, men and women in the work force who have been displaced by structural and locational changes. Even in a larger region, like the Monongahela Valley near Pittsburgh, tourism is touted as a development strategy that works, at least in the short term, to clean up industrial sites and put people to work. The Mon Valley had spawned, during the 1980s, a regional coalition of labour, church, and community groups that tried to attract new industrial investment to steel mills that were recently shut down.[11]

So cultural strategies are often a worst-case scenario of economic development. When a region has few cards to play, cultural strategies respond to the quality-of-life argument that people and investors flow to areas with the best amenities. But cultural strategies do not reverse the hierarchies of place that lead to competition for distinctive segments of capital and labour – competition that is often perceived in terms of image. Indeed, cultural strategies suggest the utter absence of new industrial strategies for growth, i.e. the lack of local strategies that have any chance of success in attracting traditional productive activity.

THE BEST CASE: NEW YORK

Painting Glasgow as the culture capital of Europe, or New York as the culture capital of the world, implies multiple levels of material and symbolic competition. In New York and other great cities, the major cultural institutions long identified with 'high culture' now take pride in representing the entire city's cultural *and economic* value. There has been, of course, since the 1970s, an enormous increase in the economic value of art. In the auction houses, there was, especially during the 1980s, an explosion in the prices paid for art, including works by living artists. There has also been an enormous escalation in competition among museums for private and governmental support. Market competition among museums has intensified their strategizing on the basis of visual attractions (and also raising revenues by turning more of their unique visual resources into postcards and gifts). It has also fed into the competition for capital investment and tourist spending among cities and regions.

From the early 1980s to the early 1990s, as the New York region grew more 'global' and its cities grew poorer, public attention centred more and more upon the arts as the essence of the region's, and especially the city's, irreducible uniqueness, its competitive edge. In 1983, the Port Authority of New York and New Jersey, an influential public agency that runs the region's infrastructure and is responsible for much economic development planning, issued a report that demonstrated how valuable the arts are to New York City's and the regional economy.[12] The report basically documented the large volume of money and jobs involved in an arts economy, and established significant multiplier effects for tourist spending connected with visits to cultural institutions and performances. So it confirmed supporters of the arts against those in government who continually reduced their grants and those in business, especially real estate developers, who tried to replace them with higher-rent uses.

Ten years later, a follow-up study showed that the size of the nonprofit sector had increased, albeit within the parameters of the continued disappearance of manufacturing and many job losses in corporations and business services.[13] The happy news was that, despite a recession that began in 1989, following a crash on Wall Street two years earlier, the arts economy seemed to hold its own. Both revenues and spending in all cultural sectors, from film and video production to art galleries, for-profit theatres, and non-profit art museums, had increased since 1983. Although there were setbacks reflecting the recession in the early 1990s, the arts were praised for luring tourists, increasing employment, and symbolizing the city's enduring dynamism. When the Republican Mayor Rudolph Giuliani, elected in 1993, was forced to retract his suggestion that city subsidies to cultural institutions be reduced, he reiterated the standard line that all public officials in New York City take, regardless of their political party: 'It really is the core of a great city to maintain and preserve the arts, certainly as part of the spiritual identity of the city but also because this is an important industry.... This is vital to our economic renewal' (*New York Times*, 25 January 1994).

Is this rhetoric or is this real? The mayor did, after all, propose a budget that reduced cultural subsidies. A careful reading of the 1993 report, moreover, suggests two important caveats about the future development of the arts economy. On the one hand, New York is really losing creative cultural producers in all fields except those connected with real estate and business services – losing them to a more rapidly gaining Los Angeles. On the other hand, the jobs created in the arts economy since the 1980s are mainly part-time and temporary jobs – and these are in the major cultural institutions that are supposed to exemplify the desired direction of growth. New York is, nevertheless, by any calculation, the biggest centre of the arts in North America. Although the city has not built a major cultural centre since Lincoln Center in the 1950s and 1960s, the largest current project of urban redevelopment – the long-awaited redevelopment of Times Square – has recently been transformed by a cultural strategy.

As in the Monongahela Valley, the cultural plan to rebuild Times Square is presented as an interim strategy, to last only past the dawn of the new millennium, to the year 2004. This gives a breathing period to the private developers and New York State redevelopment authority that have not been able to sign up corporate tenants for the commercial skyscrapers designed for the area in the mid-1980s. While prospective tenants expressed interest when the projects were first designed, the plans were delayed until after the recession began by numerous criticisms in the media that in turn delayed necessary public approvals. Significantly, the objections that stalled the standard corporate skyscraper redevelopment strategy were aesthetic objections. Historic preservationists objected to the eradication of 'traditional' 'populist' signage and electric lights, really representations of the commercial culture of the early 1900s, and also to the large scale and high density of development compared to existing, relatively rundown buildings on the site. Theatre owners led a campaign against redevelopment, based partly on preserving 'landmark' theatres, in the 1980s, but that campaign, at best, saved only a small number of theatre façades. At any rate, by the time the aesthetic objections were met, by scaling down the skyscraper plans and mandating illuminated signs on Broadway, there was too much vacant commercial space chasing a diminishing number of corporate tenants. Tragic stories of developers who lost their buildings to the banks and visions of long-term vacancies plagued the northern end of Times Square, around 50th Street. And the skyscrapers planned for the southern end, on 42nd Street, remained blueprints on paper while theatres were empty and small businesses continued to be evicted by the state.

A turning point came in 1992, when the city government gave subsidies worth $11 million to the German media conglomerate Bertelsmann to buy one of the vacant buildings. Yet the idea of using Times Square for the offices of a corporate *culture* industry fits with the idea of an 'interim' cultural strategy leaked to the press in 1991. The new plan featured outdoor art exhibits, including site-specific art linked to the area's history, a children's theatre, revitalized commercial theatres, restaurants, and a visitors' centre. It was inaugurated, with much celebration in the city's media, in 1993, when more than 20 artists and designers were commissioned to install works on 'storefronts, facades, vitrines, marquees, billboards, and even roll-down grates' (*New York Times*, June 27 1993). Many of the artists appropriated the history of sexual trades long concentrated on 42nd Street, especially pornography, prostitution, and cross-dressing, subverting the use of space by appropriating visual motifs, ironically cleaning up an area of the city where such taboo activities had traditionally been given relatively free license. During the 1993 collective exhibit, a nearby branch of the Whitney Museum led free tours of the site for adults and children.

The transition from one redevelopment strategy to another still relies on corporate locations, although the corporations, as the deal with Bertelsmann suggests, are now culture industries. In 1994, the city and state announced they were giving subsidies to the Walt Disney Company to buy a derelict theatre on 42nd Street to create a showcase for live performances of Disney products (*New York Times*, March 3 1994). Broadway's legitimate theatre owners, who initially opposed the city's negotiations with Disney, were promised financial aid in renovating their properties and became supporters of the Disney plan. The chairperson of the New York City Landmarks Preservation Commission waxed enthusiastic about Disney's opportunity to restore the theatre's decor as well as the public culture now associated, despite its raucous history, with early twentieth century urban entertainment. By 1995, even the investment banking firm Morgan Stanley, which received public subsidies to buy a vacant new office building on the northern edge of Times Square, erected a huge electric sign on its building's façade, conforming to aesthetic guidelines for the redevelopment of the area.

THE WORST CASE: NORTH ADAMS, MASSACHUSETTS

By contrast, the outcome of a cultural strategy of redevelopment under different circumstances, for a different public, tempers the conclusions we can draw from New York City. In North Adams, Massachusetts, an impoverished corner of the Berkshire Mountains, two cycles of industrial growth and decline have left a historic preservationist's dream of derelict red-brick factory buildings, on a space equivalent to 10 football fields, along a river whose lack of manufacturing activity could well lead to waterfront recreation. In the late nineteenth century after the Civil War, North Adams was a centre for printed textile manufacturing, and in the 1920s, along with the decline and relocation of the rest of New England's textile and leather producers, the town suffered. In the 1940s and 1950s, with a relocation to North Adams of electronics manufacturing, in the midst of booms for military and consumer goods production, the town revived. In the 1980s, after the major electronics employer was sold to a distant corporation, the new owner reduced employment and finally shut the plant down. By the mid-1980s, the site was unused, unemployment was high, and no businesses sought to relocate in North Adams.

At this point, an ambitious museum director who had graduated from nearby Williams College, a prestigious private institution with its own art museums, proposed transforming the unused factory into an art museum. This museum, moreover, would specialize in Conceptualist and Minimalist art of the 1960s and 1970s – forms quite foreign to the indigenous folk art and realist traditions of the area, as well as to the Impressionist collection that drew many visitors to the Clark Art Institute in Williamstown. The museum director won praise and, more importantly, political support in the area by presenting this proposal as a strategy of economic redevelopment. He succeeded in getting a state bond guarantee from the Massachusetts legislature for developing the

Massachusetts Museum of Contemporary Art (MASS MoCA), as well as some budget money to plan the museum. He also won praise in the art world and in the mass media, where he presented the same proposal as a strategy for creating the biggest museum in the world (to house some of the biggest works). It is crucial to understand that the proposal to re-use industrial space in North Adams became connected to the director's plans to make the Guggenheim Museum of New York a multinational player in the art world – for he was named director of the Guggenheim Museum one year after proposing MASS MoCA – and the controversies over the specific forms of art he chose became embroiled with controversies over the acquisition of specific pieces of art, the direction of the Guggenheim, and competition among art museums in New York.

To make a long story shorter, the plan for MASS MoCA was stalled and eventually derailed by the withdrawal of support from the state of Massachusetts, which was plagued by fiscal problems following the end of the high tech boom of the 1980s. MASS MoCA was also stopped by questions in the New York press about the appropriateness of showing Minimalist and Conceptualist art in North Adams, criticisms of the Guggenheim's expansion plans around the world, and, not least, the failure of the project team to get a financial commitment to the museum from private donors. Neither was there a sizable group of local art patrons that could commit political capital to supporting the museum.

Yet it is significant that local political leaders felt they had no choice but to accept, with great enthusiasm, a cultural strategy of economic redevelopment. The local press in North Adams never addressed the question of which art forms were to be shown, and the project team early on won over potential critics by promising to include educational space and study space for local artists. These issues were secondary, however, to the lure of jobs. The MASS MoCA proposal promised more than 400 jobs in a hotel and culture complex. The museum proposal also offered the possibility of putting the property back on the tax rolls. A cultural strategy, in brief, seemed to be North Adams's only chance.

In 1994, the Guggenheim Museum's vision of redevelopment in North Adams lost all governmental support. No private patron with deep pockets emerged to fund the museum. No Massachusetts official (even, finally, those in North Adams) wanted to be identified with a losing proposition. Nevertheless, the idea of connecting economic development to an arts complex was not abandoned. Instead, a consortium of local cultural institutions in the Berkshires (led by the administrator of Jacob's Pillow Dance Festival) was joined by a group of radical historians from New York City and an Asian cultural group from Los Angeles in proposing an alternative vision. The new MASS MoCA emphasized performances by visiting artists and groups and production by crafts workshops organized around visiting artists. Just as the previous project forecast jobs for local residents in hotels and restaurants and the museum complex itself, so the new project asserted that new jobs would be created – this time, in cultural production. While the entire tone of the project shifted from imported art to local artists, and from exhibition space to space for production and performance, it is significant that the new project did not suggest jettisoning a *museum*. No other possibility of anchoring economic redevelopment has been envisioned.

Without the cultural resources of New York City, or the same degree of elite and political support for avant-garde and metropolitan cultural forms, a cultural strategy may fall flat. North Adams may be the wrong place: too close to both New York and Boston, not sufficiently detached from its industrial history, too far from the charming pastoral landscapes and mainstream cultural tourism of the Berkshires. But it is interesting that a usually hegemonic cultural strategy would be taken seriously in such a place. Indeed, a cultural strategy of economic redevelopment is the only strategy in town.

DESIGNING PUBLIC SPACES FOR SOCIAL CONTROL

Neil Smith has written well and often about the efforts to drive the homeless out of Tompkins Square Park, in the East Village of lower Manhattan, by enforcing a new design for surveillance by park rangers and the police and for social control by homogeneous groups of park users (see Smith's chapter in this volume). Although they are often applied to populist sites, such as public parks and commercial streets, urban designs are more frequently used to 'clean up' central spaces of the city for high-class businesses, high-rent buildings, and high-income employees, managers, and shoppers. In both populist and high-class quarters, however, the common denominator is 'civility'. Urban designs try to use visual aesthetics to evoke a vanished civic order associated with an equally vanished, or at least transformed, middle class. They use civility, in turn, to evoke a vanished social homogeneity.

Thus the new design of Bryant Park, a nine-acre public park behind the New York Public Library on 42nd Street in midtown Manhattan, was calculated to repel muggers and drug dealers and encourage sitting and strolling by office workers, especially women.[14] The Victorian-style food booths, the Parisian-style park furniture, the gravel paths, and most of all, the uniformed and plainclothes guards from both private security forces and the public police department ensure a 'pacification by cappuccino' that aims to expel the widely perceived offenders against the city's quality of life. While it doesn't cost any money to enter the park, the atmosphere is that of a paying public. Retro urban designs and picnicking on the law aim to recapture this space for owners and tenants of the adjacent office buildings – tenants that include the corporate offices of the cable television network HBO, corporate offices and production studios of the cable television network MTV, and Nynex, a regional telecommunications company. The real benefits to women, and to men who were afraid to use the park during the height of drug dealing there in the 1970s, must be weighed against surveillance and social control by visual strategies.

In an experiential sense, the redesign of Bryant Park is part of a general urban discourse around central spaces and quality of life. Complaints against garish and overbearing shop displays, the persecution of street peddlers in downtown Brooklyn and on 125th Street in Harlem, and the war against the homeless are also parts of this discourse of aesthetics and social control. Also present, however, are real motivations of increasing (or maintaining high) property values, attracting (or retaining) affluent shoppers, and satisfying the complaints of middle-class residents and corporate employers. By the same token, both the experiential discourse of urban public spaces and the old Marxist shibboleth of raising land values are situated in a political context of rapidly increasing privatization. Significantly, visual strategies of redesigning urban public spaces are championed by local business groups that acquire management rights over public spaces by funding physical and aesthetic improvements.

Bryant Park is essentially run by the Bryant Park Restoration Corporation, a private-sector business improvement district (BID) chartered by the laws of New York State. A BID is a voluntary group of building owners and commercial tenants in a specific area of the city who assess their own taxes over and above existing rates, which are collected for them by governmental agencies and returned to them for funding improvements to their public spaces. Any business district can form a BID. Since assessments are based on commercial rents, the richer business districts have access to greater resources – in many ways – than poorer districts. Moreover, three centrally-located New York City BIDs won mayoral approval to issue their own bonds in 1992 and 1993. So they can leverage their rent rolls and property values, through the bond market, to increase their financial resources even more. Public officials and the press were slow to criticize the unfair advantages of rich BIDs, and their usurpation of governmental functions, while enjoying the improvements BIDs wrought in public spaces. All BIDs across the city paid for their own street sweepers, garbage removers, security guards, street lighting, and street furniture. Most of these streets were cleaner and safer than they had been since the era of chronic fiscal crisis began in the late 1970s.

In 1995, however, debate over the accountability of BIDs was aroused by accusations that one central Manhattan BID, the Grand Central Partnership, had directed its social service outreach workers to roust homeless people sleeping on streets in their district. Simultaneously, a scandal erupted over charges that the same group and its administrator, who also managed two other central Manhattan BIDs, had overstepped the bounds of their charter by investing a small amount of money in, and advising, a new BID across the Hudson River in Jersey City. Under these conditions, the widely known fact that the BID administrator was drawing large salaries from each of the three BIDs he managed – and earned more than the Governor of New York State and the Mayor of New York City earned together – became a major grounds for criticism.

The hubris of rich BIDs and their managers is only one critical aspect of this institution. Seen in the context of continuing efforts to privatize government, and redesign the Welfare State, BIDs remove public entrepreneurship from the public sector. They permit the private sector to initiate and control urban redevelopment. And they legitimize their assumption of governmental functions by designing and financing urban public space. Not only are these designs exclusionary, they confirm a relation between visual order and social control. The BIDs's ability to 'restore' a previous degree of civility in public space and control social diversity by aesthetic strategies (and private security forces) has a material effect on public culture.

The notion of 'restoration' is both implicit and explicit in this work.

On the one hand, architectural designs explicitly restore, on the basis of existing ruins or historical plans, a late 19th century image. Such contemporary designs may, of course, also fabricate a vision of the past out of pastiche, allusion, and imagination. This is the case with Bryant Park, which for most of its history was unattractive and even, in early years, an eyesore. On the other hand, the social order that is alluded to – one based on assumptions of public safety, a common level of civility, and, *en fin de compte*, citizenship – is more implicit; it is consciously embedded in the design. Such visual strategies adopt a middle-class urban order last seen around 1960 without ignoring current realities of social diversity, homelessness, and crime. Each element of danger is assigned its place in the landscape, with the public-private corporation firmly in control of the panorama. At last, many people exclaim, an urban space that works! Or as an editorial column in the usually level-headed magazine *The New Yorker* (14 February 1994, p8), says, 'Now [Bryant Park] is safe, as beautiful as a Seurat, and lovingly used.' In the sense of widening use of the park to all office workers, especially women, who had felt excluded from the old Bryant Park, this is just. In the sense of turning the park over to private control, however, and instituting a sense of the public space of the park as a consumer good, this involves a questionable redistribution of rights.

THE DEMOCRATIZATION OF HISTORIC PRESERVATION

Some public sites that are likely to be incorporated into a new visual order are fiercely contested by different social groups. In the early 1990s, the discovery in Lower Manhattan, in the course of excavating for the foundation of a new public building, of the old Negro (now African) Burial Ground led to acrimonious conflicts over who would control the site, as well as over the processes leading to its historical recuperation. In Houston in the mid-1990s, new cultural strategies of economic development focus on ethno-tourism and historic preservation, leading to struggles to designate historic African American neighbourhoods as landmarks regardless of their value to real estate developers. The area on the East Side of Houston may well be declared a landmark, and the area on the West Side may fail to get this designation, because the West Side is marked by high-class and commercial development.

Despite their reliance on governmental controls, visual strategies nonetheless tend to move the framing of public culture away from government and toward private spheres. The neighbourhood groups involved in visual strategies are often 'nonpolitical': they do not represent the 'material' interests of tenants or homeowners or workers or people of colour. Yet visual strategies, especially historic preservation, have impressed nonhegemonic no less than powerful groups with their ability to do something concrete, like raising property values. The combined material and symbolic effects of visual strategies have, then, democratized to some degree the desire to use culture for material or social ends.

When community leaders from Upper Manhattan pressed the New York City Landmarks Preservation Commission in the early 1990s to designate as a landmark the Audubon Ballroom, where Malcolm X was killed in 1965, they opposed the aesthetic values that have become the most legitimate part of historic preservation with an argument in terms of political significance. This argument also made a rather specific case for using a historic landmark to construct the political culture of a single community – 'the' African American one – rather than for constructing, and certainly not for restoring, an inclusive public culture.[15] Around the same time, community leaders from central Harlem requested that a number of apartment houses with no great architectural or historic distinction by designated as landmarks. Their argument was not merely that Harlem and other African American areas are under-represented in the list of New York City landmarks. They insisted, with some knowledge of gentrification, that historic preservation would 'stabilize' the area and acknowledge the striving for middle-class status of neighbourhood residents.

I suspect that some of the minority group neighbourhoods in Houston and other places are similarly motivated. If this is so, it suggests that visual strategies such as historic preservation can be politicized and used as tools of community development. It also suggests that culture, in the sense of the material control of symbolic resources, may eventually be seen as a public good. Community preservation was, in fact, envisioned by some activists as a goal at the origin of the historic preservation movement in the 1960s, but it has been submerged in aesthetic arguments. The point, however, is that visual strategies now provide significant means for framing disputes over public goods and moving them away from government into private spheres. Communities have become repositories of powerful visual images whose control depends on expressing and imposing a coherent vision.

THE SYMBOLIC ECONOMY, PAST AND PROLOGUE

When I wrote about an Artistic Mode of Production (AMP) structuring the redevelopment of American cities, I traced the beginning of the AMP to the 1960s.[16] I was concerned with the rising social status of the arts and artists, the aesthetic demands and desires expressed by highly visible gentrifiers, and the social power both drawn upon and communicated by artists in efforts to defend their space in the city. The issues surrounding loft living reflected much of the strategic thinking, as well as the temporizing, of bankers, real estate developers, public officials, and urban-minded intellectuals in New York City in the 1960s. In New York, in particular, the spectacular decline of small-scale, traditional manufacturing and the equally spectacular rise of corporate business shaped a planning discourse based on national (and eventually, global) priorities rather than local needs, insubstantial rather than concrete products, and the role of the arts in representing the gains of a mainly symbolic economy. Throughout the 1960s – when the acceptance of loft living was still far from being a foregone conclusion – this planning discourse crystallized the image of the city as a 'national centre', uniquely nurturant of and yet also dependent upon cultural products and cultural institutions. If the city was to 'specialize' in high-level business activities, then art galleries, performances, and philanthropic museum memberships offered the perquisites and the symbols of economic power. While this fit between, as I put it then, accumulation and cultural strategies is consistent with the materialist analyses that David Harvey has inspired, I have come to think it exposes only part of the picture.

By the 1990s, a larger picture might be framed by the symbolic economy to which business services, culture industries, and real estate development belong. These activities give a much larger creative role to the organization of consumption, since either the end product of the production processes or large part of the social reproduction ('lifestyle') functions of the men and women involved in these sectors focuses on consumer goods or services. Similarly, consumption spaces – from leisure complexes to restaurants and retail shops – play a more important role in people's lives than was thought before. Such spaces make narratives of the city's complex heterogeneous languages, constructing multiple histories and identities for both individuals and local communities. At the same time, industries that deal in symbolic products – from fashion to finance – have become powerful players on the local scene, whether that power is refracted through tourism or jobs. This framework obliges us to do much more research on the material impact of symbols than do analyses framed in terms of either postmodernism (e.g. fragmentation-simulation-pastiche) or represen-tations (e.g. multiplicity-absences-city-as-text). This approach demands a comprehensive research effort on the material impacts of the symbolic economy, its mediation of cultural practices and cultural categories (not least, ethnicity and race), and its ability to control urban spaces by 'framing' a vision.

Although we have lived through many expressions of urban visions in the last quarter century – from the demise of government-sponsored urban renewal to the heralding of private-market gentrification, from slash-and-burn Modernism to historic preservation, from ambitions of building new financial centres for worldwide trading to desperate efforts to fill empty spaces in office buildings – we do not enter the twenty-first century with a sense that cities are being guided by any vision.

The rise of new industries based on cultural consumption seems to justify visual strategies in the crassest material sense. The commercial success of Disney World, and its apparent synergy with a low-wage, mainly European-American work force and military technology and service firms in Orlando, demonstrate how the pleasures of vision co-exist with corporate cultural hegemony. While the failure of Euro Disney, at least in its first years, suggests a counter-example, it may in fact just qualify the sorts of visual strategies, their timing, and placement, that work in different circumstances for different publics.

Sometimes those who succeed in framing a coherent vision are corporations, such as Disney World or MTV; sometimes they are community groups, from either the grassroots or the real estate industry. Usually they are private institutions such as art museums and groups such as BIDs that link their vision with the public interest of a larger community: the city. In the absence of a strong collective vision including all the city's people, the power to impose a visual frame becomes the power to define a public culture.

The power to impose a visual frame also suggests new political-strategies for managing social diversity. As challenging, and challenged, as multiculturalism has been in its brief history, cultural strategies permit elites to 'take the high road' by acknowledging eclecticism and alloting each group a piece of the visual representation of a city or region. To some extent, this avoids ranking groups in terms of the justness of their claims. 'Everybody has a culture, so everybody is equal'. Every group can have its visible recognition, even a visual acknowledgment of past oppression. The emphasis is on 'past' oppression, for establishing a visual order of cultural hegemony seems to equalize by identifying and making formerly 'invisible' social groups visible, at least in their previous (sometimes romanticized, sometimes not) incarnation. This interpretation differs from the criticisms of themed developments for making history 'fun'[17] and of 'heritage' presentations because they sanitize and homogenize history.[18] Instead, cultural strategies that rely on visual representations attempt to create a new public culture that is both non-hierarchical and inegalitarian.

Because the capital city of a symbolic economy depends so heavily on cultural capital, socially marginal groups such as artists and immigrants play an important role in visualising, and thus defining, public culture. In the process, culture has lost its totalising meaning as a way of life to become a resource and a strategy to advance the interests of both dominating and dominated groups. Whether the power to frame a vision resides in the ownership of individual paintings, or the preservation of historic districts, or the development of entertainment complexes, visual power becomes the power to frame the city. As cities are built, or rebuilt, within these frames, the new uses of culture as identity, resource, and strategy have nurtured a much more specialized, and a much more marketable, set of cultural meanings than ever before. Far from suggesting a free expression of divergent identities, the flourishing of new cultural meanings in the highly competitive environment of urban space makes it more urgent to understand their material effects.

NOTES

[1] D. Harvey, 'Monument and Myth' in *Consciousness and the Urban Experience*, Johns Hopkins University Press, Baltimore, 1985.
[2] D. Harvey, *The Condition of Postmodernity*, Blackwell, Oxford 1989.
[3] J. Duncan and D. Ley, *Place/Culture/Representation*, Routledge, London, 1993.
[4] P. Wright, *On Living in an Old Country*, Verso, London, 1985.

[5] P. Mullins, 'Tourism Urbanization', *International Journal of Urban and Regional Research*, Volume 15, 1991, pp336-342.

[6] H.K. Bhabha, *The Location of Culture*, Routledge, London, 1994.

[7] S. Zukin, *The Cultures of Cities*, Blackwell, Oxford, 1996.

[8] See S. Zukin, *Loft Living*, Johns Hopkins University Press, Baltimore, 1982 and S. Zukin, *Landscapes of Power: From Detroit to Disney World*, University of California Press, Berkeley, 1991, respectively.

[9] Every country must have its own paired comparisons: the competition, on the basis of cultural resources, between Glasgow and Edinburgh; the consensus or lack of consensus among political parties and labour unions in Lancaster, Cheltenham and Sheffield.

[10] J. Urry, *The Tourist Gaze*, Sage, London, 1990.

[11] This is not necessarily an easy process. The National Park Service is not really receptive to integrating abandoned and often polluted industrial sites in a system based on the management of 'pristine' natural places.

[12] Port Authority of New York and New Jersey, *The Arts as an Industry*, Port Authority, New York, 1983.

[13] Port Authority of New York and New Jersey, *The Arts as an Industry*, Port Authority, New York, 1993.

[14] Influenced by W.H. Whyte, *The City*, Doubleday, New York, 1988.

[15] This dispute also pitted community groups against Columbia University, whose medical school planned to tear down the Audubon and build a new biotechnology complex, so there were also questions of whether community residents would benefit economically – e.g. by getting jobs – from the new use of the site. Certainly, the geographical community involved in the Audubon conflict was not exactly the same as the political community. Although the site is considered to be in Harlem, and thus African American, many neighbourhood residents are Hispanics from the Caribbean, especially Dominicans.

[16] S. Zukin, 1982, *op.cit.*

[17] See, for example, D. Harvey, 1989, *op.cit.*, pp88-98.

[18] See, for example, M. Wallace, 'Mickey Mouse History: Portraying the Past at Disney World', *Radical History Review*, Volume 32, 1985, pp33-57.

Editors' Postscript

We cannot and will not make a concluding statement to this collection. We do not wish to close down horizons, but instead want to open up new ones. Although this book has been brought together by academics, we hope its readership will not just be academics. For us, as well as for the contributors, talking about issues of social justice and emancipatory politics is fraught with all kinds of frustrations, contradictions and anxieties that go with conducting these explorations within the academy. Many are involved in daily struggles for emancipation and empowerment in a variety of environments: in the streets, the workplace, in the community and at home.

But academia has, aside from maybe a brief moment in the late 1960s, rarely been a hotbed of struggle for emancipatory social change. Still, it has been and – who knows – might become again the breeding ground for new enabling ideas, theories, strategies and organic intellectuals that can and should combine with the desire to 'reclaim the streets' – to borrow the name of a newly-founded British protest group. That, ultimately, is what we wish to deepen and keep alive to counter the *noir culture* associated with every *fin de siècle* conjuncture. We do not believe that the society we live in is as good as it can possibly get; nor do we believe that history and geography have somehow ended. Instead, we insist that it is possible to strive to make an unpredictable future meaningful and our own: scholars and academics on the left have a responsibility to be a part of that struggle to create a genuinely humanizing urbanism.

Notes on Contributors

Marshall Berman is Professor of Political Science at City College of the City University, New York.

Susan Fainstein is Professor of Urban Planning and Policy Development at Rutgers University, New Jersey.

David Harvey is Professor of Geography at the Johns Hopkins University, Baltimore and Senior Research Fellow, St. Peter's College, Oxford.

Ira Katznelson is Professor of Political Science at Columbia University, New York.

Michael Keith is Principal Research Officer at Goldsmiths College, University of London.

Doreen Massey is Professor of Geography at the Open University.

Andy Merrifield is Lecturer in Geography at King's College, University of London.

Neil Smith is Professor of Geography at Rutgers University, New Jersey.

Ed Soja is Professor of Urban and Regional Planning at the University of California, Los Angeles.

Erik Swyngedouw is Lecturer in Geography at Oxford University and Fellow of St. Peter's College.

Sharon Zukin is Professor of Sociology at the City University of New York.

.